The Orange Order

THE ORANGE ORDER

A Tradition Betrayed

Brian Kennaway

Methuen

First published in Great Britain by Methuen in 2006

Methuen Publishing Ltd
11–12 Buckingham Gate, London SW1E 6LB

www.methuen.co.uk

Methuen Publishing Limited Reg. No. 3543167

ISBN 10: 0 413 77535 6
ISBN 13: 978 0 413 77535 1

A CIP catalogue record for this book is available from the British Library

This book has received financial support from the Northern Ireland Community Relations Council which aims to promote a pluralist society and encourage an acceptance and an understanding of cultural diversity.

The views expressed in this publication are of those of their authors and do not necessarily reflect those of the Northern Ireland Community Relations Council.

Typeset by SX Composing DTP, Rayleigh, Essex

Printed and bound in Great Britain by The Cromwell Press, Trowbridge, Wiltshire

Contents

Foreword

The Rev. Brian Kennaway in this carefully researched and thoroughly documented account of the present-day Orange Order addresses the current situation within Orangeism. It is an honest appraisal and is to be commended as such.

'Where are we as an Order today?' This is a question which many inside the Institution are asking, and asking with a sense of deep sadness that an organisation which celebrated its bicentenary with high hopes and great enthusiasm just ten years ago should have so far drifted from its former place of influence and declined from its bygone strength. Of course, external forces beyond anyone's control can account for much of the decline in membership. However, many of us still within the Order have a deeply rooted conviction that we have all too often been the authors of our own misfortunes.

So far as the general constituency of the Order is concerned it is probably in much the same condition today as it was twenty or even thirty years ago. If the numbers have fallen quite considerably the general quality and calibre of the membership is not radically different from what it was in former years. This is especially evident if one is thinking of the degree of religious commitment manifested by the brethren. In rural Ulster, especially west of the River Bann, one can still assume a general, even if not a complete linkage of ordinary lodge members with one or other of the Protestant churches. That has always been the case. Belfast was and is quite different in that regard. In former days the fact that a majority of the Belfast membership had only a tenuous connection with any church was obscured by the sound core of committed churchmen who held office in most of the district lodges. These in turn made up what once was, but no longer is, the largest of the County Grand Lodges under the jurisdiction of the Grand Orange Lodge of Ireland. We need spiritual revival and renewal right across these islands, in all societies and groupings, and possibly nowhere is the need more urgent than within the Orangeism of Belfast.

It can be argued that the social mix today within the Order is not what it was. For one thing, even the lesser gentry are by and large conspicuous by their absence from its ranks. Further, the Order is no longer drawing the same proportion of its membership as it once did from business or the professions. This is reflected in the current make-up of most of the District and County Grand Lodges and that again carries on up to the Grand Orange Lodge. A variety of reasons can be given for this. It is no longer socially advantageous to be an Orangeman. Much more tellingly, the increasing politicisation of Orangeism has damaged the sense of fellowship within lodges. As a consequence, in too many instances it is no longer a pleasant experience for many men when they attend their lodge. When the floor is taken by the least intelligent and the most belligerent, it is not hard to feel that lodge-night is a waste of precious time.

Taken in the round, however, Orangeism is probably still very largely what it has always been, and particularly in country areas the quota of decent, solid sensible men in local lodges probably has not diminished. Unfortunately neither has the percentage of 'kick the Pope' reactionaries, most of whom could not give an intelligent or intelligible critique of Roman Catholicism if it were to save their lives. The antiquated language still extant in the Law Book of the Order is unfortunately taken by this vociferous minority to give succour and support to their prejudices.

What *has* changed is the character of the leadership within wide swathes of Orangeism, not excluding the Grand Orange Lodge. The book before you demonstrates that. Whereas formerly, the wilder men of the uncouth fringe were largely marginalised in the Order, and not many of that type attained even district lodge office, this is no longer the case. A fairly recent amendment to the Order's Laws and Ordinances, of questionable legality so far as its mode of introduction was concerned, gave district lodges the right of direct representation to the Grand Orange Lodge. This meant that though there was scope for some able men to be promoted more quickly, there was even greater scope for those of quite a different ilk to carry their prejudices to the highest court. Though still unrepresentative of Orangeism as a whole, too many of those who see Orangeism's role in purely negative and confrontational terms have infiltrated the district lodges and through them the County Grand Lodges. They are able to intimidate a sometimes weak and indecisive leadership. Their presence is a not inconsiderable factor inhibiting some men from taking decisions which they fear would arouse the ire of extremists.

Anticlericalism, and the 'sect' mentality, i.e. opposition to and criticism of the mainline Protestant denominations, is also an unlovely feature of some modern-day Orange gatherings. It is certainly more obvious now than it was in years gone by, when clerics in large numbers from the principal Protestant churches were members of County Grand Lodges. On the whole they provided wise counsel. Probably there has always been an undercurrent of 'anti-minister' attitudes. Naturally, it receives support from some whose problem really lies in their enmity to the radical demands of the Evangelical Gospel. These nowadays are more vocal than once was the case. The forthright challenges which some chaplains sometimes gave did not always please. For example, to be told that we *all* need to repent of our sins, or to be told that Christ demands that those who profess His Name should love their enemies, is not the route to popularity in a political Protestantism of which Orangeism unfortunately harbours quite a few adherents.

Of all present day ills afflicting our Order none is more damaging than the surrender by the leadership to the bully-boys who misused the name 'Spirit of Drumcree'. A few demagogues used the apparent triumph of Sinn Féin strategy in the Garvaghy Road stand-offs in Portadown to gather the malcontents within the ranks of Orangeism, ostensibly 'to face the enemy'. It soon appeared that their strategy was directed towards capturing the Order for a campaign of extremism which would have destroyed the Institution's credibility. They were a conspiracy aimed at intimidating those who stood for the Christian principles of toleration embedded in the Basis of the Institution. This faction ultimately commandeered the headquarters of Orangeism, and prevented the Grand Orange Lodge of Ireland having one of its half-yearly meetings in its own premises. It also flexed the muscle of bigotry at other venues, not shrinking from threatening physical assault on brethren who dared to oppose them. After promising that steps would be taken to deal firmly and decisively with the rebels, the Grand Orange Lodge, taking its cue from the Secretariat, simply caved in to the bigots' bluster. Secret negotiations had taken place in the meanwhile, the full details of which have never been disclosed, and a wrong road was taken.

Since the Referendum on the Belfast Agreement of 1998 a disproportionate amount of time and energy within lodges has been taken up by sometimes bitter political controversy. That has not been helpful to the Orange cause. The accusation has often been made that politicians have used the Orange Institution to forward their own agenda and their own personal ambition. Whatever element of truth there may be in that, the commerce between politicians and the Orange Institution was not all one way. It could be maintained that Orangeism as an organisation simply acted as an umbrella for all who adhered to moderate Unionism, whatever their particular preference might be, and certainly it once welcomed into membership any law-abiding Protestant loyal to the Crown. If that day is not quite past there has been a noticeable change of temperature. In an earlier era Orangeism was in a much healthier state. It tried hard to be inclusive of all loyal Protestants. Now, in its official publication, and by repeated assertions within Grand Lodge itself which no Orange leader has as yet repudiated, those of the membership who voted Yes in the Referendum of 1998, have been stigmatised as 'traitors'. Obviously, no voluntary organisation can long maintain a healthy condition when its leaders approve political intolerance. To stigmatise a large section of its membership as 'disloyal', because they took a conscientious stand on an issue which any intelligent observer knew would be an apple of discord if not discreetly handled, is not a recipe for progress.

Confrontational solutions to community problems and an almost pitiful willingness of the Orange leadership to jump through every hoop held up for them by the Sinn Féin manipulators, who obviously delighted in winding them up, is also part of the new temper and outlook within the Orange hierarchy. The clear evidence of the bankruptcy of the tactics devised by the Strategy Committee set up to deal with the parading issue, not to speak of some of the proposed (but thankfully not implemented) remedies, of highly questionable morality, was for a long time blithely disregarded.

The emergence of evidence that paramilitary elements were involving themselves in the earlier stand-offs at Drumcree Parish Church raised questions as to what degree of influence the paramilitary movements had in the happenings of July 1996 and in other Orange-related events since then. The questions have still to be answered. The uneasiness and pain which this wickedness creates in the hearts of law-abiding, church-going members of the Order is hard to allay while no answer is forthcoming. In former years, though attempts were undoubtedly made to seduce Orangeism into a covert alliance with paramilitarism, the leaders of the Grand Orange Lodge firmly resisted such temptation, and paramilitary influence within the membership was noticeably curbed. Much of this is to be set down to the lasting credit of the Rev. W. M. Smyth, former MP and former Grand Master. There is a strong suspicion among many members of the Order that the case in the present day is somewhat altered.

It has to be said that the doings of the Grand Orange Lodge's leadership do not figure much in the consciousness of the great majority of rank-

and-file members of the Institution, save when another request for financial support comes through from 'Headquarters'. The ordinary membership are of course the real Orange Order. When the Order was officially abolished in the nineteenth century, and there was no Grand Orange Lodge, the rank and file kept Orangeism alive. They keep it alive today and it is *their* welfare that Brian Kennaway had in mind when he produced this book. It simply tells the truth. Until a few years ago he was convenor of the Education Committee of the Grand Orange Lodge, and the work of that committee during his period of leadership gave hope to many of us who had access to some of the inner workings of the organisation. We had at least one committee which was trying to relate the Order to the real world, being vigorous in the presentation of its position as a tolerant, intelligent and consistent Protestant organisation whose great strength lay in its ability to unite men from the lay membership of the various Protestant denominations in a brotherhood which could cohere in defence of Reformation principles, but always remembering that 'the weapons of our warfare are not carnal'.

A strengthening and intensification of the Order's outreach and witness, which the Education Committee had initiated, was urgently needed in any recovery of confidence. By its publications and contacts with a wide variety of individuals and groups the committee succeeded in putting Orangeism 'on the map' in the best sense of the word. The Grand Orange Lodge's own Special Commission, of which I was convenor, noted and reported on the work of the Education Committee with high commendation. This report was of course received and approved by the Grand Orange Lodge but the plaudits offered to the Education Committee were soon muted. Whispers and mutterings behind the scenes saw to that. The resignation of the great majority of the Education Committee's membership, after a virtual vote of no confidence in their work, quenched yet another lamp which might have lighted the path for those of us who have a sincere desire for the prospering of all that genuine Orangeism stands for. It is such a desire which lies behind the publication of this present volume. Its record, which can be thoroughly vouched for, is meant to recall the Order to its essential tasks and basic principles. Important though political matters may be and necessary though they are, there is a more important calling and a higher necessity that demands the energy and obedience of Orangemen. As professed children of the Reformation we have a witness to commend, and as those who claim 'a humble and steadfast faith in Jesus Christ, the Saviour of mankind' we have a Redeemer to proclaim. *This* is our great work and to do it as an

Order we need an inner integrity. Brian Kennaway's faithful testimony ought to go a long way in helping us regain our integrity. He has spoken simple truth, 'nor has set down aught in malice', as befits his Christian calling and conviction.

Rev. Dr William Warren Porter BA, BD
Grand Chaplain, Grand Orange Lodge of Ireland 1993–8
Assistant Grand Master, Grand Orange Lodge of Ireland 1994–7

Preface

This book is not an encyclopaedic history of the Orange Order, but a personal analysis of the problems which the Institution faces today. For the benefit of both the membership who are often kept in the dark, and the wider public, it explains how the Institution, once a power within Unionism, came to nothing through a lack of vision and a complete absence of leadership.

Brought up in north Belfast, I joined 'Christian Crusaders' LOL 1339*, a lodge within the County Grand Lodge of Belfast, in 1964. I did so because I believed, as I still do, in the core values of the Orange tradition.

My interest in the religious and historical nature of Orangeism has developed over the years. I was a member of the Grand Orange Lodge of Ireland for twenty-five years. I was appointed to the Education Committee of the Grand Orange Lodge of Ireland in 1984 and became chairman in 1989 and convenor in 1992. The Education Committee, which during my tenure produced seventeen titles on various aspects of Orangeism, made an ever-increasing impact on the public perception of the Institution until its demise in June 2000, as we were demonised and driven from office to the fringes. In the last decade of its existence the committee had been active in explaining the core values of Orangeism to interested audiences throughout Ireland.

It is my conviction that in many important respects the Order has abandoned basic principles and lost its way, leading to a decline in its membership, influence and public standing. My efforts to achieve reform internally, by being proactive rather than reactive, were thwarted by a cadre of unyielding senior officers. I argue that far from being a sectarian, controversial and divisive body, the Order, properly reformed, could be a force for good and reconciliation in Northern Ireland's deeply divided society.

*LOL is the standard acronym for Loyal Orange Lodge, and is accordingly used throughout this book.

I am conscious that this is the first completely frank and authoritative 'inside' account of the affairs of the Orange Order to be written in recent years by someone whom the media describes as 'a prominent and senior member'. For that reason I am indebted to a number of individuals who have been a constant source of encouragement, including many who hold significant offices within the Institution and who share my analysis and concern, but would not wish to be named. To others like the Very Rev. Dr John Lockington, the Rev. Denis Bannerman and Cecil Kilpatrick, the Grand Lodge Archivist, along with former members of the Education Committee the Rev. Dr David Richardson and Richard Whitten, who read the original manuscript and offered helpful suggestions, I am most grateful.

I am particularly indebted to the Rev. Dr William Warren Porter, who has kindly provided a foreword to this publication. As an Orangeman of sixty years' experience, having served in some of the most senior positions within the Institution, his encouragement and assistance has been a constant driving force in the preparation of this book.

I am indebted to those who have walked this path before. Ruth Dudley Edwards, who read an early manuscript some years ago and provided helpful comments, has been a constant source of help. Chris Ryder, whose analysis of Drumcree was challenging, though disregarded by the leadership, has kindly led a novice through the labyrinth towards publication.

Many in the academic world have been a source of encouragement as I have shared this project with them. Professor Paul Bew, Professor of Irish Politics at Queen's University, Belfast, has been a constant support since I first shared the idea with him early in 1999. To the Very Rev. Dr R. F. G. Holmes, who read the manuscript and offered helpful suggestions, I am deeply indebted. Others like Eric Kaufmann, Henry Patterson and Dominic Bryan have always been willing to discuss various aspects of Orangeism from the perspective of their extensive research. I am indebted to them all.

I am indebted to my publisher, Methuen, and Max Eilenberg for accepting the manuscript for publication, and to the Community Relations Council for their financial support. My sincere thanks must go to Eleanor Rees, who skilfully edited the text to make it acceptable for publication.

Rev. Brian Kennaway
January 2006

List of Illustrations

18. Banner of 'Ireland's Heritage', LOL 1303, an Orange Lodge in Belfast County
19. Ruth Dudley Edwards (© *An Phoblacht*)
20. Grand Master Robert Saulters and others support Catholics' right to worship (© Crispin Rodwell)

This book is dedicated to the memory of all those who have endeavoured to live out the core values of the Orange tradition

Chapter One

The Place of Orangeism in Irish Society

> *'The less certain we are of our future, the more interested we become in our past.'*
>
> G. K. Chesterton

In 1685, when Charles II died, his brother ascended the throne of England as James II. James, as Duke of York, had already caused concern among the English ruling aristocracy by joining the Church of Rome, against the advice of his brother the King, his two daughters, Ann and Mary, and Mary's husband, the Prince of Orange. The House of Commons had responded in April 1679 by unanimously voting 'That the Duke of York, by coming as a Papist to the Crown, had given encouragement to the designs and conspiracies against the King and the Protestant religion'.

The national outcry which arose at the time of the alleged Jesuit conspiracy to assassinate Charles II and replace him with the Roman Catholic James, known as the Popish Plot of 1678, meant that James had to flee to Europe, and several unsuccessful attempts were made to exclude him from the succession. The succession crisis arising in 1685 on the death of Charles raised three fundamental issues – the Protestant Constitution, national liberty and the influence of the French. In the eyes of the lovers of liberty, James could not be trusted, because of both his Roman Catholicism and his closeness to the French.

After James eventually succeeded to the throne, he regarded himself as monarch by divine right. When the Privy Council ordered a Declaration of Indulgence to be read during divine service in all parish churches, the bishops promptly objected to what they saw as interference by the King in the affairs of the Church. Seven bishops of the Anglican Church who petitioned the King, pointing out that 'the Sovereign was not constitutionally competent to dispense with statutes in matters ecclesiastical', were promptly imprisoned. Such a demonstration of religious intolerance, together with the appointment of Roman Catholic officers to a large standing army, contrary to existing laws, was nationally unacceptable. The acquittal of the bishops on 30 June 1688 was greeted with the customary sign of celebration – the lighting of bonfires.

Anxious English Protestants began to consider the claim to the throne of William Henry, Count of Nassau, Prince of Orange and Stadtholder of Holland, who had married his cousin Mary, the daughter of James II, in 1677. Though William was connected to the house of Stuart, his mother Mary Henrietta being a sister of both Charles II and James II, it was his wife Mary who was the heir presumptive. This remained the case until the birth of a son, James ('the Old Pretender'), on 10 June 1688, to James II and Mary of Modena, his second wife. Accordingly, on the evening of the acquittal of the bishops, William was approached with an appeal to rescue their rights and liberties by a group of influential Protestants who were to become known as the 'Immortal Seven': the earls of Shrewsbury, Devonshire and Danby, and Richard Lumley, Dr Henry Compton, Edward Russell and Henry Sidney.

William responded to their invitation and arrived with his fleet at Torbay on 5 November 1688. The flag flying at the masthead of his ship the *Brill* carried the message '*Pro Religione et Libertare – Je Maintiendrai*'. As M. W. Dewar points out in *Orangeism: A New Historical Appreciation*, 'This is usually freely rendered "The Protestant Religion and the Liberties of England I will maintain". Strictly speaking of course it is simply rendered "I will maintain Religion and Liberty".' This was a combination of the purpose of his mission – 'The Liberties of England' – and the motto of the House of Nassau, 'I will Maintain'.

The 'Glorious Revolution' and constitutional settlement of 1689, placing William and Mary jointly on the throne of England, laid the basis for western democracy and established the liberties of the Reformation firmly on English soil. William always sought to apply the constitutional settlement with liberality, though he was often restricted by parliament. In Ireland the 'Ascendancy', the Anglican aristocracy who had so much to lose, prevented the full implementation of the terms of the Treaty of Limerick which brought the Jacobite war of 1689–91 to an end. The treaty offered Roman Catholics such privileges in the exercise of their religion as they had under Charles II, and the failure to implement it understandably caused great bitterness among the Roman Catholic population. This was far from William's wish.

The formation of the Orange Order or the Orange Institution a century later in 1795 has often been described as the coming together of various traditions which already existed at that time. Williamite fraternities such as the Boyne Society and the Enniskillen Society had been formed to keep alive the memory of William, the constitutional settlement and the battles of the Irish campaign. The Boyne Society had branches in many parts of Ireland, particularly in Ulster, and was still going strong in 1795, although in England the original Orange societies which had been formed to oppose James II were now dissipating. There was also the Volunteer movement, recognised by many historians as the forerunner of both the Orange Order and the United Irishmen. A third source was the 'Orange Boys' formed by Presbyterian farmer James Wilson of the Dyan, in County Tyrone.

These groupings all came together under the pressure of attacks on Protestants in County Armagh by the 'Defenders', a Roman Catholic group. Economic competition was being created by the influx of Roman Catholics from other parts of Ireland into Armagh, then the most densely populated county in Ireland outside Dublin, to engage in the emerging textile industry. After the 'Battle of the Diamond' on 21 September 1795, when the Defenders attacked the home and inn of local Protestant Dan Winter at the Diamond crossroads outside Loughgall, the men who repulsed them came together to form the Orange Society, later to be more correctly known as the Loyal Orange Institution of Ireland. It will be evident that the Loyal Orange Institution of Ireland was a *manifestation* of Orangeism, and not Orangeism per se.

Orangeism in itself, apart from any particular organisation, is a broad philosophical concept embracing the great principles of the sixteenth-century Reformation, and especially of William III, Prince of Orange and King of England. William accepted and affirmed the constitutional government of the three kingdoms and strictly adhered to the Declaration of Rights, later to become the Bill of Rights, which he and Mary jointly accepted from parliament. By the standards of the day he was a liberal monarch and any lack of liberality towards others during his reign can be laid at the door of a less than liberal parliament. He was a man of truly tolerant principles, who had been brought up in Holland where the wisdom of his ancestors had united the country.

Although he *conformed* loyally to the rights and ceremonies of the Church of England, of which he and Mary were joint governors, William was never *confirmed*. However, his religious convictions were the guardian of all the other values in his life. William was a Christian by conviction, not by convention. As Cecil Kilpatrick puts it in *William of Orange: A Dedicated Life*: 'William was quite unconcerned by public opinion or popularity, kept his own counsel and did what his conscience and wise judgement told him was right in the sight of God.' Many of William's personal prayers still exist. They are the epitome of personal devotion and humble submission to the will of the Almighty:

> Enable me, O Lord by thy grace, to govern all my appetites, and every inordinate lust and passion, by temperance and purity, and meekness of wisdom; setting thee always before me, that I might not sin against thee . . . Make me to love thee, as I ought, above all things; and let the interest of thy holy honour and glory be ever dearer to me than my own will, or reputation, or any temporal advantage whatsoever . . . Be merciful, also O God, to my native country; let true religion and righteousness be established among them, as the surest foundation of their peace and prosperity.

These core values of William must therefore also be the core values of all those who, in the words of the Basis of the Loyal Orange Institution of Ireland, 'associate also in honour of King William III, Prince of Orange, whose name they bear, as supporters of his glorious memory'.

Allegations of sectarianism and anti-Catholicism have plagued the Orange Institution since its foundation in 1795. The Institution has often been wrongly accused of involvement in sectarian attacks against Roman Catholics. Over two hundred years there have been examples of tolerance. When during the 1798 Rebellion many Roman Catholic churches were burned in South Antrim, leading Orangemen subscribed towards their rebuilding. In 1998, when arsonists in the same South Antrim area burned Roman Catholic places of worship, leading chaplains of the Order publicly condemned the vandalism and dissociated the Institution from such totally anti-Christian behaviour, while Lord Molyneaux of Killead followed the noble Orange tradition by contributing money towards the restoration of Aldergrove Church. Colonel Edward Saunderson, the Orange leader at the end of the nineteenth century, also supported the civil and religious liberties of his Roman Catholic neighbours, facilitating 'the growth of Catholicism by freely providing land for church-building projects'.[1]

Allegations of anti-Catholicism have often focused on the 'Qualifications of an Orangeman'. Mistakenly held by some to be 'secret', these are in the public domain, and assent to them is required by everyone joining the organisation. The Qualifications state that an Orangeman 'should strenuously oppose the fatal errors and doctrines of the Church of Rome, and scrupulously avoid countenancing (by his presence or otherwise) any act of Romish Worship'. To put this in context, let us note the doctrinal standards of the main Protestant churches. The Westminster Confession of Faith of the Presbyterian Church speaks of the Pope as 'that Antichrist, that man of sin, and son of perdition, that exalteth himself, in the Church, against Christ and all that is called God' (Chapter 25). Article 31 of the Thirty-Nine Articles of the Anglican Churches (Church of Ireland) refers to the Mass as '*blasphema figmenta sunt, et perniciosæ imposturæ*' – 'blasphemous fables, and dangerous deceits'. Similarly the Methodist Church in its foundation documents, 'Standard Doctrines of the Methodist Connection', which include John Wesley's *Sermons* and *Notes*, also makes reference to the Church of Rome. Wesley in his *Notes* on 2 Thessalonians 2:3–9 writes:

> In many respects the Pope has an indisputable claim to those titles. He is in an emphatical sense, the man of sin, as he increases all manner of sin above measure. And he is, too, properly styled, the son of perdition, as he has caused the death of numberless multitudes both of his opposers and followers, destroyed innumerable souls and will himself perish everlastingly.

In this respect therefore the present Qualifications of the Grand Orange Lodge of Ireland cannot be judged to be any more 'anti-Catholic' than the doctrinal standards of the three main Protestant Churches in Ireland.

In spite of the Orange Institution presenting an image of being reluctant to change, what is often not stated, and perhaps not understood, by both the leadership and the rank and file of the Institution, is that the Qualifications have changed materially since the formation of the Institution. As the County Grand Master of Belfast, John McCrea, wrote in *The Twelfth 1988*: 'When the Orange Order was established in 1795, the object of the Order was to aid all loyal subjects of every religious persuasion.' The specific anti-Roman Catholic declaration so familiar today was not part of the original substance of the Qualifications.

The original handwritten minutes of the second meeting of the Grand Orange Lodge of Ireland on 20 November 1798 contain the 'Qualifications requisite for an Orangeman' as follows:

> He should have a sincere love and veneration for his Almighty Maker, productive of those happy fruits, righteousness and obedience to His commands; a firm and steady faith in the Saviour of the world,

> convinced that He is the only Mediator between a sinful creature and an offended Creator. Without these he can be no Christian – of a humane and compassionate disposition, and a courteous and affable behaviour. He should be an utter enemy to savage brutality and unchristian cruelty; a lover of society and improving company; and have a laudable regard for the Protestant religion, and sincere regard to propagate its precepts; zealous in promoting the honour of his King and country; heartily desirous of victory and success in those pursuits, yet convinced and assured that God alone can grant them; he should have a hatred to cursing and swearing, and taking the name of God in vain (a shameful practice); and he should use all opportunities of discouraging it among his brethren. Wisdom and prudence should guide his actions; honesty and integrity direct his conduct; and honour and glory be the motives of his endeavours. Lastly he should pay the strictest attention to a religious observance of the Sabbath, and also of temperance and sobriety.

It is regrettable that, to some modern authors, to 'have a laudable regard for the Protestant religion, and sincere regard to propagate its precepts' carries with it an implied anti-Catholicism. Protestants, as Protestants, cannot avoid opposing the errors of the Church of Rome. However, it is stressed in the Basis of the Loyal Orange Institution of Ireland that the Institution 'will not admit into its brotherhood persons whom an intolerant spirit leads to persecute, injure, or upbraid any man on account of his religious opinions'.

The Grand Orange Lodge of Ireland had dissolved itself on 18 March 1825 as a result of the implementation of the Unlawful Societies (Ireland) Act of 9 March that year. The practical effect was minimal as the interests of Orangeism were kept alive by a newly formed group, 'The Benevolent and Loyal Orange Institution of Ireland'. The Orange Institution was revived in Ireland when the 1825 Act lapsed. The Grand Lodge met in Dublin on 15 September 1828 when it adopted the English system and elected the Duke of Cumberland as Grand Master.

On 14 April 1836 the Grand Orange Lodge of Ireland dissolved itself once again, 'in consequence of the recent vote of the House of Commons and the reply of the Sovereign to an Address from that body, expressing His Majesty's disapprobation of the continuance of the Orange Association, and his determination to take such measures as might appear to him to be advisable for its effective discouragement'. The resolution to dissolve was passed by seventy-nine votes to fifty-nine. There was therefore no Grand Lodge between the years 1836 and 1846. The result of this was minimal, as lodges continued to meet, hold services of worship and keep their traditional parades going. The 'head', if such it was, may have been removed but the body continued to be active.

It was following the second re-formation of the Grand Orange Lodge of Ireland in 1846 that a significant material change appears in the Qualifications, which had been only slightly revised in 1830. The 'Laws and Ordinances of the Loyal Orange Institution of Ireland', newly revised and adopted by the Grand Orange Lodge of Ireland at Monaghan in May 1849, include these words:

> [An Orangeman] should strenuously oppose and protest against the errors and dangerous doctrines of the Church of Rome – he should, by all lawful means, resist the ascendancy of that church, its encroachments, and the extension of its power – but he should abstain from all uncharitable words, actions, or feelings towards his Roman Catholic brethren.

The introduction of this explicit reference to the Church of Rome was a response to the rise of Roman Catholic anti-Evangelicalism, itself a reaction to the very successful missionary enterprises in Connaught by the Church of Ireland.

A further material change is discernible in the Qualifications revised and adopted by the Grand Orange Lodge of Ireland on 3 June 1885, which include the requirement to 'scrupulously avoid countenancing (by his presence or otherwise) any act or ceremony of Popish Worship'. The Qualifications of today are substantially the same as those of 1885, with the exception of the substitution of 'Romish' for 'Popish', and of 'any Roman Catholic' for 'his Roman Catholic brethren'. Both these changes were made on 9 December 1998.

In recent years the high moral content of the Qualifications has been an embarrassment to some members, leading some to state that the Qualifications are 'aspirational'. This contradicts the words used in the initiation of a new member. After hearing the Qualifications read, the candidate is asked whether he is prepared to 'assent' to them, not whether he will merely 'aspire' towards them.

The question to be addressed is whether or not the present Qualifications truly reflect the core values of Orangeism as witnessed in the life of William III, Prince of Orange. If what is already affirmed is true – that the Loyal Orange Institution of Ireland was a *manifestation* of

Orangeism and not Orangeism per se – that raises a further and more fundamental question. Is the Orange Institution at the beginning of the twenty-first century, a true manifestation of historic, traditional Orangeism?

Senior officers often stress the Qualifications of an Orangeman as the fundamental principles of the Institution, but these Qualifications expose, by their specific statements, the multiple contradictions tolerated in current practice. These contradictions are found not only in the rank and file but in the leadership team of Grand Lodge. If the Qualifications indeed are the expression of its core values, then the Orange Institution has drifted badly from its moorings.

As pointed out in the Institution's leaflet *What is the Orange Order?*, the Qualifications stress a love for God – 'A sincere love and veneration for his Heavenly Father . . . He should never take the name of God in vain.' In practice this is perhaps one of the most widely abused statements of the Qualifications. Sadly God's name is all too frequently abused. Such behaviour is not just contrary to the Qualifications; it is to act contrary to the mindset of the Ulster Scots as the people of the Word. Dr John Dunlop pointed out in his book *A Precarious Belonging*, 'The name of God is held in reverence. A Presbyterian will be reluctant to use the name of God in a loose or familiar way. Seldom will you hear a Presbyterian say "God bless." God's name is not used as a method of saying farewell.'

Faith in Christ is listed in the Qualifications: 'steadfast faith in Jesus Christ, the Saviour of mankind'. This is an expression of the Institution's commitment to the Reformed faith. *Sola Fide* (Faith alone) and *Solo Christo* (Christ alone) were the cries of the sixteenth-century Reformers. Yet it would appear that many within the Orange Institution have fallen into the trap of the medieval church. They have placed the Orange Order as a substitute for or addition to Christ in terms of personal loyalty and obedience. By the Institution's own declaration of allegiance to the Reformed Faith, the Church should come first! The authority of Scripture alone – *Sola Scriptura* – is held to be supreme, as opposed to the Roman Catholic 'joint authority' of Scripture and tradition. The Qualifications prescribe that an Orangeman 'should honour and diligently study the Holy Scriptures and make them the rule of his faith and practice'. This sounds very hollow when individuals are confronted with the truth and relevance of the Word. It is the working out of this Reformed principle of 'Scripture alone' which has in recent years exposed the Institution collectively and privately to the greatest criticism.

Within the ritual of the Institution, the Holy Bible is referred to as that which 'contains the precepts on which our Order is founded . . . whereby all men, particularly Orangemen, should govern and regulate their conduct and actions through life'. The ambivalent attitude to Scripture seen in recent years in the failure of the leadership to apply these principles to issues both external and internal makes these affirmations a sham. Not only have the Scriptures been disregarded, but also the clear instruction of the Qualifications to 'make them the rule of his faith and *practice*' (italics mine). For example, the Qualifications state that an Orangeman 'should remember to keep holy the Sabbath day, and attend the public worship of God'. While this was never interpreted as a strict sabbatarianism, participation in Sunday sport is an offence under Law 18: 'Members are required to honour the Lord's Day. It shall be deemed an offence for any member to take part in organised games, sports, entertainments and dances on a Sunday.' But a blind eye has often been turned to breaches of this law.

Expanding on the spirit of the Qualifications, an information leaflet produced by the Institution explains: 'The brotherly bond which unites the members is based on a spirit of tolerance, tolerance toward those within the brotherhood with whom there may be differences of emphasis and towards those outside the brotherhood who differ from us in religious persuasion.' Sadly, the 'brotherly bond', which was once strong within the organisation is fast disappearing. This has become particularly evident since the Referendum on the Belfast Agreement on 21 May 1998. Members who were in the Yes camp have been given the special 'cold shoulder' treatment or been victims of a whispering campaign.

While Orangeism claims to be an international organisation, not all the other national jurisdictions embrace the same Qualifications. The Orange Institutions in both England and Scotland would appear to have taken the lead from Ireland. The English Qualifications of 1815 are identical to the 1798 version adopted in Ireland. Their present Qualifications, like those in Ireland, reflect the Order's opposition to the Church of Rome, as do the present Qualifications of the Institution in Scotland.

Orangeism in Canada developed under the influential and energetic leadership of Wexford man Ogle Robert Gowan, who emigrated there in 1829. The Canadian Institution's' 'Purpose Statement' and 'Mission Statement', as given on their website, make no reference to Roman Catholics, either as a church or as individuals, and do not display anything which could be misinterpreted as anti-Catholic. Canadian

Orangemen have also abandoned their Law about members marrying Roman Catholics, a Law which did not come into Irish Orangeism until 1863.

In the United States there has been a similar approach, as described by an American delegate quoted by Ruth Dudley Edwards in *The Faithful Tribe*:

> Over the past number of years . . . we've changed a number of things that were in our constitution, in our rules and regulations. Basically we've gone to a pro-Protestant stand and taken out all the anti kind of stuff that has been there for years. We have a multi-religious country so we're not faced with the Catholic–Protestant problem.

This is reflected in the Qualifications of US Orangeism.

North American Orangeism, it could be argued, is a more accurate reflection of original Irish Orangeism than its Irish counterpart, as it has distanced itself from the conflict of Irish politics. It is the Irish Orangeman's North American cousins who, by their broad and inclusive nature, are creating an 'acceptable face of Orangeism', and, as Ruth Dudley Edwards suggests, it is the Irish who are caught in the time warp.

As we have seen, following the Battle of the Diamond on 21 September 1795 Orange lodges spread across Ireland, into Scotland and then further afield. The Institution was always particularly strong in the county of its foundation, Armagh. So rapid was its growth that an all-Ireland structure was established in Dublin only three years later. The support which the various lodges had given to the government in suppressing the United Irishmen in their rebellion of 1798 was recognised, and the Orangemen of the day had a renewed confidence. Lodge meetings were no longer conducted in isolated areas for fear of being discovered by crown forces.

The moving of the Grand Lodge to Dublin from Armagh may not have pleased those of the premier county, but Dublin was the capital and the seat of government until the Act of Union closed the Irish parliament and united it with Westminster. In the words of Colonel Robert Hugh Wallace, Grand Secretary of the Grand Orange Lodge of Ireland from 1903 to 1910:

> The removal of the Grand Lodge to Dublin was not intended to disparage the valuable services rendered to Orangeism by the Dyan and Loughgall. It was a purely strategic movement dictated by

> circumstances, the city being then the metropolis of an independent kingdom, the seat of legislative and executive power. Unfortunately, it was also a hotbed of conspiracy, which Orangeism was competent to check. Besides, the Orange system found favour with the nobility and gentry, who spent much of their time in their town residences.[2]

Dublin was therefore the natural headquarters for the Orange Institution and remained such until the Headquarters building, the Fowler Memorial Hall, was seized by the IRA and severely damaged in the Civil War between the Treaty and anti-Treaty forces in 1922. Following its evacuation by the IRA all the books and documents which had survived the siege were removed to Belfast.

Some people have suggested that in the early days of the Institution only members of the Church of Ireland were permitted to be members. While no evidence can be found for such a statement – the idea may have had its origin in forged rules which were circulated in 1798[3] – it is easy to understand the sentiments expressed. Though Wolfe Tone and other leaders of the rebel cause were undoubtedly Episcopalian in their church background, many Presbyterians, particularly in the North, had been supporters of the radical thinking of the Society of United Irishmen and had taken part in the 1798 Rebellion. This no doubt led to difficulties in the relationships between some members of the Church of Ireland and the Presbyterian Church. However, it should be remembered that Presbyterians were also subject to some Penal Laws at this time. Though these laws were not applied as stringently as those against Roman Catholics, Presbyterian marriages were not officially recognised until the middle of the nineteenth century and the arrogance of a small minority of Church of Ireland rectors protracted a sense of injustice for several decades after that. However, as Colonel Wallace points out:

> The founders of the Orange Boys Society were all, or nearly all, Presbyterians, and they joined the Orange Men's Society after the Battle of the Diamond. Wilson, Master of Number One of the Dyan, was a Presbyterian, and the members of the Presbyterian Church took well to the Institution. Many Methodists, at that time attendants at the services in the Established Church and the Presbyterian Church, were Orangemen. The Quakers were not excluded by any Rule of the Society. They excluded themselves. In later days, some of the most worthy Orangemen were members of the Society of Friends.[4]

Ian McBride, in *Scripture Politics: Ulster Presbyterians and Irish Radicalism in the late Eighteenth Century*, makes reference to one Presbyterian minister who associated himself with the new fledging Orange Association:

> The correlation between evangelical commitment and loyalism is further strengthened by the fact that one of the three ministers of the Synod who joined the ESU (Evangelical Society of Ulster, formed in 1798), Thomas McKay of Brigh, County Tyrone, was the only minister of the Synod to publicly associate himself with the Orange Order at this period.[5]

Relationships between the Church of Ireland and Dissenters were not helped by the remarks of the Church of Ireland Archbishop of Dublin, William Magee, as he inaugurated the 'Second Reformation' in St Patrick's Cathedral on 24 October 1822: 'We, my reverend brethren, are placed in a station in which we are hemmed in by two opposite descriptions of professing Christians; the one, possessing a Church, without what we can properly call a religion; and the other, possessing a Religion, without what we can properly call a Church.'

One can well understand how long memories are in small communities like Ireland. Aiken McClelland, in *William Johnston of Ballykilbeg*, refers to Johnston's father-in-law, the popular Belfast Orangeman and Church of Ireland clergyman the Rev. Thomas Drew, who died in 1870, as 'typical of one school of thought which opposed the admittance of Dissenters into the Orange Order'. 'Dissenters', in the language of the nineteenth century, were those who did not belong to the established Church of Ireland. The two most notable groups of 'Dissenters' were the Presbyterians and the Methodists. The attitude of Dr Drew towards Presbyterians, if true, is difficult to understand in the light of the fact that support for the Church of Ireland, as an Established Church, came from many Presbyterians, two of the most notable being the great Unionist and Evangelical churchman the Rev. Dr Henry Cooke, acknowledged leader of Irish Presbyterianism for half a century, and the Rev. Hugh Hanna. The Rev. Hanna was an active and outspoken Orangeman, but Dr Cooke never joined the Institution. The ailing Cooke had attended and addressed the famous Hillsborough Demonstration, held in opposition to the disestablishment of the Church of Ireland in October 1867.

The Orange Institution has always been a very conservative body. Conservatism by its nature seeks to preserve the status quo, and saying no comes naturally to Ulster Protestants. This conservatism was displayed in three ways in the nineteenth century. The first, and most serious, was the strong opposition to the extension of the franchise to Roman Catholics, not because of any purely religiously sectarian motive but as a question of loyalty: could the Roman Catholic population of Ireland be trusted in the light of their loyalty to their church, and therefore to Rome? The issue was hotly contested throughout the United Kingdom as it also applied to the voting franchise for the Westminster parliament. This might appear a little strange in a day and age when religious convictions matter so little, even to those in high office in the land, but in the mid-nineteenth century it was a burning issue. As the twenty-first century opens, one of the last remaining positions in the kingdom which excludes Roman Catholics is the monarchy. Even this exclusion is under review, but it is so far causing much less debate than Catholic emancipation did 150 years previously.

The genuine fear, in the mid-nineteenth century, was that Roman Catholics would return Roman Catholic members to parliament, who would unbalance the question of the constitutional settlement. The Orangemen of Dublin took this matter seriously, as is evidenced by a 'Bottle Riot' at the Theatre Royal in Dublin on 14 December 1822, when Orangemen threw a bottle at the Lord Lieutenant, Richard Wellesley, because he had expressed support for Catholic emancipation. They also hotly opposed Daniel O'Connell's formation of the Catholic Association in the following year.

Secondly, the Orange Institution, in the middle of the nineteenth century, came out in opposition to the disestablishment of the Church of Ireland, which it saw as a bulwark of Protestantism against the encroachments of Rome. The disendowment of Church lands, some £7 million being confiscated by the government, which accompanied the disestablishment was also seen as a threat to 'Protestant' lands. There was also the fear, expressed both in resolutions of the Grand Orange Lodge of Ireland and in addresses to parliament, that this would have some effect on the question of legislative union, notwithstanding that fifty years previously at least half of the membership of the Institution had opposed the Act of Union.

Thirdly, the Institution opposed the introduction of the secret ballot. Secret voting was anathema to Orangemen, who assumed that Roman Catholics would vote according to the instruction of their parish priests unless overseen by their landlords. William Johnston of Ballykilbeg caused consternation within the Orange Institution when he announced that he intended to support a bill to introduce a secret ballot.

Considering that Catholic emancipation was passed in 1829, the Irish Church Act was passed in 1869 and the Secret Ballot Act was introduced in 1872, the Orange Order did not have a very successful track record of opposition to things it perceived as 'liberal' in the nineteenth century. It has always seen itself as fighting a rearguard action and giving in to as little as possible. It has enshrined within its ritual the statement: 'Meddle not with them that are given to change' (Proverbs 24:21). Change is inevitable, but whether any change is a legitimate development or not depends on its nature. If it is evolutionary rather than revolutionary it will comply with its own fundamental substance.

Changes in attitude within society have taken their toll within the Institution. Leadership in the early days came largely from the aristocracy. Examining the list of Grand Masters of the Grand Orange Lodge of Ireland we can count one duke, four earls, one knight and two baronets among the holders of that office, over a period of two hundred years. Since then there has been as clear a shift in terms of leadership within the Institution as there has been within society at large. We no longer live in a society where the doctor, the schoolmaster and the clergyman are the only educated people in a rural community and are thus the 'natural' leaders. The Order has correspondingly shifted from being led by the aristocratic and the business classes to being driven by the populace, becoming much more of a working-class movement. There are a variety of reasons for this, but one consequence became tragic at the turn of the twentieth and twenty-first centuries. Individuals coming up through the structures of the Institution lacked the ability to lead, though they sometimes had the gift of speech in the style which Shakespeare described as 'full of sound and fury signifying nothing'. There was a tendency to appoint such individuals to office at district and county level, with the inevitable resultant rise to Grand Lodge level, simply because they could speak. Little consideration was given to whether they could think through what they actually said. The quiet sensible Orangeman was therefore even more reluctant to take office in the Institution. The local Orange lodge is still a focal point for the community in rural Ulster, but even there some of the discernment exercised in the selection of members in previous years has gone.

The Institution is no longer the thing to join if you want to get on in society. In the closing years of the nineteenth century, when there were over twenty lodges in Dublin, many were made up of the professional classes. Solicitors were more than willing to advertise their membership, because it was perceived to be a way of promotion within the judiciary.

Today in Belfast many business people no longer belong to, and in many cases have no sympathy for, the Orange Order, largely because of the confrontational image which the Institution has projected. Business and professional people are reluctant to be identified with an Institution which is perceived in the public mind as an organisation dedicated to 'walking where they are not wanted'.

This movement of the class structure within the Institution has produced an inverted snobbery, or what sociologists would call 'status envy'. When Robert Saulters was appointed Grand Master in December 1996, a well-known officer of Derriaghy District damned him right away as 'a millionaire from the Malone Road' – a prosperous area in south Belfast. William Sibbett, who resigned from LOL 148 of the Institution in March 2001, once said, 'In my opinion if you can read a book you are not wanted.'

Another aspect of status envy is shown by the anticlericalism evident in some areas within the Institution. While in many areas there is a warm welcome for members who are ministers in the main churches, elsewhere there is a scarcely disguised distrust of 'the clergy' and an unwillingness to listen to their advice. This anticlericalism is really anti-intellectualism in disguise, and has been one of the most destructive elements within the Orange Institution in recent years. It is seen most notably in the failure to get the Institution off the hook over the Drumcree debacle. A Church of Scotland minister commented to an Orange chaplain in January 2000, 'Northern Ireland must be the only place in the world where "smart" is regarded as a derogatory term.'

Had the leadership of the Institution sought out and encouraged those of ability, its subsequent history could have been very different. The Rev. John R. W. Stott made the point, speaking at the Inter-Varsity Fellowship's annual public meeting on 'Evangelism in the Student World' in September 1959. He said, 'The majority of the world's leaders in politics, education, medicine, the law and the church are university graduates. Today's leaders are yesterday's students; today's students will be tomorrow's leaders.'

Another clear shift within the Institution in the twentieth century has been the Northern Ireland dominance of the membership. While this has been the direct result of the depletion of Protestants in the Republic of Ireland since Partition, it has also led directly to a 'separatist' attitude. The Institution is perceived, even by its membership, to be an Ulster organisation as opposed to an all-Ireland body. Instead of the Institution being an inclusive and all-embracing organisation of Protestants, as was the intention of the founding fathers, it is becoming a restricted organisation characterised not so much by 'tunnel vision' as by an increasingly narrow 'funnel vision'.

There would be little sympathy today for the strong opinions expressed by the first Grand Secretary of the Grand Orange Lodge of Ireland, John Claudius Beresford. Speaking against the proposed Act of Union at a meeting in Dublin on 10 January 1799, he declared, 'Proud of the name of an Irishman, I hope never to exchange it for that of a Colonist.'[6] Even at the turn of the twentieth century, in the midst of the Home Rule question, there was a much broader vision within both Unionism and the Orange Institution. Partition has had the result of making individuals and organisations more insular, entrenched and embittered. The Order has long since abandoned the broad vision of the acknowledged leader of Unionism, Edward Carson, who told the House of Commons on 29 April 1914:

> . . . if Home Rule is to pass, much as I detest it, and little as I will take any responsibility for the passing of it, my earnest hope, and indeed, I would say my most earnest prayer, would be that the Government of Ireland for the South and West would prove, and might prove, such a success in the future, notwithstanding all our anticipations, that it might be even in the interests of Ulster itself to move towards that Government, and come in under it and form one unit in relation to Ireland.[7]

The last piece of advice which Carson gave to the Ulster Unionist Council, as he relinquished his leadership on 4 February 1921, was this:

> We used to say that we could not trust an Irish Parliament in Dublin to do justice to the Protestant minority. Let us take care that that reproach can no longer be made against your Parliament, and from the outset let them see that the Catholic minority have nothing to fear from a Protestant majority . . . Let us show them that while we were always determined to maintain intact our own religion and all that it means to us, we consider that they have a right to expect that all that is sacred to them in their religion will receive the same toleration. When we are represented as bigots, intolerant towards those that differ from us in religion, I believe it to be false. What has driven us asunder is not the religion itself, but the fact that the majority of those who differ from us in religion would not accept loyalty to the King and Constitution [applause] and if they had, I believe there never need have been the

> acute differences between us at all. And so I say from the start be tolerant to all religions, and while maintaining to the last your own traditions and your own citizenship, take care that similar rights are preserved for those who differ from us.[8]

Had those who regarded themselves as 'loyalists' in the winter of 1996–7 remembered those words, nothing so shameful as the Harryville Church protest would even have been contemplated, not to speak of the wholesale burning of Roman Catholic houses of worship in July 1998.

Edward Marjoribanks, in his life of Edward Carson,[9] says that he was 'initiated as an Orangeman at the age of nineteen', but there is no evidence to substantiate this, and more recent biographies make no reference to Carson's membership of the Institution. Carson addressed many Orange gatherings, at which he was referred to as 'Brother', but there are no known photographs of him wearing Orange regalia. In fact one famous photograph reproduced in *The Twelfth 2001*, a publication of the County Grand Lodge of Belfast, shows him speaking to Colonel R. H. Wallace, then Grand Master of the Grand Orange Lodge of Belfast. Wallace is wearing an Orange collarette but Carson is not.

In contrast to Carson's vision, which was influential in the Order of the 1930s even if he himself was not a member, very many Orangemen today claim allegiance to breakaway Protestant sects, of which some maintain a narrow exclusiveness in their own truth and others have little or no connection to any church. Even as late as 1951 the Grand Lodge indicated its commitment to the main churches by listing those it recognised for the purpose of appointing chaplains. On 9 December 1998 this resolution was rescinded, in a clear demonstration of the shift in the direction of the Institution and a further indication of the 'funnelling' of attitudes. There is today a narrowness of theological perspective not evident either in the nineteenth century or the early years of the twentieth.

Further evidence of 'funnel vision' is seen in the equating of Orangeism exclusively with the Ulster Scots heritage. In the March 1999 edition of the *Orange Standard*, the Executive Officer, George Patton, was quoted as saying with reference to the Orange Festival at the Waterfront Hall: 'This is an extremely important moment in our history and we must stand proudly together in our Orange and Ulster Scots heritage.' What of our Anglo-Irish heritage? On page 10 of the same edition of the *Orange Standard* R. G. McDowell writes that: 'The United Irishmen got their name as they were supposed to be an alliance between the Irish, the Scots-Irish and some radical element of the now extinct

Anglo-Irish.' Even given the Ulster dominance within the Institution in the twenty-first century, it should be remembered that the Plantation stock of Ulster was made up of both Ulster Scots Presbyterians and English Episcopalians. The Anglican Church of Ireland influence appears to have been forgotten by some, even though Drumcree parish is the annual focus of conflict in the present sectarian climate.

The confusion has been further compounded lately by the equation of the erection of Orange Arches with the Ulster Scots tradition, and the danger of narrowness and sectarianism grows even greater as elements within the Ulster Scots tradition seek to elevate the Ulster Scots dialect to the status of a language. An even more radical element of the tradition finds itself sitting comfortably with the British Israelite Movement.

The present situation of falling numbers and political confrontation is not simply a product of the years since the signing of the Anglo-Irish Agreement in 1985. A senior clerical chaplain told me on 24 May 1999: 'We are reaping a harvest of many years. The growth was not tended and we are now reaping a harvest of weeds.' As the Institution entered the new millennium it had just over forty thousand members. There are now probably more former members who have resigned than actual practising members.

The Rev. Dr John Lockington, Moderator of the General Assembly of the Presbyterian Church in Ireland (1999–2000) and an Orangeman then of forty-six years' membership, confessed his preference for holidaying in recent years rather than walking on the Twelfth – the celebration held annually on 12 July to commemorate the Battle of the Boyne.[10] In the *Irish News* on 12 July 1999, he wrote: 'As time has gone on so things have changed . . . The Twelfth is different too. The political and sadly sometimes violent overtones are not what I remember or want. Has a family day out gone for ever? I hope not.'

This general malaise, combined with the reluctance of many able individuals to ally themselves with the Orange cause, has had an overall impact on the leadership of the Institution. In the very early days of the Institution wise and clear-headed thinking was evident. During the controversy within the Institution concerning the proposed union of parliaments after the suppression of the 1798 Rebellion, salvation came from the wise advice of the Grand Orange Lodge of Ireland, who counselled the brethren:

> strictly to abstain from expressing any opinion pro or con upon the question of a Legislative Union between this country and Great Britain,

> because that such expression of opinion, and such discussion in Lodges could only lead to disunion; that disunion might lead to disruption; and the disruption of the Society in the existing crisis would but promote the designs of the disaffected, and, in all human probability, lead to the dismemberment of the Empire.[11]

R. M. Sibbett comments, in *Orangeism in Ireland*:

> At the same time, the brethren were informed that, as citizens of a free state, they were at liberty to act as they pleased in regard to the question. Again on 5th January, 1799, another meeting of Grand Lodge was held, and the Address issued after alluding to the happy effects attending their former advice, and from the evils likely to result from the discussion of the question of such magnitude as that of the proposed Union, proceeded: 'It is, therefore, recommended to all Orangemen to keep in mind the great object for which they have associated, and to avoid, as injurious to the Institution, all controversy not connected with their principles.'[12]

Judging by the opposition of the Orange members of parliament for Dublin in the Irish House of Commons, we might well conclude that the majority of Orange opinion was against the union of the two parliaments, and saw the proposed measure as injurious to Protestantism. One hundred years later it was the leadership of the Orange Institution who saw a Home Rule parliament for Ireland as injurious to Protestantism.

The impact of the Institution in society at large, historically, has been enormous. It has encouraged many from a variety of walks of life to play their full part in the communities in which they lived and, in two world wars, to serve the nation in the forces of the Crown. The Institution acted as a cohesive unifying force within the Protestant community, because it was seen to be inclusive. It gave a sense of personal identity and community, particularly throughout the traditional parading season. In the early days of 'the troubles' which have plagued Ireland and Great Britain since 1969, many young men were kept from involvement in serious inter-community strife through the wise counsels of their elders within the Institution, though sadly some did not listen or take the advice offered to them.

Of course there have always been those who use organisations to serve their own particular agendas, and the Orange Institution has not been exempt from this. It has been used, and even abused, by politicians to suit their own particular ends. It could be argued that even Colonel Edward Saunderson, whose statue graces the centre of Portadown, used the Institution for his own ends, for he was 'no friend of the Institution' until his politics determined otherwise. In 1870, in the House of Commons, speaking *in favour* of the Party Processions (Ireland) Bill, Saunderson attacked the Orange Order:

> Upon the general question he might say that, as far as he himself was individually concerned, he regretted these party processions and exhibitions, and had invariably tried to put them down, and nothing more offended him that to see the house of God made a flagship for a party emblem.[13]

After being defeated by a Home Rule candidate in 1874, Saunderson joined the Order he had previously disowned in 1882.

The confrontations over parades, especially in the 1990s, have created a negative public image. Clear warnings of this have been delivered to the leadership, including one from a most significant source. In a private letter to the Grand Master, Robert Saulters, on 18 February 1997, Sean O'Callaghan, a former member of the IRA, warned that the Orange Order was being led into the Provisionals' trap: 'More importantly it is their [the Provisional IRA's] objective to force the Orange Order into conflict with the RUC, the British army and therefore the government and majority of public opinion in the rest of the United Kingdom.' Regrettably, this has all come to fulfilment.

The spirit of confrontation of recent years has effectively worked against the affirmation of Unionist principles espoused by the majority of the population in Northern Ireland. In the first place, the tension over parades has made traditional supporters first ambivalent and then agnostic. It has in effect been self-defeating. As the Irish journalist Eoghan Harris wrote in the spring of 2000: 'I have reluctantly come to the conclusion that the current leadership of the Orange Order is now an obstacle to everything that is decent in Unionism.'

Chapter Two

Religion or Politics?

> *'Like some other Protestant institutions many of our Orange Lodges have lost their pristine spiritual power. Without the Spirit, the reading of the Scriptures and the saying of prayers can be lifeless formalities.'*
>
> Jock Purves[1]

One of the most relevant and important questions concerning the Orange Order, over the two hundred years of its existence, is that of its relationship to politics. Is the Orange Institution a religious organisation with a political element or a political organisation with a religious element?

The formal structure of the Orange Society which arose following the Battle of the Diamond revealed the objectives of this new Protestant group. The primary emphasis was on the Protestant religion; 'King and Constitution' followed. The original Qualifications of 1798 highlight the positive Protestant aspects of the Christian faith before progressing to the need to promote 'the honour of . . . King and country'. This connection between religion and politics, in the broad sense, must be understood within the context of eighteenth-century Ireland. For Irish Protestants it was the British throne and constitution which enshrined the Protestant religion as an article of the state and therefore, in the hostile environment of an overwhelmingly Roman Catholic Ireland, offered them protection.

In the pamphlet *Orangeism: Its Religious Origins, Its Scriptural Basis, Its Protestant Principles*, the Rev. Dr Fred. C. Gibson, Superintendent of the Irish Mission of the Presbyterian Church in Ireland, wrote:

> While the Orange Order, generally, has been closely associated with the political party which has been loyal to the Protestant Succession to the Throne, and the maintaining of the union between Great Britain and Ireland, nevertheless there is something more fundamental in the order than this, and that is the adherence to the principles of Protestantism.

Two early episodes establish the credibility of the Orange Order as fundamentally a religious organisation. In November 1798 the Grand Orange Lodge of Ireland took out an advertisement in *Sanders' Evening Post*, the *Hibernian Journal* and the *Freeman's Journal* to refute a pamphlet which had purported to contain 'Orange Songs' while 'really containing expressions directly opposite to the fundamental principles of the Orange Institution'. The advertisement reproduced the Order's '5th General Rule', 'That no person do persecute or upbraid any one on account of his religious opinion, but that we will on the contrary be aiding and assisting to every loyal subject of every religious description,' and made it known that 'a song to the tune of "Croppies lie down" in said publication, the chorus of which is changed to "Papists lie down", meets with our strongest disapprobation being directly contrary to our principles as reflecting on a part of our fellow subjects for their religious persuasion'. If the same resolute action had been taken against the 'Spirit of Drumcree' faction, the slide into disorder and chaos of recent years could have been avoided. The resolution of the Grand Lodge leadership in these early days is all the more commendable given that this took place a few months after the failed 1798 Rebellion, when tension was high and feelings were strong.

A second example is the question of the prohibition of marriages to Roman Catholics. In the early years of the Institution it was not an offence for a member to marry a Roman Catholic. Neither was it considered to be an offence for someone having been married to a Roman Catholic to apply for membership of the Orange Order, as in the case of Dr Patrick Duigenan (1735–1816), who was born to Roman Catholic parents but converted to Protestantism, entered Trinity College, Dublin, and went on to have a distinguished career in law and politics. Duigenan's marriage to a practising Roman Catholic neither reduced his commitment to Orange principles nor decreased his prominence within the Orange Institution of his day. He was the second Grand Secretary of the Grand Orange Lodge of Ireland, elected in succession to John Claudius Beresford in 1801.

The early Rule Books of the Orange Institution make no prohibition of marrying a Roman Catholic. Records reveal that in the period 1853 to 1860 members were expelled for 'marrying a Papist', but not under a specific rule to that effect. They were expelled under the catch-all rule of 'behaviour unbecoming of an Orangeman'. The rule prohibiting members marrying Roman Catholics first appears in Irish Orangeism in 1863. It still forms part of the Constitution, Laws and Ordinances of the Loyal

Orange Institution of Ireland (1998), but is not always enforced. In Canadian Orangeism, this rule has been removed. Grand Master Robert Saulters was probably unaware of the existence of Patrick Duigenan when in 1996 he accused Tony Blair, then leader of the Labour Party in opposition, of betraying his faith by marrying a Roman Catholic.

The first direct foray into politics by the Institution was in relation to the Act of Union. The politics of the day are reflected in the personalities of the first two Grand Masters of the Grand Orange Lodge of Ireland. Thomas Verner (1774–1853) was Grand Master of the counties of Tyrone, Londonderry and Fermanagh, and was elected as first Grand Master of Ireland in 1798, retaining the position until 1801. He is remembered for his contribution to the foundation, development and growth of the Orange Institution. After the formation of the Institution in 1795, he founded an Orange lodge (LOL 162) on the family estate of Churchill, County Armagh, in 1796; his brother David was the first Worshipful Master. He also founded the first Orange lodge in the city of Dublin (LOL 176) on 4 June 1797. The membership of LOL 176, which totalled over three hundred, included some of the most distinguished men in Ireland at that time.

Verner supported the Act of Union, which united the Irish and British parliaments and created the Union flag consisting of the cross of St George and the saltires of St Andrew and St Patrick. Through his wise political skill and leadership he prevented the differences of opinion over the Act of Union from becoming a cause of division within the Institution. In this both he and the Grand Lodge were supported by Killylea District in County Armagh, who declared: 'That we highly approve of the opinions set forth in the Publications issued by the Grand Orange Lodge, advising all Orange Men to abstain from discussion of Politics in their Lodges.'[2]

George Ogle (1742–1814) became the next Grand Master of the Grand Orange Lodge of Ireland in factious circumstances. Three Dublin lodges, who held influence and power because of their numerical and political strength, protested against the Grand Lodge injunction forbidding discussion of the Act of Union. They demanded that a Grand Lodge be elected which would 'support the independence of Ireland and the Constitution of 1782', stating that 'as Orangemen we consider the extinction of our separate legislature as the extinction of the Irish nation'. (Of course for them, the 'nation' only consisted of those whom they regarded as 'loyal Protestants', an attitude not entirely unknown even in the twenty-first century.) LOL 253 from County Armagh joined them in these demands. Opposing Verner, they suggested George Ogle as Grand Master because of his 'uniform support of the interests and independence of Ireland'.[3] On 12 July 1801 Ogle was elected Grand Master by fourteen votes to twelve. He held the position until his death on 10 August 1814.

George Ogle was something of an Irish patriot. He had been elected to the Irish parliament in 1768 as a member from County Wexford, where he strenuously supported the legislative independence of the Irish parliament, eventually achieved in 1782. When the Irish parliament raised the Yeomanry in 1796 as auxiliaries to the regular army, in the face of a threatened invasion by the French, Ogle, according to his godson Ogle Robert Gowan, 'raised and equipped solely at his own expense a Yeomanry Corps, called Ogle's Blues'. After the Act of Union he went on to represent the city of Dublin in the Westminster parliament.

The political positions of Thomas Verner and George Ogle could not have been more different for the times in which they lived. Verner was a pro-Unionist and Ogle an anti-Unionist (Home Ruler), though both were pro-British.

Though the Orange Institution over its two hundred years of existence has remained loyal and supportive of 'King and Constitution', the same cannot always be said for its relationship to 'His Majesty's Loyal Government'. There has always been something of a suspicious relationship between the Institution and various governments, but it has remained wedded to the Union since 1800, albeit with various periods of distrust such as in 1871 over the issue of the disestablishment of the Church of Ireland. As the Church of Ireland was established within the terms of the Act of Union, the Institution argued that a disestablishment of the Church would weaken the Union. When the Irish Church Act was passed on 26 July 1869 (to be effective from 1 January 1871), such was the sense of betrayal that one prominent member of the Institution at that time, J. H. Nunn, a resident magistrate and Deputy Grand Master of Dublin Orangemen, proposed at the meeting of Grand Lodge on 27 December 1871 that the members of the Order should no longer be obligated to maintain the Union. Though his proposal failed and he subsequently resigned from the Institution, he may have been something of a visionary, a man before his time.

This sense of betrayal was to be repeated in succeeding years as various Home Rule bills were presented to the Westminster parliament, culminating in the compromise of Partition. During these years the Orange Institution became even more wedded to the 1801 Act of Union, which some of their predecessors had bitterly opposed. This was not purely because of political ambition but rather because of a genuine fear that 'Home Rule means Rome Rule', and that the Protestants of Ireland would fare poorly in a Roman Catholic-dominated state. John F. Harbinson therefore rightly maintains, 'The emergence of Orangeism as a political force in 1885 is the second factor which contributed to a coherent Unionist movement.'[4] More recent analysts put it succinctly: 'The Orange Order took on a distinctively Unionist flavour when Home Rule threatened in the 1880s. The effective beginning of the Ulster Unionist Party was a meeting of seven Orangemen, elected as MPs at Westminster in 1886.'[5]

At the turn of the twentieth century the Protestants of Ireland were not putting their politics before their religion, but seeking the maintenance of the freedom of their religion through politics. The Covenanting forefathers of the Ulster Presbyterians had taken a similar stand in the seventeenth century, and those with knowledge of the Old Testament Children of Israel knew that there was a connection between religion and politics.

In the early years of the twentieth century this blend of religion and politics was joined by the added dimension of social prejudice. One of the most consequential events in the history of the Institution took place on 12 July 1902 at the Twelfth demonstration of the County Grand Lodge of Belfast at Castlereagh. It led to the foundation of the Independent Loyal Orange Institution on 11 June 1903. The Belfast Protestant Association, described by Kevin Haddick-Flynn as 'a politico-religious organisation whose brand of muscular Christianity soon became notorious',[6] arose out of Sunday afternoon preaching at 'The Steps', the equivalent of London's Speakers' Corner established on the steps of Belfast's Custom House.

Thomas H. Sloan, a Belfast Orangeman and 'semi-skilled shipyard worker with a talent for public speaking',[7] had taken over the leadership of the Belfast Protestant Association while Arthur Trew and Richard Braithwaite served prison sentences for attacking a Corpus Christi procession. The Rev. Dr Warren Porter, in a paper delivered to the Loyal Orange Lodge of Research on 28 October 1995, commented that Sloan 'had also other talents and a gift for persistent heckling was among them, not greatly circumscribed by any strict regard for factual accuracy'.

At the Castlereagh demonstration Sloan led a group of hecklers against the Belfast County Grand Master, Colonel Edward Saunderson, MP for North Armagh. Saunderson's 'crime' was that he had voted for the exclusion of convent laundries from the Factory And Workshops

Amendment and Consultation Bill (1901). No evidence was ever presented to support the allegation, and in fact the record of the debate in the House of Commons for 13 August 1901 reveals that Saunderson 'ventured to say that the great majority of hon. Members, whether on this side or the opposite side, would agree with him that all institutions of this kind ought to be inspected'.[8] Saunderson went on to vote in favour of the amendment, which was defeated, along with six other Protestant members including William Johnston of Ballykilbeg. Edward Carson, however, is listed as having voted with the Noes!

The accusation launched against Saunderson was therefore entirely without foundation, but it served a political purpose. However, even if Saunderson had voted against, as Carson had, that would have been a very weak reason to cause a split within the Orange Institution. The denial of the right of an elected member of parliament in a representative democracy to exercise his vote as he saw fit was a denial of the civil and religious liberty often affirmed by the Orange Institution.

George Dawson, the Imperial Grand Master of the Independent Orange Order, acknowledged in his Centenary Paper, delivered in Sandy Row Community Centre on 10 June 2003, that there was more to the split than a vote in the House of Commons. Class consciousness played an important element in the attitudes of the time. Saunderson was one of the last of the landed gentry and could trace his lineage back to the influx of settlers following the defeat of the rebellion led by the Earl of Tyrone in 1603. The Saunderson estates eventually covered some eleven thousand acres in counties Monaghan and Cavan. He was opposed by the working-class Belfast Protestant Association, who in their inverted snobbery despised those who 'had'. This attitude, like the denial of Saunderson's right to exercise his vote, was contrary to Orange principle. One of the noble claims of the Orange Order is that it embraces all social classes.

Thomas Sloan was charged under the law of the Institution and sentenced to two years' suspension, to be remitted if he apologised in writing to the Grand Orange Lodge of Belfast. He refused to apologise and appealed the sentence to the Grand Orange Lodge of Ireland. When this appeal failed at the Grand Lodge meeting in Armagh in June 1903, Sloan and others formed the Independent Orange Order.

R. M. Sibbett records in *Orangeism*: 'By a resolution of the Grand Orange Lodge of Ireland in 1903, all members of the Orange Order who had identified themselves in the past, or who should do so in the future, with the Independent Institution, were *ipso facto* expelled from the Loyal Orange Order.'[9] Sloan and those who joined him were therefore expelled from the main body of Orangeism. The Independents are not recognised within world Orangeism, although the resolution was rescinded by the Grand Lodge on 7 February 1968, on the proposal of the new County Grand Master of Antrim, the Rev. John Brown, supported by James Molyneaux.

In the midst of the Sloan affair, William Johnston of Ballykilbeg, MP for South Belfast, died on 17 July 1902. Sloan availed himself of the opportunity and was nominated by the Belfast Protestant Association to fight the seat as an Independent Conservative candidate. He subsequently defeated the official Unionist candidate nominated by the Belfast Conservative Association, Charles W. Dunbar-Buller, a fellow of All Souls College, Oxford, and the Master of a Belfast lodge. Although the Order in Belfast was evidently divided on the issue, the County Grand Lodge of Belfast supported Dunbar-Buller. Meanwhile, Kevin Haddick-Flynn comments, Sloan 'soon offended his plebeian supporters by wearing a fur-trimmed overcoat and smoking small cigars'.[10]

George Dawson omitted to mention in his Centenary Paper two significant elements in the early history of the Independent Institution. The first was the 'Magheramorne Manifesto', issued on 13 July 1905 in Magheramorne, County Antrim. The Manifesto, which has never been withdrawn, made reference to Unionism as a 'discredited creed' and stated that the Independent Orange Order stood 'once more on the banks of the Boyne, not as victors in the fight nor to applaud the noble deeds of our ancestors . . . but to . . . hold out the right hand of fellowship to those who, while worshipping at other shrines, are yet our countrymen – bone of our bone and flesh of our flesh'. These sentiments are at some distance from the behaviour of the Independent Institution as later observed by Kevin Haddick-Flynn: 'In 1996/97 its members participated in a picket on the Catholic Church at Harryville, Ballymena, when Orangemen sought to intimidate Mass-goers as part of a protest against Catholic opposition to Orange Parades.'[11]

The flirtation with Home Rule in the Magheramorne Manifesto and the bitterness of the resultant division had a lasting effect on the Protestant and Unionist cause. In spite of their avowed hostility to politicians, their opposition to Unionist Association candidates led to the defeat of William Moore in North Antrim and of Captain Smiley in West Belfast.

The second omission in Dawson's paper was any reference to Robert Lindsay Crawford, the Independents' Grand Master and the draughtsman of the Magheramorne Manifesto. He and other officers who had signed the Manifesto stuck to their principles when Thomas Sloan attempted to distance himself from it, claiming that it was misunderstood. The rank and file of the Order refused to go along with Sloan, as they began to see that the contents of the Manifesto were indistinguishable from the Home Rule policy being advocated by nationalists. In 1908 Lindsay Crawford was expelled from the Independent Orange Order. He went to New York where he became a trade representative of the Irish Free State.

While the Independent Orange Order regarded political interference in the old Order as detrimental to the principles of Orangeism, the Independents today are the more political of the two Orders. This is borne out by the presence of Ian R. K. Paisley on their Demonstration platform making political speeches every Twelfth, and the nomination of their Imperial Grand Master, George Dawson, as a DUP candidate in 2003. The Independent demonstration in Ballymoney in 1904 was estimated to have attracted ten thousand; the membership presently stands at about one thousand.

Sectional interest, separation, and sectarianism stand in opposition to authentic Orangeism. Authentic Orangeism is broad and inclusive of all the Protestant churches. In Ireland it embraces the membership of all the Protestant Denominations including the Non-Subscribing Presbyterian Church. It is not Trinitarian in outlook and may include those of a Unitarian theological perspective, though in Scotland Unitarians are excluded from membership.

While the religious aspects of Orangeism prevailed up to the mid-twentieth century, with minutes of Grand Lodge meetings revealing a preponderance of ministers of religion, this was also a period of marked connection between the Institution and the Unionist Party which had ruled Northern Ireland since the foundation of the state. Every prime minister of Northern Ireland during the period 1921–72 was an Orangeman, and John M. Andrews, for example, prime minister from 1940 to 1943, was Grand Master of the Grand Orange Lodge of Ireland from 1948 to 1955.

The relationship between the Orange Institution and the Ulster Unionist Party has not always been clearly understood. The Orange Order is, along with many other groups, an affiliated body of the Ulster Unionist Council. As a result of this affiliation seven of the eight County Grand Lodges in Northern Ireland (Belfast, Antrim, Armagh, Down, Fermanagh, County of Londonderry and Tyrone) have the right to send up to 122 delegates to the Ulster Unionist Council, according to the council's constitution. Delegates are elected annually from their various counties, and must be members in good standing in their Unionist Party branch.

As the new millennium dawned discussions continued, in the media if not within the Institution, concerning this relationship between the Orange Institution and the Ulster Unionist Council. The Orange Institution continued to take up their entitlement of 113 delegates to the council, distributed as follows: twelve from Armagh, twenty-four from Antrim, twenty-four from Belfast, twenty-two from Down, ten from Fermanagh, ten from Londonderry County and eleven from Tyrone. In 2002 all the counties took up their full entitlement of delegates, with the exception of Down who returned seventeen. If the Ulster Unionist Council had strictly adhered to its constitutional requirement to allot delegates 'on a county basis according to membership', the distribution would have looked very different. Given the numerical strength and distribution of membership within the Institution, as the Grand Orange Lodge of Ireland entered its third century, the distribution of the 113 delegates should have been twenty-six from Antrim, sixteen from Armagh, eleven from Belfast, twenty-two from Down, eight from Fermanagh, thirteen from Londonderry County and seventeen from Tyrone. The Central Committee of the Grand Orange Lodge of Ireland also continued to send twelve of those elected from their County Grand Lodges to the Executive Committee of the Ulster Unionist Party until 2005, when it severed all links with the Ulster Unionist Council.

For many years no check was made by the Ulster Unionist Council to ascertain if those delegated from the Orange Order were in fact branch members, and it has been rumoured that some of these delegates were not Party members. This is highly probable, as one incident within the County Antrim Grand Orange Lodge will illustrate. At the annual election of officers on 12 November 1997, when the Council delegates were being nominated, the presiding officer, the Rev. Dr Warren Porter, enquired if those nominated were members of a branch of the party. The response was that they were Orangemen and that was sufficient! Dr Porter pointed out that they must be branch members or they could not be nominated. Had he not challenged this, it would have passed without anyone being any wiser.

It seems incredible that there is no mechanism within the administration of the Ulster Unionist Party to ascertain the validity of delegates. A simple nomination form to be signed by the branch secretary would be a simple and effective security.

When on 5 February 1999 the County Antrim Grand Lodge passed a resolution calling for the Institution to disaffiliate from the Ulster Unionist Party, it was not the first time the county had been the source of such expressions. In 1969 Cloughfern District passed on a resolution to County Antrim Grand Lodge asking that the Institution should disaffiliate from the Ulster Unionist Council. This resolution got no further than the County Grand Lodge level, where it was marked 'read'. Significantly, thirty years later its sentiments were endorsed at County Grand Lodge level.

When the 1999 resolution from County Antrim was passed on to Grand Lodge to be dealt with at its next meeting on 27 March, it was not processed by way of a resolution and discussion. Instead the Grand Lodge was informed that 'The matter is currently being dealt with by a committee established by the Grand Master.' Had strict procedure been adhered to, the resolution would have been tabled for a vote from the Grand Lodge, and had strict adherence to the Constitution, Laws and Ordinances of the Grand Orange Lodge of Ireland been observed, the County Antrim representatives in Grand Lodge should have been informed that this matter was not within the competence of the Grand Orange Lodge of Ireland but was a matter for their County Grand Lodge. Neither the Ulster Unionist Council nor the Ulster Unionist Party is mentioned in the Constitution, Laws and Ordinances.

No one from County Antrim Grand Orange Lodge pressed the case for their own resolution. Neither did they follow the logic of their own decision, continuing for some years to send delegates to the Ulster Unionist Council. The council is adamant that it is the County Grand Lodges who send the delegates, not the Grand Orange Lodge of Ireland. The County Antrim Grand Orange Lodge resolution was therefore flawed on two counts. In the first instance the decision of the county should not have been directed to the Grand Lodge of Ireland, as the matter is evidently within the competence of the county itself. In the second place, the decision should have been directed to the Ulster Unionist Council, and it would have been up to the council to grant the request of the County Antrim Grand Orange Lodge and officially disaffiliate them. In spite of all their bluster, the County Antrim Grand Orange Lodge failed to implement their own decision.

The question of the relationship between the Orange Institution and the Ulster Unionist Council arose during a debate at the autumn 1995 conference of the Ulster Unionist Party, when the party leader, David Trimble, announced that he wanted to create a modern political party. This would have meant the dissolving of the present 'federation' of the Ulster Unionist Council. To the dismay of many present, Drew Nelson, one of the delegates, personalised the issue in terms of the relationship with the Orange Institution. While this was not the intention of the Unionist leadership, it had the effect of focusing attention solely on this aspect of the modernisation.

Subsequently on 6 October the Central Committee of the Grand Orange Lodge of Ireland authorised the creation of a delegation to meet with officers of the Ulster Unionist Council so that Grand Lodge could be fully briefed. The Ulster Unionist Council was not written to until 26 October. One might well ask why the delay of twenty days, particularly in the light of the fact that disaffiliation was one of the demands being made by what at that stage was an 'anonymous faction', later calling itself the 'Spirit of Drumcree'.

The committee appointed to liaise with the Ulster Unionist Council consisted of the Grand Secretary, John McCrea, the Rev. Dr Warren Porter, Canon Dr S. E. Long and myself. We met representatives of the Ulster Unionist Council, David Trimble, Josiah Cunningham, and Jeffrey Donaldson, on 11 December 1995. No further meeting took place until 21 November 1997. This meeting, called 'as a matter of urgency', coincided with a meeting of the Education Committee and so I could not attend. John McCrea, as an *ex officio* member of the Education Committee, would have known this. A third meeting, of members of the committee only, was arranged for 2 December 1997. Canon Long and I were only able to attend this meeting for part of the time, and Dr Porter was unable to attend at all. None of the members ever received notification to attend the committee again.

It was therefore surprising to read in *Sunday Life* on 9 May 1999, under the headline 'Time to bring order to divorce talks', that talks about restructuring the links between the Orange Order and the Ulster Unionist Party 'were resurrected at the start of this year, and both groups selected three-man talks teams. The Orange Order's trio are Willie Ross, the Unionist MP for East Londonderry, Denis Watson, County Grand Master in Armagh, and John McCrea, former Grand Secretary of the Order.'[12] At the Grand Lodge meeting in Londonderry on 2 June 1999, William Ross confirmed that he was on this committee. The minutes of the Grand Lodge Meeting of 27 March 1999 state, 'The matter is currently being dealt with by a committee established by the Grand Master'.

At the subsequent meeting of the Central Committee on 21 May, the Grand Master was asked if the committee referred to in *Sunday Life* was new. He replied, 'Not that I know of . . . I am not aware of any committee.' It did however transpire that there had been a meeting of this new committee on 12 February 1999, without reference to the one established on 6 October 1995. Evidently, the make-up of the original committee did not now suit some individual or individuals, and a new committee had been created to present a much more hardline approach.

Many members of the Central Committee thought that the matter was now resolved and that 'someone had got their fingers burned'. In fact it was far from resolved, as at the meeting of the Grand Orange Lodge of Ireland on 2 June 1999 things were further confused and no clear explanation was offered.

Another meeting was called for 11 May 2000, in the House of Orange, of a composite committee consisting of John McCrea and myself from the original committee, William Ross from the second committee, the Grand Master Robert Saulters and David Brewster. How and when these others were appointed it is not known. Following my resignation from the Education Committee on 14 July 2000 I was not notified about further meetings. Some people were evidently not only making up the rules as they went along, but were also effectively bypassing the already established system under the authority of the Grand Lodge. In any event it was a most inadequate and unbusinesslike way of dealing with these matters.

The actual power and influence of the 113 Orange delegates to the Ulster Unionist Council is, like many things within the Orange and Unionist community, largely overstated. The Cadogan Group of academics, in their 2003 pamphlet *Picking up the Pieces: Northern Ireland after the Belfast Agreement*, reflected the position more accurately than most: 'The Orange Order does not control the UUP, its financial contribution is negligible, and its allocation of votes in the Ulster Unionist Council is not huge.'

When the Grand Master Robert Saulters summoned all the Orange delegates to the House of Orange prior to a crucial meeting of the Ulster Unionist Council on 26 November 1999, significantly only thirty-five turned up. This thirty-one per cent response was to be expected, for the typical Ulster Protestant Orangeman was not going to be told how to vote, even by the Grand Master of the Grand Orange Lodge of Ireland. This was the second such meeting to be called since the autumn 1995 conference of the Ulster Unionist Party at which the restructuring had been discussed. On 6 October 1995 the Central Committee had also suggested that a meeting of Orange delegates be called, and this took place in February 1996 in Brownlow House, Lurgan. There a majority favoured a restructuring of the relationship between the Institution and the Ulster Unionist Council, but this conclusion was not communicated to the membership.

Effective methods were subsequently employed to ensure a more hardline delegation which would toe the party line the Orange leadership was now demanding. These methods however did not result in a much greater response to the Grand Master's diktat. When the 113 delegates were again called to meet on 7 May 2002, only forty-three were present.

The substance of the discussion at this latter meeting reveals the true state of affairs within the Institution at this time. The seven County Grand Lodge delegations involved met with the Grand Master beforehand and expressed two concerns: that they should stay within the party, and that they objected to paying the new £100 fee which the council had set for each delegate. The thirty-eight per cent of the delegates who were present can hardly be regarded as representative of the delegates as a whole. However, those in attendance clearly regarded the Order as the backbone of Unionism, with corresponding leverage. They failed to recognise the reality that they had not been paying their way as delegates for many years, and that as numbers within the Institution continued to fall, an increasing financial burden was being placed on an ever-decreasing membership. This was particularly true of Belfast.

Some expressed the desire to address the Ulster Unionist Party delegation as county delegates. This revealed a lack of confidence in the Grand Lodge representatives, and was rejected, as the hierarchy clearly would not take the risk that each county might not put forward the same views as Grand Lodge.

The question of the relationship of the Orange Institution to the Ulster Unionist Council demonstrates the ability of the Orange leadership to lead from behind. While it is always good to consult and take soundings, this can often be a cloak to hide behind, as we will see again later in relation to the 'sounding' taken over the relationship to the Parades Commission. The February 1996 meeting of delegates had not provided the answer the leadership wanted. They therefore employed their well-worn tactic of calling a multiplicity of meetings until that answer was achieved, hiding behind democracy in order to protect their office within the Institution.

In the midst of all this confusion leadership was given by the County Master of Tyrone, Edward Stevenson, who at the meeting of the Grand Lodge on 16 June 2004 proposed a Notice of Motion 'that the Grand Orange Lodge of Ireland severs all links with the Ulster Unionist Council'. This received overwhelming – but not unanimous – support on its first and second readings and was passed by a majority at its final reading at the March 2005 meeting of the Grand Lodge. Edward Stevenson was well aware that the Constitution, Laws and Ordinances did not require either a Notice of Motion or three readings on this subject, as it did not fall under the competence of the Grand Lodge, but he was informed by senior officers at the meeting on 16 June 2004 that this was the procedure to be followed. Was this ruling by senior officers ignorance or malevolence? (Ironically, according to Ed Moloney in *A Secret History of the IRA*, Gerry Adams used similar manipulation tactics in order to control the Sinn Féin Ard Fheis and the Army Council of the IRA.)[13]

In spite of this decision of the Grand Orange Lodge of Ireland to sever 'all links with the Ulster Unionist Council', and the media hype that the Orange Order had 'broken the link', that link will remain until the Ulster Unionist Party changes its constitution, which lists 'The County Grand Lodges (within Northern Ireland) of the Grand Orange Lodge of Ireland' as affiliated bodies.[14]

The accusation is often made, particularly in Orange circles, that politicians have used the Orange Institution for their own ends. While this may well be true in some cases, the converse has equally been true. There are many examples of individuals joining the Orange Order when they decided to enter politics, even though they were not religious in any meaningful sense. Ulster Unionist Party MLA Duncan Shipley Dalton wrote in *Ireland on Sunday* on 27 July 2001, 'I was born and raised as a Protestant but I no longer worship; my relationship with God is, at best, distant, at worst, non-existent.' Dalton had joined the Orange Order when he stood as a candidate in South Antrim for the Northern Ireland Assembly in 1998. His proposal form would have required him to state his religious denomination and name the church at which he regularly worshipped. If his position had changed since, the honourable thing would have been for him to resign.

Just as the Order's relationship with politicians has occasionally been stormy, so has its relationship with some of the churches, particularly as regards the use of church buildings for services. The Institution has at times seemed to have an inflated view of itself in relation to the mainstream churches, with an air of arrogance when it comes to organising 'Orange Services'. This stems from an identity crisis. Is the Orange Institution a religious organisation with a political element or a political organisation with a religious element? The cynic might argue that the Orange Order is evidently not political, on the grounds that politics is the art of compromise, which the Orange Order is clearly not good at.

The Rev. S. E. Long correctly assesses the situation in *Orangeism: A New Historical Appreciation*:

> It is historically unarguable that the Ulster Unionist Party came out of the Institution. It is equally true the party has never been without the leadership of men who were Orangemen before they became politicians. It has always been true, though, that Orangemen have belonged to other political parties and that a great number of them belong to no party.[15]

John M. Andrews, the former prime minister of Northern Ireland, speaking as Grand Master of the Grand Orange Lodge of Ireland in June 1950, gave what Canon Long regards as 'the official Orange attitude to politics':

> I observe from reports in the press that there are a few Orange Brethren who feel that we are exclusively a religious Order. While I agree that we are mainly a religious body, the Order has been in the front rank for generations in preserving our constitutional position. The Orange ritual lays it down that it is the duty of Orangemen to support and maintain the laws and constitution. It is fundamentally important that we should continue to do so, for if we lost our constitutional position within the United Kingdom 'civil and religious liberty for all' which we are also pledged to support would be endangered.[16]

Canon Long, as senior Grand Chaplain of the Institution, continued to hold to this position, as is evident from the various contributions he has made over the years to statements and resolutions of the Institution. This was made particularly clear in a paper read at a Chaplains' Conference on 3 May 1997, in which he stated: 'The Orange Order is a Christian Organisation with political aims and aspirations.' Another Grand Chaplain, the Rev. Dr M. W. Dewar, expressed a similar opinion in *Why Orangeism?*:

> Hitherto we have tried to show that the Orange Institution is a religious Order, with its foundations firmly laid in the history of Protestantism in general and of Ulster Protestantism in particular. But in Northern Ireland, for reasons that have been made clear, it is almost impossible to separate 'religion' from 'politics'.[17]

It is therefore understandable that Chris Ryder and Vincent Kearney, in *Drumcree: The Orange Order's Last Stand*, appraise the situation as follows: 'In the complex anatomy of Orangeism, the twin devotion to God and Ulster provides a seamless link between the Protestant religion and Unionist politics,'[18] but this is an over-neat description. In the underlying anatomy of Orangeism politics are secondary to religion. In a press statement on 13 December 1995 the Grand Orange Lodge of Ireland said that 'any political action necessary to be taken must always be subservient to and supportive of its primary evangelical concern'. The Chaplains' Report presented to the Grand Orange Lodge on 11 June 1997 affirmed that 'the Christian witness of Orangeism must not be compromised, however provocative the circumstances may be. Our commitment to Christ as Lord and Saviour over-rides all else.'

In spite of this, the clear historical position of the Institution is not always understood by the membership. Writing in the *Belfast Telegraph* on 21 July 2003, Lord Kilclooney (formerly John Taylor) called for people to join the Orange Order as an effective means of halting the involvement of 'the Dublin government in the administration of Northern Ireland'. The religious affairs correspondent, Alf McCreary, asked, 'Is he simply underlining what most of us have expected all along, that the Orange Order is a political institution and little else?' Similarly, on 22 July 2003, Lord Laird of Artigarvan (formerly John Laird), the chairman of the Ulster Scots Agency, wrote in the *Belfast Telegraph* of the 'religious dimension' of the Twelfth. He failed to understand the historical position of the Institution as, in Dr Dewar's words, 'a religious Order, with its foundations firmly laid in the history of Protestantism in general and of Ulster Protestantism in particular'.

A former Assistant Grand Secretary of the Grand Orange Lodge of Ireland, Melvyn Hamilton, who resigned following the death of Constable Frank O'Reilly in October 1998, is quoted in *Drumcree: The Orange Order's Last Stand* as saying that 'in addition to becoming more and more political', the Order 'has also lost its credibility and influence'.[19]

In 1951, at a high point in the relationship between the Institution and the main Protestant churches, Grand Lodge resolved:

> . . . realising the harm being done by our continuing divisions, we call upon all Orangemen to do their utmost to promote better understanding and a closer union between our various Protestant denominations. To this end we strongly advise that facilities be refused for holding

> religious services in Orange and/or Protestant Halls except in the case of representatives of such Religious Bodies as are recognised by the Grand Orange Lodge of Ireland, as the indiscriminate granting of such facilities has helped to increase divisions amongst Protestant people.

The purpose behind this resolution was to keep Ian Paisley from continuing on the path of division on which he had embarked in 1951 with the formation of his own church, the Free Presbyterian Church of Ulster. Sadly this was 'whistling in the wind'. As any observer of the religious scene in Northern Ireland will be aware, not only Paisley's church but all sorts of 'religious' groups, some of whom would not be recognised as within the Reformed tradition, still use Orange Halls. (Paisley was to continue his crusade of division politically, as well as religiously. In 1969 he formed the Protestant Unionist Party, later renamed the Democratic Unionist Party.)

The 'Religious Bodies recognised by the Grand Orange Lodge of Ireland' in 1951 did not include the Free Presbyterian Church of Ulster. This situation changed in 1998, reflecting a shift towards extremism within Grand Lodge. The position of the Free Presbyterian Church in terms of relationships with other churches of the Reformed tradition was one of complete separation. In 1992 Alexandra Presbyterian Church in Belfast offered to allow the Rev. Ronald Johnstone, a Free Presbyterian minister, to conduct a pre-Twelfth Service for the Clifton Street Orange Hall Management Committee. He was forced to decline as a result of pressure from within his own denomination, because to take a service would have meant a compromise with the 'apostate Presbyterian Church in Ireland'. Logically, the members of the Free Presbyterian Church of Ulster who adopt this strict separation policy of 'Come out from among them' (2 Corinthians 6:17) are derogating from their declared doctrine by being members of the ecumenical Orange Institution.

Clerical chaplains within the Orange Institution, though not as numerous as in previous years, were still up to the end of the twentieth century concerned about the spiritual emphasis of the Institution. This was revealed at various Chaplains' Conferences in recent years. One such meeting of twenty chaplains was held on 3 May 1997, following two Drumcree stand-offs. A letter was read from the Rev. Roy Vallely, minister of Ballylinney Presbyterian Church, expressing his concern about the present spiritual state of affairs within the Institution. (The Rev. Vallely later resigned from the Institution in the wake of events in the summer of 1998.)

The Rev. William Bingham then presented a paper in which he addressed the question 'Why are we in the Orange Order?' He expressed concern at the way the Institution was going and gave two horrific examples from Drumcree in the previous year, when the Royal Ulster Constabulary was regarded as the 'enemy'. He highlighted the religious conviction of the Institution and stressed that as far as parades were concerned, 'what we do in a majority community affects those who live in a minority community'.

Canon S. E. Long delivered a paper called *The Orange Order in Crisis*, reminding the chaplains, 'The declared intention of the leadership is to prevent the recurrence of the horrific happenings of the summers of 1995 and 1996.' He wisely pointed out, 'The refusal to accept any restriction on Orange Order marches is not sustainable, if in the wake of that resolution there is certain to be violent confrontation, injuries, destruction of property and maybe deaths.'

Throughout this crucial period the chaplains of the Order endeavoured to make a positive contribution to Christian principle and common sense, but to very little avail. Their contribution was restricted when their number was reduced by half in October 1998, contrary to the expressed wishes of the Rules Revision Committee. This reduction was by implication downgrading the religious emphasis of the Order, as was the fact that when the leadership visited Downing Street on 7 May 1998 to meet Prime Minister Tony Blair, they failed to take even one chaplain with them.

In December 1997 the Commission on the Loyal Orange Institution of Ireland, set up by the Grand Orange Lodge of Ireland two years previously, recommended the formation of a Religious Affairs Committee. The leadership have evidently been in no hurry to implement this decision, as eight years later it has yet to be established.

At the meeting of the Grand Orange Lodge of Ireland on 13 December 1995, the spiritual priority of the Institution was still being emphasised. After the presentation of the report on the Ulster Hall Rally of 14 November 1995 (organised by the Spirit of Drumcree faction) the resolution released to the press declared that 'our Order's principal concern is for the maintenance of the Protestant and Reformed Religion . . . any political action necessary to be taken must always be subservient to and supportive of its primary evangelical concern.' In an article the same year in the bicentenary publication *Steadfast for Faith and Freedom*, the Executive Officer, George Patton, wrote, 'Once Orange-men allow themselves to betray Biblical Protestantism they deny their *raison d'être*.'[20] The glossy information booklet distributed at the time of the US presidential visit to Belfast on 4 September 1998 sets out 'The Religious Basis of the Order': 'The Orange Institution is a Christian organisation . . . As Orangemen our trust is in God and our faith and dependence is in Jesus Christ, the Saviour and Lord of mankind.'

Yet in recent years there has been a subtle shift away from defining the Order in primarily religious terms to defining it in almost exclusively 'cultural' terms, as in the July 2001 edition of the *Orange Standard* when the Grand Master, Robert Saulters, stated that 'the July parades celebrate our cultural traditions', or when in a meeting with the prime minister towards the end of 1998, Grand Lodge representatives called for the Institution's 'recognition as a cultural organisation'. A petition organised by the Parades Strategy Committee, to be delivered to the prime minister or the new Assembly on 'Ulster Day', 28 September 1998, did not mention religion, instead arguing that 'There is no place for cultural apartheid in a democratic society' and asking that 'our culture and role in society be officially recognised'. While the religious and political natures of the Institution are not necessarily exclusive, it is the focusing of different aspects for different audiences which leads to accusations of duplicity.

The religious nature of the Institution was undoubtedly compromised by the violence associated with the consecutive Drumcree stand-offs. Significantly, during this period we can observe a shift in the language of press statements issued by Grand Lodge, away from the religious nature of the Institution towards 'cultural rights' and 'heritage'. The revamped website of the Grand Orange Lodge of Ireland however continues to affirm the authentic, traditional position of the Institution: 'The Order with its proud history is primarily a religious organisation that also expresses the culture of a people. An organisation involved in social and charitable work that also accepts its political responsibilities.'

Sometimes those within the organisation have added to the general confusion. Alistair Simpson, Governor of the Apprentice Boys of Derry and an Orangeman who has done much to deal with the confusion over what the Apprentice Boys of Derry stand for in his own native Londonderry, was one such person. Speaking on the BBC Northern Ireland programme 'Looking for Lundy' on 29 November 2000, he said, 'You have the Apprentice Boys being the historical organisation, you have the Orange Order being the political organisation and you have the Black Perceptory being the religious organisation.'

The crisis facing the Institution following the death of the three Quinn children in a petrol-bombing house fire on 12 July 1998 raised the question of the religious nature of the Order to a level of acute importance. In a presentation to County Down Grand Lodge, published in the *Belfast News Letter* on 13 November 1998, the Rev. Denis Bannerman, then an Orange Chaplain and a member of a lodge in County Down, said:

> Disputes over parades, and particularly the problems associated with Drumcree, have done incalculable damage to both the reputation of the Institution in the wider world and the morale and commitment of many of our best and most conscientious members.
>
> We fail to take any account of the consequences that this particular dispute is having virtually everywhere else. Civil and religious liberty is an individual thing. To abuse that liberty by forcing it upon others is a very different matter – we cannot claim a right to do that!
>
> The Institution has permitted demonstrations of civil disobedience which have been hijacked by more sinister elements who have perpetrated actions for which the Institution has been blamed, at least in part.
>
> It is important that our Institution remembers that civil rights are for all people; as we protect the rights that we value so we must also protect the rights of others whose culture and religion might differ from ours.
>
> Politics (bordering on sectarianism) has become the master rather than the servant of the Institution; and matters of faith and Christian witness have been sacrificed or abandoned in the pursuit of a perceived right to parade down a particular piece of roadway in Portadown – and for no other reason than 'we have always done it'.
>
> The Institution must declare itself to be, either a political organisation with an interest in Christianity; or a Christian organisation with an interest in politics. It is, in effect, decision time. The Institution must declare itself and be clearly identified with whichever priority it sees.
>
> How much better it would be to stop fighting battles we cannot win; or even if we should win, the victory would be a hollow one if we have caused irreparable damage to the reputation of the Institution as a professed Christian organisation.

It was not surprising that the Rev. Bannerman received a very positive response from those who read this article. The *Belfast News Letter* has a wide circulation in rural Ulster, among Orangemen who would hold to the high moral principles he expounded.

The difficulty for the present leadership is that to come out as predominantly religious would mean placing their personal lives under scrutiny. It is much easier to play politics than to take religion seriously, except that in this case they are playing at politics without having the popular mandate of the electorate. The determination of some chaplains within the Order to present clearly the unadulterated Gospel of personal faith and trust in Christ alone for salvation, witnessed in both word and deed, has become an embarrassment to some members of the Orange Institution. Meanwhile, to some the Orange Institution has become a substitute religion and an alternative to a church affiliation. 'Andy', the unnamed Orangeman quoted by Glenn Jordan in *Not of this World? Evangelical Protestants in Northern Ireland*, says, 'Within the city [of Belfast] a lot of them aren't churchgoers, the vast majority aren't, so we can't call it a solely religious organisation. There is a religious dimension to it, but that doesn't make it a religious organisation.'[21] Yet the Qualifications state that an Orangeman 'should remember to keep holy the Sabbath day, and attend the public worship of God'.

Some believe, as David McNarry told Denis Watson on 5 July 1999, 'The trouble is that the churches are setting the spirituality for the Institution. What we need to do is to get our chaplains together and create our own spirituality.' Canon S. E. Long, addressing a Lodge of Research Conference on 13 April 1991, maintained the traditional position: 'It would be a betrayal of Orangeism if it was to become another denomination or even if it were made a substitute for church affiliation.'

On 18 May 1999 the Church of Ireland Archbishop Dr Robin Eames, in an address to the General Synod of the Church of Ireland, said: 'The real question for members of the Orange Order to address is whether *they* wish to be regarded as members of a religious or a political movement. In the light of events over the past four years at Drumcree most outside observers would regard the Order as a political rather than a religious movement.' He went on to summarise the present conflict facing those with Christian convictions, though the media missed this significant point:

> I have always recognised that the vast majority of members of the Orange Order are decent, respectable and law-abiding men and women.*

* Women are not admitted to the Orange Order, but have a parallel organisation, the Association of Loyal Orangewomen of Ireland. Initially founded in the mid-nineteenth century, it quickly lapsed, but was revived in 1911.

> They have never found a conflict between Church membership and membership of the Order. Many of them hold key positions in their local parishes. There are also many who have told us of their moderation and disgust at the scenes on Drumcree Hill. Their responsibility is immense. Have they the courage to speak out and to witness to their moderation? Which is more important to them the policy of a lodge or the teaching of Jesus Christ? Their choice is clear – is the Order to be a means of enriching the Kingdom of God – or an obstacle?

In the *Belfast News Letter* the following day the past Grand Master, the Rev. Martin Smyth, disputed the right of the Archbishop 'to dictate to the Orange Order that it should distinguish whether it is a political or a religious organisation . . . Primate Eames confirmed that he had a political-religious dimension when he was elevated to the House of Lords, a political post, while still remaining head of his church.' The East Londonderry MP William Ross complained that the Archbishop had ordered the Orangemen 'to honour three pledges, but not the nationalist residents of the Garvaghy Road'. Was Mr Ross not aware that it was the Orangemen and not the Garvaghy Road residents who were occupying the property of the Church of Ireland?

In an interview in the *Belfast Telegraph* on 30 June 1999, the Grand Master, Robert Saulters, is quoted as feeling 'betrayed' by the leaders of the main Protestant churches – Dr Eames, the Primate, and Dr John Lockington, the Moderator of the General Assembly and a lifelong Orangeman. Such public attacks were unprecedented, but they indicated the direction in which at least the leadership of the Institution was now going.

A further attack took place on 15 November 2001 during a public seminar at the Institute for Irish Studies at Queen's University, Belfast, attended by a number of senior officers of the Institution including Denis Watson, the Grand Secretary, and George Patton, the Executive Officer. After a paper was delivered on 'The Place of Orangeism in Irish Society', the discussion degenerated into an attack on the Protestant churches by several including William Smith, the Master of Derriaghy District, Dawson Bailie, the Master of Belfast County Grand Lodge, Thomas Ross, the Master of Glenavy District, and the Rev. Victor Ryan, County Chaplain of Belfast! Both Denis Watson and George Patton remained silent. The complaint was made that 'some Protestant clergy and ministers do not stand up for their people the way that the Roman Catholic priest stands up for his people'. This argument displayed a fundamental lack of knowledge of the respective roles of the Roman Catholic priest and the Reformed minister. In the Reformed tradition it is the primary function of the minister to represent God to the people, not the people to God. The Roman Catholic priest represents the people to God when, in the Mass, he offers a sacrifice on behalf of the people.

While the Protestants of Ireland at the beginning of the twentieth century looked at their politics through their religious eyes, it would appear that many of the present generation of Ulster Protestants look at their religion through political eyes. The Institution therefore now reflects a less 'religious' Protestantism than it did at its foundation – even a secular Protestantism. The last hundred years have seen the rise of this 'political Protestant' as opposed to the 'religious Protestant'. What Glenn Jordan said of some evangelical Protestants in Northern Ireland could equally be said of some Orangemen: 'For many their politics have influenced their Christianity rather than the reverse'.[22]

With this renewed emphasis on politics, and the inability of the Orange leadership to cope with the new situation, Jock Purves' statement in 1968 that the Institution's members had 'lost their pristine spiritual power' was even more true as the Institution entered the twenty-first century.

Chapter Three

Decisive Discipline

'Anyone convicted of a criminal offence is automatically expelled from the Institution.'

Denis Watson, Grand Secretary, Grand Orange Lodge of Ireland[1]

It is no easy thing to establish discipline in an organisation which is voluntary in membership and fraternal in its internal allegiance, and where the ultimate sanction is expulsion. In the Loyal Orange Institution of Ireland, the threat of expulsion meant much more in the past, when membership of the Orange Order was seen by society as a mark of personal integrity. When the Protestant principles of the Order commanded the adherence of the vast majority of the Protestant population, expulsion from the Order was viewed as a disgrace.

Writing of the situation in Canada in the nineteenth century in *The Sash Canada Wore*, Cecil J. Houston and William J. Smyth comment:

> Through the obligations imposed upon candidates at initiation and extended by a series of by-laws the lodges maintained a code of discipline that, on the surface at any rate, appeared comprehensive . . . The latter penalty [expulsion] was particularly severe, not only because it placed the individual beyond the Orange fold, but also because the accused could be placed under censure by the community at large in areas where the majority of adult males were in the Order.[2]

There is of course, no sense in pretending that we are living in the nineteenth century, when membership of the Order was a badge of respectability and discipline was accepted with grace. The context in which the Institution now operates is the laissez-faire society in which respectability is denounced and discipline is disregarded. The wisdom of King Solomon is ignored: 'He who ignores discipline comes to poverty and shame, but whoever heeds correction is honoured' (Proverbs 13:18).

It would however be wrong to suggest that the writ of the Grand Orange Lodge of Ireland was always obeyed. There are some notable historical exceptions. When Grand Lodge at the end of 1798 counselled the brethren 'strictly to abstain from expressing any opinion pro or con upon the question of a Legislative Union', that instruction was not universally followed. The situation was confused by the creation of Union Lodges, which R. M. Sibbett describes as 'the work of the enemy'.[3] Although not in any way associated with the Grand Orange Lodge of Ireland, their very existence created an atmosphere of uncertainty.

While some Orange Lodges supported the Grand Lodge directive, many did evidently discuss the Act of Union and submitted resolutions accordingly. LOL 500 in the City of Dublin was foremost in opposition to the Grand Lodge directive and the proposed legislative union. They were joined later by Charlemont LOL 253 in County Armagh, and by 'a large meeting of the Orangemen of Antrim and Down held at the Maze', who considered 'Legislative Union with Great Britain as [the] inevitable ruin to the Peace, Prosperity, and Happiness of this Kingdom'.[4]

During the second dissolution of the Grand Lodge between 1836 and 1846, private lodges continued to function. The evidence for this is seen in the minute books of many lodges of the time.

William Johnston of Ballykilbeg, the Orange folk hero, defied the policy of the Grand Orange Lodge of Ireland on a number of occasions. After defying the Grand Lodge in its opposition to the Grand Black Chapter, he went on to lead a procession from Newtownards to Bangor in 1867, contrary to Grand Lodge policy. He further defied Grand Lodge policy when he announced his support for a bill to introduce a secret ballot for parliamentary elections. No disciplinary proceedings were taken against him. Indeed his more modern counterparts, like Newtownbutler District in County Fermanagh, who talked to the Parades Commission in contravention of Grand Lodge policy, were not to be disciplined either. As we shall see, it was virtually impossible to enforce discipline in relation to either policy or, more importantly, the Constitution, Laws and Ordinances of the Loyal Orange Institution of Ireland.

In more recent years the public's attention has been drawn to various individuals whose lives do not demonstrate the high ideals and values of Orangeism as expressed in the Qualifications of an Orangeman and the Basis of the Orange Institution. Orangeman Jeffrey Shields was one who did not fulfil the virtue of 'setting a good example in our daily lives, by living up to the high principles of the Order'. A member of 'Star of Ulster Temperance' LOL 1085 in Belfast's No. 6 District, Shields sued glaziers

John Frackelton & Son over an accident in July 1994 which he claimed left him housebound and unable to walk. He dropped his claim for compensation in May 1997 when lawyers produced a photograph of him walking with his lodge, seven days after the alleged accident.

In the March 1999 edition of the *Orange Standard* an advert appeared on page 2 from William Parkinson of 'Whitewell Temperance' LOL 533, seeking sponsorship for running the London Marathon on Sunday 18 April 1999. Law 4 of the Constitution, Laws and Ordinances of the Loyal Orange Institution of Ireland states: 'It shall be deemed an offence for any member to take part in organised games, sports, entertainments and dances on a Sunday whether as promoter, spectator, player or participant. Members are required to honour the Qualifications of Candidates for membership in the Institution as to Sunday Observance.' Not only was William Parkinson's participation in the London Marathon a clear breach of the Law of the Institution, but he also held office in Belfast's No. 2 District as a district lecturer, a position that called for the instruction of members in the principles and values of the Institution. It could be argued that the editor of the *Orange Standard*, Billy Kennedy, made matters worse by publishing Parkinson's intention to break the Law of the Institution. The irony of this proposed breach of principle was highlighted when it was noted that a strongly worded article on page 12 of the same edition was entitled 'Preserving the Ulster Sabbath'. This point did not go unobserved by the *Sunday Times*, which made reference on 11 April 1999 to 'falling Orange Standards'. William Parkinson can still be seen in the prominent position of the colour party of the County Grand Lodge of Belfast on Twelfth parades through Belfast.

These double standards concerning the Lord's Day reached a new depth of hypocrisy when, following the Grand Orange Lodge meeting on 12 December 2001, a press release was issued and published on its website expressing Grand Lodge's 'strong opposition to the idea of Sunday Soccer' and calling 'on those directly involved in this to avoid further movement towards a secular Sunday which is contrary to Holy Scripture'.

The traditional values which are to be the objective of all Orangemen were restated in the Education Committee's publication *The Order on Parade* in 1996:

> We must all endeavour to disarm suspicion and antagonism. This can best be done by setting a good example in our daily lives, by living up to the high principles of the Order so that every section of the

> community will be compelled to admit that there is something in the Orange Society that elevates a man and raises him above the average of humanity. Something that makes him a better man morally, socially and intellectually.

Since the middle of the twentieth century, the discipline question has been raised largely, though not exclusively, in connection with political violence and paramilitary activity. In October 1966, Augustus 'Gusty' Spence, a member of 'Prince Albert Temperance' LOL 1892, was found guilty of the murder of Peter Ward on 26 June that year. The Constitution, Laws and Ordinances in operation at that time stated: 'Expulsions shall be limited to criminal convictions or to offences against morality' (Law 17). The general interpretation was that once a person had been convicted in the courts, he was automatically expelled. There was no need to have another trial, which after all would be impossible if the person in question were in prison.

In the case of LOL 1892, there was the added difficulty of close family ties. It would be a brave man who would propose such action when brothers, uncles and cousins sat in the same lodge. It was therefore left to the County Grand Lodge under the Master, the Rev. Martin Smyth, to pressurise the district and the lodge to have Spence removed from the books. This took some time and it did not stop the lodge from paying 'respect' to 'Brother Gusty' on the Twelfth of July morning, by stopping outside Crumlin Road Prison where he was serving his sentence.

A well-known Lodge in No. 3 District in Belfast is 'Old Boyne Island Heroes' LOL 633. They are known for their generally unruly behaviour and the fact that they have had within their ranks, at one time or another, a number of individuals who have spent time in Her Majesty's prisons. One such person was Davy Payne, a leader of the UDA in North Belfast. Payne was caught on 8 January 1988 with a consignment of rifles in the overloaded boot of a hired Ford Granada car outside Portadown. He was later sentenced to nine years' imprisonment.

'Old Boyne Island Heroes' are known locally as the 'UVF Lodge', for good reason. Peter Taylor in his book *Loyalists* lists their 'proud' tradition:

> The only bomber on Lodge 633's banner, under the words 'In fond memory of our fallen brethren', is one of the names of five UVF Lodge members killed in the current conflict listed on the Lodge's smaller bannerette. Aubrey Reid was one of four UVF men blown up in 1975

> when the bomb they were carrying in their car exploded prematurely; Noel 'Nogi' Shaw was 'executed' as a result of an internal UVF feud, also in 1975; John Bingham was a UVF commander shot dead in his home by the IRA in 1986; Brian Robinson was killed on 'active service' by undercover soldiers in 1989; and Robert 'Basher' Bates was shot dead in a revenge attack in 1997. A sixth name, that of Colin Craig, gunned down by the INLA in 1994, was once listed on the bannerette but removed when it was thought he had been an informer.[5]

Taylor quotes the Master of LOL 633, Eddie McAdam, as saying: 'We don't throw them out because they're brethren . . . We could throw out house burglars or sex offenders and the like, but to us these guys are not criminals, they're victims of circumstances.'[6]

Much of this information about this lodge came into the public domain in the mid 1980s, but it was revived when the *Belfast Telegraph* reported on 27 February 1999 that LOL 633 had commemorated Bobby 'Basher' Bates, one of the 'Shankill Butchers' and a former member of the lodge, on their newly commissioned bannerette. The Grand Lodge, of course, was 'not aware of the bannerette'.

On 14 September 1986, the IRA shot dead in his home John Dowey Bingham, an alleged leader of the UVF and a member of LOL 633. In 1983 Bingham had received a twenty-year jail sentence on the word of the UVF 'supergrass' Joe Bennett. He was freed in December 1984 when the Court of Appeal quashed the conviction.

Bingham's funeral on 16 September 1986 was an 'Orange funeral', with members of his lodge flanking his coffin wearing traditional regalia. Three gunmen had fired a salute of shots over his coffin the night before. Prominent politicians such as Ian Paisley visited the Bingham home and some also attended the funeral, including North Belfast MP Cecil Walker and the liberal ex-Lord Mayor of Belfast John Carson. The *Belfast News Letter* next morning carried the headline 'UVF leader buried', between two photographs. One showed the coffin draped in the UVF flag and escorted by Orangemen wearing regalia. The other showed the coffin being given a UVF salute of gunfire.

Barry White, writing in the *Irish Independent* on 18 September, saw the implications of the attendance of politicians, which he said had "shocked Unionist moderates". But it also shocked and saddened ordinary respectable Orangemen who wanted nothing to do with the paramilitaries. The Roman Catholic Bishop Cahal Daly, who said, 'They owe the public an explanation,' also challenged the presence of Unionist politicians. Bishop

Daly was of course inconsistent. He did not call for an explanation when nationalist public figures took part in IRA funerals. However, all this reduced the respectability of the Orange Institution in the eyes of a discerning world, and did nothing to 'disarm suspicion and antagonism'.

George Seawright, a Belfast City Councillor, had carried Bingham's coffin wearing Orange regalia and had called for 'revenge'. The following evening, in the grounds of Holy Cross Roman Catholic Church in Ardoyne, North Belfast, Raymond Mooney, who had been chairing a church meeting on a project called 'Living Faith', was shot dead. The North Belfast Sinn Féin spokesman Gerard McGuigan was reported in the *Belfast Telegraph* of 17 September as saying, 'Loyalist councillor George Seawright should share part of the blame for what happened, after his comments about revenge in the wake of the murder of John Bingham.'

Seawright had been expelled from the Democratic Unionist Party in 1984 after expressing views which were too extreme even for that party. On 29 May 1984, during a debate of the Belfast Education and Library Board in Belfast City Hall, he made the following remarks, reported in the *Irish News* on 31 May: 'Taxpayers' money would be better spent on an incinerator and burning the lot of them. The priests should be thrown in and burnt as well.' This caused widespread revulsion and he was suspended from the Council for a time. He was also prominent in the aftermath of a loyalist band parade through the largely Roman Catholic village of Castlewellan on 27 June 1985, and in the Obins Street disturbances in July 1986 in Portadown.

Seawright was a member of the Orange Institution, which expressed high ideals and Christian values. His private lodge was 'Ballysillan Temperance' LOL 1891, in Belfast's No. 3 District. His standing as an Orangeman went unchallenged, and indeed was confirmed by the Grand Master, the Rev. Martin Smyth. The *Irish Times* of 8 July 1986 reported that at an 'Official Unionist' press conference, when questioned about whether Seawright was 'in good standing within the Orange Order' following his remarks on burning Catholics, Smyth answered, 'To the best of my knowledge he is. How long do you punish a person?'

By any standards, the opinions expressed by Seawright stood in stark contrast to the Basis which states that the Order 'will not admit into its brotherhood persons whom an intolerant spirit leads to persecute, injure, or upbraid any man on account of his religious opinions'. But the revulsion expressed by society at large, which resulted in Seawright's removal from Belfast's Education and Library Board, was not replicated in the Orange Institution. No disciplinary action was taken against him.

Seawright was shot by the INLA on the Shankill Road on 19 November 1987 and died on 3 December. At his funeral members of the Institution flanked his coffin wearing Orange regalia. Ian R. K. Paisley also attended and helped to carry the coffin. The following year, on 4 December, a memorial service was organised by the Apprentice Boys of Derry, of which Seawright was also a member, held in the Stadium Recreation Centre on the Shankill Road and conducted by the Rev. Hugh Ross, a member of the Orange Institution, minister of Newmills Presbyterian Church near Dungannon in County Tyrone and chairman of the Ulster Independence Committee. According to press reports at the time, the service was held in the stadium because the main Protestant churches were unwilling to be involved. Seawright's widow accused the churches of hypocrisy, but one of the ministers approached pointed out that Seawright 'had no links' with his church.

UVF man Brian Robinson, shot on 2 September 1989 by an Army undercover team, was another member of 'Old Boyne Island Heroes' LOL 633. He and his accomplice, David McCullough, had just shot dead a forty-three-year-old Roman Catholic, Patrick McKenna, in the Ardoyne. He also was given an 'Orange funeral', and death notices appeared in the local press from his lodge. This caused some controversy at the time and led to at least one letter of complaint to the *Belfast Telegraph*.

Kevin Magee, writing in *Sunday Life* on 24 September 1989, said, 'The Orange Order last night defended its position over members' attendance at the funeral of a UVF volunteer.' He quoted the then County Grand Master of the Grand Orange Lodge of Belfast, John McCrea, as saying:

> The Orange Order has always condemned violence from all sources . . . Funerals of lodge members are a personal matter and a lodge will only attend a funeral at the request of a family . . . The death notice inserted in the newspapers was from an individual lodge and not the Orange Order as a whole.

If this was an attempt to distance the Institution as a whole from paramilitarism, it failed, and the Secretary of LOL 633 was forced to defend the position in a letter to the *Belfast Telegraph* on 6 October 1989, stating that Robinson's 'private life was his own affair'. This contradicted not only the words of the Basis of the Institution, that it 'will not admit into its brotherhood persons whom an intolerant spirit leads to persecute, injure, or upbraid any man on account of his religious opinions', but also the aim of 'setting a good example in our daily lives, by living up to the high principles of the Order'.

Robinson's was not the first, nor sadly the last, death notice to appear in the local press identifying the deceased as both an Orangeman and a member of a paramilitary organisation. Over the years of the 'troubles' this embarrassing connection was publicly displayed with regularity, making the statement attributed to the Executive Officer, George Patton, in the aftermath of the police raid on Stoneyford Orange Hall on the evening of 1 November 1999, all the more incredible: 'Our rules are quite explicit. If anyone is involved in paramilitary activity they will be disciplined by expulsion from the Order. You can't be a member of the Order and a loyalist paramilitary group.'

The behaviour of 'Old Boyne Island Heroes' did not result in any disciplinary action. In fact the prevailing attitude throughout Belfast County Grand Lodge was that they had to be 'kept on board'.

An annual parade is held to 'commemorate' Brian Robinson on the first Saturday in September, including over forty bands which have previously led Orange lodges on the Twelfth. On Saturday 2 September 2000, the parade was held in north Belfast to the memorial erected in his name. As well as the usual UVF paramilitary presence there was also a delegation from LOL 633, wearing Orange regalia, who laid a wreath in Robinson's memory. This caused an outcry in the media, but no one had the courage to raise this matter in the higher echelons of the Orange Order.

Dawson Bailie, the County Grand Master of Belfast, was interviewed by David Dunseith on the BBC Northern Ireland programme 'Talk Back' on 4 September 2000. In the interview he refused to condemn the Orange presence, describing the Institution as 'a broad church' and saying that he had 'no axe to grind whatsoever' with those who took part in the parade. Jacqueline McIntyre, writing in the *Irish News* on 5 September, did not miss the point: 'For a second time, County Grand Master, Dawson Bailie yesterday contradicted an Orange Order statement issued last year categorically stating that any member found to be involved in paramilitary activity would face instant dismissal.'

The media were beginning to spot the duplicity at the heart of this behaviour. This shameful conduct by both the members of this Lodge and the County Grand Master raised the question, in the minds of many within the Institution, of the growing links between Orange Lodges and paramilitary activists. One of the major problems in recent years, particularly in Belfast, has been that many of the 'contentious Orange parades' are escorted past flashpoint areas by leaders of loyalist paramilitary organisations. This has been an excuse if not a reason for confrontation.

'Old Boyne Island Heroes' LOL 633 was seldom out of the media limelight. On 28 June 2003 they walked with Belfast's No. 9 District in the controversial Whiterock Parade. Following the parade a photograph appeared in the local paper, the *North Belfast News*, showing one of the 'Shankill Butchers', Eddie McIlwaine, who was sentenced to eight years for his part in the Butchers' campaign of terror, carrying the lodge's bannerette dedicated to the memory of Brian Robinson. The photograph was reproduced in *Sunday Life* on 20 July. Whether Eddie McIlwaine renewed his membership on release from prison, or continued his membership throughout his imprisonment is unknown.

While it is often stated in Orange circles that it is up to private lodges to initiate discipline against members, in some instances, as with LOL 633, the very opposite takes place. This was also seen in the case of Ken Wilkinson, the PUP spokesperson in Antrim and a member of Loanends LOL 585. In September 1999 Wilkinson refused to pay a fine of £815 for offences arising out of Drumcree-related disturbances in Antrim in July 1998. He was detained in Maghaberry Prison for refusing to pay his fine and could have been held for fourteen days. His lodge paid the fine for him and he was released. He was quoted in the *Antrim Guardian* of 29 September 1999 as saying, 'I hope the County Lodge steps in to make up the loss.' Ken Wilkinson, still a member of LOL 585, was to appear later in court in September 2002 on charges of assaulting a police officer, and in February 2004 he was convicted of disorderly behaviour. This is certainly not the way to convince people that 'there is something in the Orange Society that elevates a man and raises him above the average of humanity. Something that makes him a better man morally, socially and intellectually.'

Twenty-seven-year-old Norman James Coopey was still a member of LOL 357 in County Down, when on 8 January 1999 he was jailed for life for the brutal sectarian murder of sixteen-year-old James Morgan. Coopey pleaded guilty to murdering the schoolboy with a hammer on the afternoon of 24 July 1997, after offering him a lift in his car. Coopey and an accomplice then set fire to the boy's body to try and destroy evidence before dumping it in a pit full of animal carcasses in a field near the boy's home in Annsborough, outside Castlewellan. Coopey was not expelled from his lodge but allowed to resign after he was found guilty. He was later released under the terms of the Belfast Agreement.

In the *Sunday Times* on 28 February 1999, Liam Clarke wrote:

'Norman James Coopey, an Orangeman convicted last January of a sectarian murder, is still a member of the Order.' In the *Irish News* on 1 March 1999, Martin Anderson reported:

> Justin Morgan, James's father, said he was unaware that his son's killer was a member of the Orange Order. He said: 'When James was killed a local Unionist councillor who is a member of the Orange Order came and expressed condolences on the Order's behalf. I appreciated that at the time but nobody told me he (Coopey) was a member.'

Later in the year the *Irish News* revealed the fact that Coopey had been allowed to resign rather than be expelled.

In late 1996 and early 1997 one of the most shameful demonstrations of religious intolerance in the recent history of Northern Ireland took place in Ballymena, a market town in Country Antrim. Roman Catholic worshippers attending Saturday evening Mass in the Church of Our Lady in Ballymena's Harryville estate were subject to verbal and sometimes physical abuse from a crowd of 'loyalists' protesting at the RUC's refusal to allow a church parade in the nearby village of Dunloy. Some protesters wore Orange collarettes, and other Orangemen were present among the loyalists, but not wearing regalia. The Law of the Institution expressly forbids the wearing of regalia without permission. Not only were Orangemen who took part in this protest in breach of Law 23 if they were wearing regalia, but they were 'endangering the honour and dignity of the Institution', an offence covered in Law 17.

Gary Kent, interviewing the Grand Master, Robert Saulters, for the *Irish Post* on 15 March 1997, reported: 'Disciplinary action is also promised against any Orange Order members who participated in Harryville pickets whilst wearing their Orange collarettes. Saulters has himself studied the photographs but has said he couldn't identify any participants. There would be definitive action by June, if not before.'

A number of those involved in the Harryville picket were members and supporters of the Spirit of Drumcree group. They were easily identified from photographs. Many made no attempt to hide their Orange membership; one member tauntingly displayed his collarette identifying LOL 438, evidently not a lodge in County Antrim. Joe Anderson, a Ballymena Council employee, was prominent in the Harryville pickets, as he was in the Spirit of Drumcree, and had taken part in the occupation of the Dublin Road headquarters of the Orange Order on 9 and 10 December

1997. Anderson, a member of Slatt LOL 475 and former member of the Ulster Defence Regiment, was later to book Ballymena Town Hall for a 'Protestant Rally' on 28 September 2001, at which the 'Grand Protestant Committee' was to be inaugurated.

Photographs taken at the time, some of which appeared later in the press, revealed other interesting participants such as David Tweed, whom Ruth Dudley Edwards called 'a leading light in the intimidation of Harryville Catholics'.[7] Another photograph, which appeared in *Sunday Life* on 4 July 1999 in connection with a story on the Long March, showed both Ballymena loyalist Billy Houston and William McCaughey at Harryville. McCaughey, by any standards, must rank as one of the most notorious policemen to serve with any force. He first came to notoriety when he was charged with stealing a table from the home of the Mayor of Lisburn, Elsie Kelsey, on 4 June 1977. He had been on escort duty with the former minister of home affairs in the Northern Ireland government, John Taylor, who had been attending a party at Mrs Kelsey's home.

Later appearances in court were to be of a much more serious nature. In June 1980 McCaughey was jailed for life for the murder of Roman Catholic grocer William Strathearn in Ahoghill on 19 April 1977. This became known as the 'Good Samaritan Murder' because Strathearn had been lured to open his shop on the pretence of a caller requiring medication for a sick child. The following month McCaughey was brought from prison to appear in court along with four other members of the RUC, charged with a catalogue of terrorist offences of which he was found guilty. These offences included intent to cause grievous bodily harm and the causing of an explosion at the Rock Bar near Keady in County Armagh on 5 June 1976, for which he received seven years and four years respectively. He was also found guilty of the kidnapping of Ahoghill Roman Catholic parish priest Father Hugh Patrick Murphy on 18 June 1978. He received a three-year jail sentence for this kidnapping. McCaughey was to appear in court yet again in December 1980, where he was sentenced to ten years for armed robbery in Coleraine on the night of 24 June 1978.

The 'life' sentence given in June 1980 meant that McCaughey was released in 1993 with 'the co-operation of the authorities at the Free Presbyterian Bible College'.[8] In 1997 McCaughey called for the Harryville protest to be called off because 'the Orange Order in County Antrim has proved itself incapable of solving the Dunloy problem'.[9]

Within the Orange Order no discipline was even attempted against McCaughey. The only effort at discipline came from outside the

Institution, from Ken Maginnis, the MP for Fermanagh and South Tyrone, who called for him to be put back behind bars.[10]

Despite all McCaughey's convictions in the criminal courts, including armed robbery, kidnapping, intent to cause grievous bodily harm and the causing of an explosion, and murder, he remained a member of 'Abraham's Chosen Few' Derryadd LOL 230 in Lurgan District. The Secretary of Lurgan District Lodge during these years was Denis Watson, who would later declare, as Grand Secretary of the Grand Orange Lodge of Ireland, that 'Anyone convicted of a criminal offence is automatically expelled from the Institution.' Had the media made the connection, McCaughey's presence at Harryville wearing his Orange collarette would have exposed the Institution to enormous criticism. McCaughey himself said:

> I expected to be expelled from the Orange Order. I expected the letter to land on the floor of my prison cell when I was convicted but I wasn't and I have to say I was surprised. I knew I had broken the rules.[11]

McCaughey was still a member of the Institution in 2005 when he paraded in Ballymena on the Twelfth as a member of Ballymarlow LOL 637.

On BBC Radio Ulster on 27 August 2002, William Ross, the former Ulster Unionist MP for East Londonderry and one of the two Assistant Deputy Grand Masters appointed by the Grand Master Robert Saulters, made an astonishing claim. In a discussion of why no one had been disciplined in relation to Harryville, he said that the Rules in existence at the time did not enable the Grand Lodge to take action. He also claimed that the Rules had now been changed to enable the Grand Lodge to exercise discipline. In fact Rule 94 of the Constitution, Laws and Ordinances of the Loyal Orange Institution of Ireland, which prevailed at the time of the Harryville dispute, stated: 'Any Member offending against the Institution as a whole may be tried, as prescribed by Law 12, by the Grand Lodge or that of the County to which he belongs, provided he has not been previously tried for the same offence by his Private Lodge.' The new Rules which came into force on 8 December 1998 transferred the contents of the old Rule 94 into the new Rule 13, which states: 'Notwithstanding anything contained elsewhere in these laws the Grand Lodge of Ireland or the County Grand Lodge or the District Lodge to which a member belongs shall be entitled to try any charge against any member who has offended against the Institution as a whole.'

Most people learn by their mistakes. Not so Grand Master Robert Saulters. After failing to keep his promise to Gary Kent that disreputable members would face discipline, a press release was issued by Grand Lodge following disturbances on 21 June 2002 during the 'Tour of the North' Parade in Belfast:

> 'We condemn unreservedly any violence towards Catholic residents,' said Robert Saulters, Grand Master of the Orange Order. 'This kind of mindless hooliganism serves no purpose whatever. We are confident that no Orangeman took part in the attacks but we shall be carrying out an internal investigation to make sure – and if any Orangeman is implicated they will face disciplinary action.'

As will be seen, no discipline was exercised against the Spirit of Drumcree group whose activities included the disruption of County Antrim Grand Orange Lodge meetings in March and April 1997 and the occupation of the Grand Lodge offices on 12 September and 9 and 10 December that year. The consequences of this failure to act are described in Chapter Six.

This inertia in relation to discipline was to have other consequences. In the words of the American pulpiteer with an apt turn of phrase, Vance Havner, 'The alternative to discipline is disaster.' A shadowy group called the 'Orange Volunteers' emerged publicly in November 1998 when they put on a stunt for Ivan Little and an Ulster Television film crew at an undisclosed location. They claimed responsibility for a number of pipe bomb attacks and were eventually banned by the Secretary of State, Mo Mowlam, in March 1999.

While not all those involved with the Orange Volunteers were necessarily members of the Orange Institution, some evidently were. In this case the Institution was quick to condemn their activities. In a statement on 21 January 1999, the Grand Orange Lodge of Ireland said: 'Members of the Orange Institution are . . . distressed and angry to find that a group engaged in violent activity has the audacity to use the title Orange in their name. The "Orange Volunteers" have no connection with the Orange Institution. We unreservedly condemn their acts of violence.' These were wise words indeed, but, as is seen throughout the recent history of the Institution, there is a vast difference between words spoken and the implementation of the ideology behind the words.

On the evening of 1 November 1999 Stoneyford Orange Hall in south Antrim was searched by the security forces, who discovered copies of security files on over three hundred Republican suspects. Reports circulating at the time revealed that the police knew exactly where to go in the Hall in order to retrieve the documents. This raised suspicions that either there was a 'mole' within the organisation or the premises were bugged. A report in *Sunday World* on 21 November 1999 added credibility to the later suggestion. Writing under the headline 'Politicians taped by police in Orange Hall', Hugh Jordan claimed, 'Two loyalist politicians are caught up in a police probe into a rebel anti-ceasefire paramilitary gang.' *Sunday World* also reported that the two politicians were members of the Orange Order.

This search followed the arrest on 26 October of self-styled 'Pastor' Clifford Peoples (sometimes spelt 'Peeples') and James McGookin Fisher. The arrests took place outside Dungannon in County Tyrone, when a pipe bomb and two grenades were discovered in the boot of a car. Peoples, who had once been a member of the Orange Order, had first come to prominence in 1986 when, along with George Seawright, he placed a caravan at Maryfield, the centre for the Anglo-Irish Secretariat, in protest against the Anglo-Irish Agreement. Later in 1996, then a member of the Ulster Independence Movement, Peoples alleged that his florist's shop had been wrecked by the UVF because he refused to pay 'protection money'. The following year he was involved in such bizarre activities as painting the word 'Ichabod' on the Stadium Recreation Centre on the Shankill Road. He claimed in his defence that 'God had told him' to do so. In 1998 he became an opponent of the Belfast Agreement and addressed an anti-Agreement rally in Antrim town on 24 April. Sharing the platform with him were the DUP's Jack McKee from Larne and former Lord Mayor of Belfast Sammy Wilson.

Justice was to catch up with 'Pastor' Clifford Peoples, described in *Sunday Life* on 10 August 1997 by a 'FAIT [Families Against Intimidation and Terror] source' as 'a good Christian man'. On 8 March 2001 Peoples, who changed his plea to guilty, was sentenced to ten years' imprisonment for possession of arms. James McGookin Fisher was given eight years' imprisonment for 'aiding and abetting and possession of explosives'. With the fifty per cent remission on sentences, Peoples was released from prison in November 2004.

Quickly following the arrest of Clifford Peoples, other arrests were made in Antrim. Two brothers, Paul and Mervyn Armstrong, were arrested after a car chase in which a rifle was discovered. Stuart Wilson of Glenavy and Alan Lynn of Antrim were also arrested.

The editorial in the *Irish News* on 5 November said, 'The onus is now on the leadership of the Orange Order to convince the general public that it wants nothing to do with extreme loyalism in any shape or form.'

The next day in the same paper Alan Erwin, under the headine 'Orangemen held in RUC swoops arrested', reported George Patton's statement that 'If anyone is involved in paramilitary activity they will be disciplined by expulsion from the Order', and revealed that 'Lisburn DUP councillor and Stoneyford Orange Lodge member Cecil Calvert last night admitted some of those in custody were members of the loyal institution. "I can confirm some of the men arrested are members of the Orange Order," he said.'

Henry McDonald, writing in the *Observer* on 7 November, did not name the suspected leader of the Orange Volunteers, who had escaped police custody following the seizure of the documents, but reiterated that 'Several of those charged were members of the Orange Order.' He also reported George Patton's assurance that 'Orangemen would be dismissed if found guilty of paramilitary involvement'.

While Patton may have been engaging in an act of public relations, it was also a feat of duplicity. As the Executive Officer of the Grand Lodge he ought to have been well aware of the remarks of Eddie McAdam, the Master of 'Old Boyne Island Heroes' LOL 633: 'We could throw out house burglars or sex offenders and the like, but to us these guys are not criminals, they're victims of circumstances.'

At a meeting of Central Committee on 26 November, questions were asked concerning the membership of those who had been arrested a month previously. Thomas Ross, the District Master of Glenavy District Lodge, stated that Stuart Wilson was not a member, but nothing was forthcoming on the others. Specific questions were asked of the County Antrim Grand Secretary, William Leathem, about the Armstrong brothers. He responded that he was 'still making enquiries'. This answer was no surprise. It was typical of the mindset. Many members present were aware by this stage that Paul and Mervyn Armstrong were members of 'Boyd Memorial' LOL 312, sitting in Burnside Orange Hall, Antrim.

When all four were to appear in Antrim Crown Court on 21 December 2000, there was wide coverage on both the local BBC and UTV News bulletins, which reported that the Armstrong brothers were members of the Institution. According to some press reports, during the trial the defending counsel told the court that 'the four accused had joined Stoneyford Orange Lodge in sympathy for the events at Drumcree'. Magheragall District Lodge, to which Stoneyford LOL 1253 was affiliated, quickly denied this. It was apparently a case of distancing the

Institution when you could and hiding when you could not. Sixmilewater District Lodge, to which Boyd Memorial LOL 312 was affiliated, did not make any statement to the press.

Duplicity was to be revealed again with contradictory statements coming from the Executive Officer, George Patton, and the Lodge Secretary, John McGrath. Stephen McCaffrey, in the *Irish News* on 27 December, reported that:

> Mr Patton said both now faced trial by the organisation and that the crimes were such that expulsion from the Order is virtually certain. Mr Patton said the Order had rules and procedures that would be followed. 'When they were arrested, they were suspended pending an investigation. What happens now is that they have been found guilty and they will be formally tried and disciplined accordingly,' Mr Patton said. Asked if he thought that would mean expulsion he said: 'I would have thought so.'

George Patton did not explain how they could be 'formally tried and disciplined' while remaining in prison. Neither did he point out how irrelevant the suspension was. Suspension of membership means that the individual is not allowed to walk in parades or attend lodge meetings, something he would be unable to do anyway while he remained in prison. His statement also conflicted with what the Grand Secretary, Denis Watson, had said on 17 October 2000: 'Anyone convicted of a criminal offence is automatically expelled from the Institution.'

Henry McDonald wrote in the *Observer* on 24 December 2000:

> John McGrath, Boyd Memorial's secretary, repeatedly refused to confirm or deny that the brothers, both terrorists with the Orange Volunteers, had been expelled . . . Asked why the Armstrongs were allowed to stay in the Order, McGrath said: 'I don't think it's any of your business. I am not making any statement on it at all; those two lads have been through enough.'

The Institution was undoubtedly sending conflicting messages to a disillusioned membership and a sceptical world.

The secretary of state may have banned the Orange Volunteers in March 1999, but they reinvented themselves under cover of the 'Loyalist Voice' website which carried the motto 'AUDACES FORTUNA JUVAT – VOLUNTEERS'. On 6 July 2001 there was a daring public show of strength at a traditional 'Arch Opening' parade in Crumlin village in County Antrim. Twelve individuals assembled wearing orange polo shirts with the 'AUDACES FORTUNA JUVAT – VOLUNTEERS' motto, put on various Orange collarettes and joined with the assembled Orangemen, with their own colour party of two flags and two supporters carrying swords. Present at this display was Mark Harbinson wearing his personal Orange collarette of Stoneyford LOL 1253 on top of his orange polo shirt. They paraded through the village as part of the Orange parade. When the colour party was approached by a Parades Commission Authorised Officer and asked who they represented, they replied that they were 'Derriaghy 135'. When the parade finished this group received a separate order to dismiss.

This event was alarming in many ways and would have caused great distress for many genuine Orangemen had it come to public attention at that time. The startling thing was that the person legally responsible for the parade, the Master of Glenavy District, Thomas Ross, who had signed the official notice for the parade, made no apparent attempt to stop them.

This parade was led by some of the most senior Orangemen of County Antrim, including Ross, William Thompson, the Secretary of Magheragall District, and William Leathem, the Grand Secretary of County Antrim Grand Orange Lodge. Ironically, the previous day the *Belfast Telegraph* had carried a letter from William Leathem, signed in his official capacity, stating: 'We have no association with any paramilitary organisation. To do so would betray our principles and precepts.' Presumably he did not understand the inconsistency of his behaviour. He was to repeat the above statement after the event in a letter to the *Ulster Star*, a Lisburn weekly paper, on 17 August 2001.

Sixmilewater District did not take any action in the case of the Armstrong brothers, but they were quick to act in another case. Jim Wilson, the chief whip of the Ulster Unionist Party, was suspended from membership of the Order for refusing to obey a summons to attend the Sixmilewater District to explain his voting in the Assembly. Wilson, along with some others, had not supported the DUP motion to allow 'automatic representation' for the Orange Order on the Civic Forum.

Ironically, on 16 February 2001, around the same time as Sixmilewater District was concerning themselves with Wilson's misdemeanours, Burnside Orange Hall, where Boyd Memorial LOL 312 meets, was being used for a UFF rally. This sent out a clear message to the world that the Orange Institution was more concerned with how an individual voted in a representative democracy than with its own association with paramilitaries.

None of this is mentioned in the 'Factfile' for LOL 312 in the October 2004 edition of the *Orange Standard*, 'the official newspaper of the Grand Orange Lodge of Ireland', which boldly states, 'In modern times Boyd Memorial LOL No. 312 is highly active in the local community and a fine example of Orangeism at its best.' It is little wonder that some members refer to the *Orange Standard* as '*Pravda*'!

Ivor Deane Knox Young, or 'Stick Young' as he is known locally, is familiar in loyalist circles in mid-Ulster. Ivor Young is the Worshipful Master of LOL 9, 'The Earl of Beaconsfield Primrose League, Clounagh', in Portadown District. In the 1970s he was the self-confessed 'Commander' of the UDA's Portadown Brigade and appeared in court on a number of charges.

Young's photograph has appeared more recently in the press on a number of significant occasions. When the Spirit of Drumcree group occupied the headquarters of the Orange Institution on 10 December 1997, he was photographed standing beside Walter Millar, wearing his Worshipful Master's collarette of Clounagh LOL 9. This photograph was reproduced in the *Belfast News Letter* of 11 December.

On 15 April 1998, prior to the referendum on the Belfast Agreement, there was a picket on the home in Dungannon of Ken Maginnis, MP for Fermanagh and South Tyrone. A photograph of those involved appeared in the *Belfast Telegraph* next day. Ivor Young appears again, along with David Moore McAllister, wearing Orange regalia and carrying a poster declaring 'TRIMBLE AND CO MUST GO'.

As Master of a lodge within Portadown District, Ivor Young was to the fore in the Drumcree protests. He was pictured in the *Sunday Times* on 3 January and the *Belfast News Letter* on 4 January 1999, leading a protest parade in Portadown the previous Saturday, wearing his usual Orange regalia but also sporting his blackthorn stick from which he received his nickname. Not being one to hide from the cameras, Ivor Young appears again in still photographs and video footage taken on the evening of 3 July 2000. Walking under a banner proclaiming 'SHANKILL ROAD UFF 2nd BATT C. COY', on this occasion he is wearing not Orange regalia but a t-shirt carrying the message 'Simply the best – Their only crime LOYALTY'. In video footage broadcast on the BBC Northern Ireland 'Spotlight' programme on 17 October 2000, he is seen sharing a beer with Johnny 'Mad Dog' Adair, whom he accompanied in a protest march down Drumcree Hill. With this kind of publicity it became increasingly difficult for Portadown District to argue that the parade down the Garvaghy Road was simply a 'walk home from morning prayer in Drumcree Parish Church'.

On the Twelfth of July 2000 Lagan Valley MP Jeffrey Donaldson spoke at the Orange demonstration in Ballinderry: 'The Orange Order stands for higher ideals than this and must at every opportunity condemn the illegal activities of the paramilitaries and of all those who engage in acts of violence. There can be no room for equivocation lest the Orange Order's reputation is dishonoured by some kind of moral ambivalence.' Wise words and well spoken, but Donaldson must have known, given the events of recent years, that this 'moral ambivalence' had already dishonoured the Orange Order's reputation. His emphasis only added to the confusion in the minds of many, and led to the conclusion that this was an exercise of duplicity on the part of the Institution. Public statements and private practice stood in stark contrast.

This moral ambivalence is seen nowhere more clearly than in the events at Drumcree in 1998. The *Belfast Telegraph* of 18 July 1998 had reported Portadown Orange leaders' warning that 'any members convicted of criminal offences arising from rioting at Drumcree could be expelled from the Order', and quoted David Jones as saying: 'It would be a matter for each lodge but there would certainly be disciplinary action.' As expected, it was only a matter of time before Orangemen were arrested. On 10 July 1998 a number of members of lodges in nearby Lurgan were charged with criminal offences. The *Observer* of 14 February 1999 reported on their appearance at Craigavon Magistrates Court: 'The eight include [Richard] Monteith (LOL 63); Geoffrey Morrison, Mark Greenaway and David Hanlon (LOL 48); Philip Black and John Saville Black (LOL 42); Roy Graham (LOL 372) and Paul Johnston.' Robert Neil Anthony and Bryan John McDowell had also been named in the *Belfast Telegraph* on 6 February.

Richard Monteith, a Portadown solicitor, was fined £250. He may have been disciplined by the state, but the Orange Institution certainly did not discipline him. On the contrary, after being charged and before the case came to court, he was elected Deputy District Master of Lurgan District. This makes it the more incredible that Denis Watson, also a member of Lurgan District, could state on the BBC 'Spotlight' programme on 17 October 2000 that 'anyone convicted of a criminal offence is automatically expelled from the Institution'. When questioned on 14 February 1999 by Henry McDonald, the Northern Ireland correspondent of the

Observer, as to 'why the Lurgan eight are still in the Orange Order despite their convictions', Watson is reported to have responded, 'I am not aware of the circumstances; that would be a matter for the men's private lodges, not the county or the Grand Lodge.'

The Grand Chaplain of the Grand Orange Lodge of Ireland, Canon S. E. Long, wrote on the 'Devastating Consequences of Drumcree' in *The Orange Torch*, the official journal of the Loyal Orange Institution of Scotland, in September 1998:

> We hope that those found guilty of criminal acts will be punished. Orangemen who broke the rules of the Order in conduct unbecoming to Orangemen must be made to face the consequences of such behaviour as agreed in the Constitution, Laws and Ordinances of the Orange Institution. The Order if it is to be true to itself must not have in its membership any whose conduct has brought discredit upon themselves and the organisation. We must be seen to be what we are, law-abiding citizens, anxious for the well being of the country and determined to do what we can to make it peaceful and prosperous for everyone regardless of class, creed or race.

This was evidently, as Samuel Johnson put it, 'the triumph of hope over experience'. Had this been written by a relatively inexperienced member of the Institution one could well understand his misplaced hope, but Canon Long had been involved in the affairs of the Orange Institution long enough to know that the chances of any kind of discipline being exercised over these events were very slender indeed.

The reality of the Order's duplicity was beginning to be seen, not only by the respectable membership but by an increasingly disillusioned world. The continual promises by senior officers assuring expulsion of those involved in criminal activity were becoming more and more unbelievable. This had not passed the notice of the 'Unionist Non-Orangeman' who wrote in the *Belfast News Letter* on 22 December 1999:

> In Lurgan a number of prominent Orangemen recently pleaded guilty to causing criminal damage, apparently in support of the protest at Drumcree. Do members of the Orange Order not swear an oath pledging to obey the law? Were they disciplined for breaking it? Apparently not. It is this attitude that has caused the Orange Order to lose the support of what could be called 'middle Ulster'.

It would be wrong however to suggest that throughout the twentieth century there was no exercise of discipline at all within the Institution. One interesting case concerned the Hon. Phelim R. H. O'Neill DL, a minister in the Northern Ireland government, and Colonel A. J. H. Cramsie DL. Both these Orangemen were members of lodges in County Antrim when each was accused of 'attending a Roman Catholic Service in breach of his obligations as an Orangeman aggravating his offence by defying the County Grand Lodge'. Their respective private and district lodges had taken no action; nevertheless the County Grand Lodge of Antrim expelled them from the Institution on 12 June 1967. Neither man appealed this decision through the procedure of the Institution or through the civil courts. It was a good thing for the Institution that they did not instigate procedure in civil law. The Grand Orange Lodge of Ireland took counsel's opinion from the Rt Hon. Anthony Babington QC, a brother Orangeman, who advised that they would not be able to confirm the expulsions. The summary of his opinion was that 'the offence is that of *giving countenance* and not of *attending* . . . there is no offence of *attending*'. He concluded: 'The High Court of Justice would be very slow indeed to hold that Her Majesty's Deputy Lieutenant by attending a Roman Catholic Service as part of his Public Duty would have thereby committed an offence of any nature.'

In many organisations, an inability to read the rules carefully leads to misunderstandings as to what they actually mean. The Orange Institution is no exception. Law 17 of the new Constitution, Laws and Ordinances of the Loyal Orange Institution of Ireland, adopted in 2000, states: 'Members participating in a Roman Catholic or other non-Protestant Worship shall be in breach of Law 16.' This takes up the point of Babington's opinion, placing the offence of participating in unreformed worship clearly within the category of offences against religion and morality, and therefore subject to expulsion. However, the reader will note that the word used is 'participating', not 'attending'. There is still no offence of 'attending'.

After hearing Babington's opinion, the Grand Lodge referred the expulsions back to Central Committee 'to clarify the situation'. However, at the subsequent meeting of the Loyal Orange Institution of Ireland the Grand Lodge ignored counsel's opinion and expelled O'Neill and Cramsie, in spite of an attempt by the former Grand Master Sir George Clark to reduce their sentence to suspension.

Other high-profile incidents of members attending Roman Catholic Churches at this time were dealt with in a different manner. Sir Robin

Kinahan and Senator John Drennan, who had apparently attended a wedding and funeral respectively, went through the appeals procedure and were suspended for two years.

A second interesting example of discipline took place in the 1970s when 'Banner of the Cross' LOL 1310 in Belfast's No. 6 District, which drew its membership largely from the Free Presbyterian Church, had its warrant suspended for a year. Members had heckled the Rev. Donald Gillies on an Orange platform because he had 'aligned himself' with the Roman Catholic priest at Holy Cross, Ardoyne. What they meant by 'aligned' was that the Rev. Gillies had publicly and in the presence of the priest expressed his sorrow at the damage caused to Holy Cross Church by a bomb on 7 July 1972. Such has been the dramatic change within the Institution since the 1970s that LOL 1310 could retell this story in *The Twelfth*, published by the County Grand Orange Lodge of Belfast in 1999, as a badge of honour.

Strange as it may seem, 'Banner of the Cross' LOL 1310 did not make a similar protest when Lord Molyneaux was one of the first to contribute to the repair of Aldergrove Roman Catholic Church when it was burned down by loyalists in July 1998. One can only speculate as to why they did not protest at this similar act of Christian charity.

As the twenty-first century dawned the Institution was to come under continued pressure to address the problem of discipline. The media sometimes put pressure on the leadership, which continued to fob them off with promises of 'dealing with it'. The embarrassment of various events being reported in the press did not even exercise the Grand Lodge officers into taking action to preserve the good name of the Order. Instead they were more concerned about who had 'leaked' information. Living in their secretive world, they did not appear to understand that a good investigative journalist could obtain information from a number of public sources, including court records.

The press did not always notice lapses in discipline. One such incident went unnoticed when sixteen-year-old Glenn 'Spacer' Branagh was killed by his own pipe bomb on 11 November 2001. His friends and relatives immediately claimed that he died a hero, alleging that he was attempting to return a pipe bomb thrown by nationalists. The *Belfast Telegraph* of 13 November carried a death notice from 'Northern Temperance' LOL 1252 in Belfast's No. 1 District, referring to 'brother Branagh', although he was not old enough to join. If this death notice was a spoof, no attempt was made to deny it. The same day, the UDA announced that Branagh had been a member of its youth wing, the Ulster Young Militants.

The media pressure increased with successive Drumcree stand-offs and reached its height following the scenes on Sunday 7 July 2002 at Drumcree Hill, when the world saw overwhelming evidence of the involvement of Orangemen in violence. The usual banal statements were issued promising discipline against those who may have been involved. One writer to the *Belfast Telegraph* on 11 July 2002 perceptively stated: 'Let us not hear "washing of hands" statements from the Orangemen who will claim this was caused by a few "hangers on".'

The Executive Officer, George Patton, said on BBC Radio Ulster the following morning, 'We will be investigating . . . We will deal with this.' On the Radio Ulster 'Talkback' programme later that morning I stated that 'acts of public disorder should be followed by acts of public discipline.' Yet on 6 August the Grand Master, Robert Saulters, wrote in the *Belfast News Letter*, 'This will be done in private because that's how companies, political parties and most other organisations deal with disciplinary matters.'

In years gone by, the leadership were conscious of the public image of the Orange Order. In 1798 the Grand Lodge published its disciplinary action against William Mackenzie in the three main newspapers of the day. In the nineteenth century, the Grand Lodge stated in reference to the continuation of illegal degrees that an offender 'shall be publicly expelled and his name sent to every Lodge in the Kingdom'. In 2003 the Institution's response to the need to improve its image was to hire a public relations company. This appeared to do nothing to counter the information now coming into the public arena.

On 10 November 2003 the 'Drumcree Fifteen', as they had become known, all pleaded guilty at Belfast Crown Court to charges of riotous behaviour and received suspended prison sentences. On leaving the court, one of the fifteen, Mark Harbinson, thanked the Orange Order for its support and said that the DPP and the PSNI should be trying to convict criminals rather than pursuing 'fifteen law-abiding citizens'.

Such support had been evident the previous Saturday, 8 November, when the Grand Master, Robert Saulters, and the Grand Secretary, Denis Watson, led a parade in Portadown. Following the Drumcree disturbances of 6 July 2002, the *Belfast News Letter* of 6 August contained a letter from the Grand Master summarised with the headline 'Troublemakers will be thrown out of Order – if proven guilty'. This confirmed that the words of denunciation previously issued by the Grand Master were nothing but words – promises which were not kept. The support of the leadership for such criminal behaviour was without precedent in the history of the Orange Institution. The public statement by William Ross on 27 August 2002 that the Rules had been changed to enable the Grand Lodge to exercise discipline appeared very hollow in this light.

The Grand Master attempted to justify his actions in an interview in the *Belfast Telegraph* on 22 November, saying that the convictions, self-confessed though they were, were a 'set-up'. This interview led directly to the resignation of at least one Deputy Grand Chaplain, the Rev. Denis Bannerman. The Rev. Dr Warren Porter wrote personally to Robert Saulters, while I had this response published in the *Belfast Telegraph* on 29 November:

1. Those who confessed their guilt have no one to blame but themselves.
2. It is untrue to say that 'We do not hear what disciplinary action is taken whenever other organisations or churches are involved in an investigation.'
3. It is unprecedented in the two-hundred-year history of the Orange Institution that the leadership should support criminals, and self-confessed criminals at that.
4. The behaviour of the 'Drumcree Fifteen' flies in the face of the 'Particular Qualifications of an Orangeman'.

On 24 November 2003, a public and courageous act again brought the Orange Institution to the attention of the media. John Allen, a member of 'Kilbride Bible & Crown Defenders' LOL 1107, whose son of the same name had been murdered, allegedly by the Ulster Volunteer Force, left his orange collarette at Schomberg House, the new headquarters of the Orange Institution in Ireland. He was quoted in the *Sunday World* of 23 November as stating: 'I have now discovered since my son's murder that I am in the same organisation as the person who prompted and organised Jock's killing . . . I can no longer be a party to any organisation which includes murderers – especially the murderer who set up my son.'

A spokesman for the Grand Orange Lodge of Ireland said in the same edition: 'We would expect all Orangemen to stand by the Ten Commandments. Especially the one which says Thou Shalt Not Kill.' Given the toleration of convicted murderer William McCaughey within the membership, one wondered just where this 'spokesman' had been.

One further wondered, when a 'spokesman' was quoted in the *Irish News* on 25 November as saying, 'The Institution will now mount a full and thorough investigation into Mr Allen's claims.' Since the Institution was unwilling to exercise discipline on those who were convicted in the courts, there was little possibility of them exercising discipline on those who were not. There is no evidence that the Institution conducted a 'full and thorough investigation into Mr Allen's claims'. The only correspondence to follow from Grand Lodge was a letter to John Allen, acknowledging receipt of his letter and stating that the information contained therein had been passed on to the police.

In the same month Roy Thompson JP, an Independent Unionist Councillor on Antrim Borough Council and a member of 'Johnstone's Own Ballyhill' LOL 484 in Killead District, pleaded guilty to fraud in Belfast Magistrates' Court for making a false subsidy claim for twenty-six sheep. Roy Thompson was not just a local councillor, Orangeman, Blackman and JP. He was also Treasurer of Killead District LOL 17 in County Antrim, as well as being Deputy County Grand Master of County Antrim Royal Black Chapter. Attempts to have Thompson expelled, in keeping with the stated policy of the Orange Institution that 'Anyone convicted of a criminal offence is automatically expelled from the Institution', failed. The failure lay not in the moral stand of LOL 484, which initiated proceedings, or Killead District, which supported them, but with the County Antrim Grand Orange Lodge who failed to support these actions. It is often affirmed in Orangeism that discipline must begin in the private lodge. Here was a classic example of a private lodge being thwarted in its attempts to be true to Orange principles.

The year 2003 did not give any encouragement to decent and respectable Orangemen, in spite of the efforts of the media consultants who encouraged the Grand Master to raise £124,000 on behalf of Cancer Research Northern Ireland as a publicity stunt. 2004 was not to hold out any greater hope either, with first the revelations of the involvement of an Orangeman in a sectarian murder. On 23 March 2004 Harry Speers, along with a nineteen-year-old accomplice, Ronald Craig, was convicted of the murder of Trevor Lowry, kicked to death in Harmin Parade, Glengormley on 31 March 2001. The father of two had been mistaken for a Roman Catholic. Forty-four-year-old Speers, the District Master of Carnmoney District Lodge, who was described as having 'UDA connections',[12] was sentenced to life imprisonment for what the judge described as a 'callous murder'. He was expelled from the Royal Black Institution on 4 December 2004. His private Black Perceptory had initiated the expulsion in May, following his conviction. Whether or not he has been expelled from the Orange Institution is not known.

On 20 April the International Monitoring Commission, established in May 2003 by the Joint Declaration of the British and Irish governments, issued its first report. Although it did not name the Orange Institution, it came so close that the media had no difficulties in drawing that conclusion. The report concluded in its recommendation 8.7:

> No organisation, statutory, commercial or voluntary, should tolerate links with paramilitary groups or give legitimacy to them. In particular, societies and other similar organisations should make every effort to satisfy themselves that none of their members are linked to paramilitary groups. If there is any suspicion that they might be, then the onus should be on the person concerned to show there is no basis for that suspicion, not on the organisation to act only if it is proved. We will examine this whole issue in future reports.

All these instances, coming into the public domain, left those members of the Institution who adhered to its authentic core values in despair. The by now obvious unwillingness of the leadership of the Orange Institution to take action against those within its ranks who failed to live up to its traditional high standards meant that the Order was now a danger to its own principles, as it gratuitously gave propaganda victories to its enemies.

Chapter Four

A Prelude to Disaster

'Taking responsibility for the past is fundamental to escaping from its clutches.'

Marianne Elliott[1]

'Parading' or 'walking', not 'marching', has long been the tradition of Orangeism, even before the Loyal Orange Institution of Ireland was formed in September 1795. There is an abundance of evidence that Irish Protestants had commemorated both William's birthday on 4 November (old style) and on the Twelfth every year since 1690. (Prior to 1752 the 'Twelfth' celebrations were held on 1 July.[2])

In his Review of the Parades Commission and Public Processions (Northern Ireland) Act 1998, issued on 27 September 2002, Sir George Quigley said:

> The origins of the Orange parading culture as ritual social behaviour can be traced back to the first birthday of William III after the Battle of the Boyne, celebrated in Dublin on 4 November 1690. Throughout the eighteenth century (and not least during the period of the Volunteer movement which ante-dated the formation of the Orange Order in 1795) it was the King's role in the Glorious Revolution rather than his military campaign that was commemorated, although it was not long before there were separate celebrations linked to the famous battles.[3]

The *Belfast News Letter* of 3 July 1750 reported from Dublin on the celebrations in the city and throughout County Wicklow:

> Last Sunday being the anniversary of the Battle of the Boyne in the year 1690, when the late King James was defeated by King William of Glorious Memory, the morning was ushered in with the ringing of bells and the displaying of flags on the several towers and steeples of this city . . .

> At 12 noon the last stone of the new spire of St Patrick's Cathedral was laid with a schedule of entertainment arranged by the Dean and Chapter. A high table was laid on the top of the spire for the workers while the last stone was crowned with an orange garland and the British flag. Once again loyal toasts were drunk. Pupils from schools in the city attended church wearing orange cockades in their bonnets.
>
> In County Wicklow Protestants assembled at Newtown Mount Kennedy and marched under arms to church at Newcastle where they heard an excellent sermon preached appropriately enough by Rev. George Derry. They fired three volleys and returned to Mount Kennedy for a banquet at the home of Robert Livesey. The Earl of Meath contributed a buck to the banquet.
>
> The celebrations began that night with the firing of guns, bonfires and other demonstrations of joy.

Kevin Haddick-Flynn says in *Orangeism: The Making of a Tradition*:

> The Protestant peasantry had never forgotten the events of the Williamite Wars. Crude paintings of William's crossing of the Boyne hung in every home and each twelfth of July was treated as a Day of Remembrance. When they gathered to commemorate the old victories, they were often known as 'William's Men' or sometimes as 'Orangemen'. On 12 July 1791 a few hundred gathered at Aghaderg in County Down and marched along the road behind a fife and drum band.[4]

On 14 July 1795 Sir Edward Newenham wrote to the Rt Hon. Thomas Pelham, Chief Secretary at Dublin Castle:

> Last Sunday being the 12th July, was duly celebrated in this village [Rathdrum, County Wicklow]. Early in the morning every Loyal Protestant House and . . . many cabins were decorated with Orange Lilies . . . at Church, Men, Women and Children, except 3 Democrats, had their loyal emblems affixed to their Persons. In the evening 32 Protestants paraded in the Market place opposite the Tavern.

The Orange Institution as we know it was not formed until after the Battle of the Diamond on 21 September 1795. The events referred to above therefore pre-date the Order, and serve to remind us of the indissoluble connection between parading and Orangeism as distinct from the Orange Institution.

Armagh, being the foundation county of the Orange Order as we know it today, takes not only a particular pride in the Institution but a special interest in 'parading' or 'walking'. Some of the largest Twelfth parades took place in County Armagh in 1796, the year after the Orange Order was founded. The following report appeared in the *Belfast News Letter* of 15 July 1796:

> We understand that, on Tuesday last, being the anniversary of the Battle of Aughrim, a great body of Orange Men amounting to upwards of 2,000 assembled in Lurgan, and spent the day with the utmost regularity and good order. It unfortunately happened in the course of the afternoon that some words took place between Mr McMordie, at Aghalee, near Lurgan, and one of the Queen's County militia, when coming to blows McMordie received a stab of which he died.

The following year a second great Orange demonstration was held in County Armagh, again in Lurgan, some five miles from Portadown, and noted in the papers of Colonel Robert Hugh Wallace:

> 'I have heard', said Mr Stewart Blacker, an aide-de-camp of General Knox who was present at the meeting, 'General Owen states that he went on that occasion from Belfast to Lurgan and that his impression of the state of the country was that it was in a most frightfully disturbed condition; that passwords were prevalent among the peasantry such as "Are you up, are you up?" On their way from Belfast to Lurgan they saw several bodies of Orangemen in procession. In Lurgan Park . . . they received a body of nearly 20,000 Orangemen, who marched past before them; and on returning the next day to Belfast, a proper feeling of confidence seemed to be restored to the country . . . and the general expression that seemed to come from the peasantry was God Save the King.' The next day dawned on a spirit of distrust among the public; but the Orange Demonstrations made a desirable change.[5]

Bands to lead the Orange walks and processions have been with us since the creation of the Institution, but too many bands have taken on a more aggressive tone in the present climate. If there is one area today where both the duplicity and inertia of the Institution is most exposed, it is here. When challenged by the media about the falling numbers on parade, the excuse is often made that 'many of the band members are also members of the Institution'. While this may be true of large areas in the west of the

Province it is not universally the case. On the other hand, when those in bands misbehave they are quickly disowned with 'That is nothing to do with us, they are not members.'

Early bands leading Orange parades consisted of 'fife and drum' – a Lambeg drummer and one or two flautists. More formal bands developed during the nineteenth and early part of the twentieth centuries. From the 1960s many bands took on a life of their own as they became part of 'loyalist culture'. This was perpetuated by the demise of the more traditional band, particularly in and around Belfast. Traditional bands required both commitment and finance, and with the reduction of the population in Belfast – by thirty per cent in the last thirty years of the twentieth century – this proved difficult to sustain. Many of the old 'great' bands were replaced by what became known as 'blood and thunder' or 'kick the Pope' bands. To add to the difficulties, many of these were associated with paramilitaries. In one appalling case, members of the 'Pride of the Village' band were involved in the exceptionally brutal murder of Margaret Wright in their Band Hall in Meridi Street off the Donegall Road in Belfast on 6 April 1994. The 'Pride of the Village' band led various lodges in Belfast's No. 5 District, Sandy Row. They also had connections with an outlawed paramilitary group, the Red Hand Defenders. When the accused in the case came to trial, television pictures showed this band parading within the County Grand Orange Lodge of Belfast along the Lisburn Road on the Twelfth. This image did nothing either to enhance the credibility of the Institution or to endear it to respectable people.

Private lodges, especially in Belfast and the larger urban areas, are under pressure to engage bands for Twelfth parades, on grounds of tradition or because a neighbouring lodge has a band and 'We cannot let the side down.' In practice, the band which leads a parade sets the tone of that parade and symbolises its significance. If a parade is led by a well-organised pipe or brass band the public response is vastly different from that provoked by a 'blood and thunder' band. The general public are unable to distinguish between the band and the Orangemen parading behind it, and the media have often referred to 'Orange parades' when there was no Orangeman in sight. What they were really looking at was a band parade.

Since 1986 the Grand Orange Lodge of Ireland's regulations for bands have required all bands engaged by an Orange Lodge to sign a contract stipulating good behaviour. Expelled Orangemen are prohibited from parading with bands, and uniformity and dignity on parade, twin drumming, the abuse of intoxicating liquor, the use of hymn tunes and 'Sacred March arrangements' at church parades and flags are all covered in the contract. But as in many other areas within the Orange Institution, this contract is often honoured in the breach rather than in the observance.

The Education Committee of the Grand Orange Lodge of Ireland addressed the implications in their publication *The Order on Parade* in 1995, reminding readers that 'The behaviour of Brethren on parade is of paramount importance and it is on that behaviour that the eyes of the public and our media will concentrate.' Later the same year a sub-committee of the Commission on the Loyal Orange Institution of Ireland reported on band discipline, considering the problem of 'guilt by association', but, like so many other good reports, it came to nothing. In the political language of the twenty-first century, there were promises but no product.

Parades throughout the nineteenth century followed the pattern established in the foundation years of the Institution. Some of the parades in Portadown, particularly in the 'Tunnel' area, resulted in confrontation from time to time, most noticeably in the latter half of the century as tension mounted over Home Rule. Disturbances of various intensity are recorded in 1873, 1884 and 1886, with rioting continuing for several days in 1892.

Throughout the twentieth century parading was a feature of the Orange tradition, with the exception of the war years when the Twelfth parades were suspended and some church parades were curtailed as many members were away in the armed services. In Portadown the now customary flashpoint of the Obins Street/Tunnel area saw various confrontations. In the early years of the century before the foundation of the State tensions ran high, as they did again in the 1930s and 1950s. A more prolonged period of confrontation arose during the years of the 'troubles', but it was in 1985 and the years following that parades became a defining issue for the Order.

The Orangemen of Portadown, being a short distance from Loughgall, the foundation place of the Orange Institution, have always regarded themselves as the 'citadel' of the Institution. Since 1807 they have held a July church parade to Drumcree Parish Church, which does not appear to have been particularly contentious until the 1970s. On Sunday 9 July 1972, prior to the parade to Drumcree Parish Church, hardline Republicans barricaded both ends of Obins Street. The Army removed these in the early hours of the morning and the parade passed through the

Tunnel, escorted by a detachment of the newly formed Ulster Defence Association (UDA).

Harold McCusker MP said in the House of Commons in July 1985:

> When the men of North Armagh try to walk in Portadown it will be over a route they and their forefathers have traversed since 1796. They are not motivated out of a desire to break the law, but a sense of historic necessity to express, as they have always done, their legitimate pride in possession of their lands and liberties. They know instinctively that they only survive by their solidarity and determination.

In the mid-1980s, having been for years on the receiving end of IRA violence, the Protestant community in general felt fearful for the future and alienated from mainland British thinking, especially in view of inter-governmental discussions in 1985. The opposition of Protestants to a nationalist St Patrick's Day Parade on 17 March and the increased tension during local council elections in May created an atmosphere of confrontation for the 'marching season' that year. This posed a real threat to the Drumcree church parade. When the Action Committee set up by Portadown Orangemen examined the alternative routes given to them by the police, it was Obins Street which was the problem. The Garvaghy Road was not an issue at this stage.

The Drumcree church parade on Sunday 7 July 1985 proceeded after Obins Street had been cleared of protesters. There was a larger than usual attendance that year, including the Grand Master, the Rev. Martin Smyth, and Harold McCusker as well as George Seawright, the Belfast City Councillor who had been expelled from the Democratic Unionist Party because of his extremist views. The parade returned by way of the Garvaghy Road, with a few stones thrown at the Orangemen as they passed the Churchill Park estate.

Other parades were hotly contested in Portadown in 1985. The parade on the Twelfth was prohibited from going through the Tunnel, which was blocked by RUC Land Rovers. Members of 'Breagh Leading Heroes' LOL 7 led a confrontation which was to last two days, resulting in sporadic clashes with the police. LOL 7 and 'The Earl of Beaconsfield Primrose League, Clounagh' LOL 9 were to exercise a strong hardline influence throughout the years of the Drumcree dispute.

In 1985, Portadown District decided that they would remain in the town on the Twelfth and not join the main County Armagh parade at Tandragee. This decision was evidently not supported by many of the membership who stayed at home or joined the main demonstration. Not for the last time did the 'grass roots' reject the decision of officers of the district.

Similar problems occurred in 1986, perhaps exacerbated by the dismay felt among the Unionist and Protestant population after the signing of the Anglo-Irish Agreement on 15 November 1985. Violence associated with the Easter Monday Apprentice Boys' parade resulted in the death of Lurgan man Keith White, struck in the face by a plastic bullet. Various other incidents in Portadown and the surrounding district increased the general tension prior to the Drumcree church parade.

Permission was given by the RUC for Portadown District to parade through the Tunnel on Sunday 6 July 1986, while a counter-parade by nationalists was eventually permitted to take place in the afternoon. District officers had apparently given an undertaking that only Orangemen who were members of the district would participate. There was confrontation with the RUC on the outward journey to the church, as the police attempted to remove non-local Orangemen including George Seawright from the parade. On the return journey the newly-formed 'Drumcree Faith and Justice Group' objected by holding up placards. Some bottles and abuse were hurled at the Orangemen. According to Chris Ryder in *The RUC: A Force under Fire*, 'undertakings to the police that there would only be local participants were broken by the organisers'.[6]

On the Twelfth morning seven of the eight lodges belonging to the Corcrain Orange Hall were escorted down the Garvaghy Road to the centre of Portadown, where they joined the district. This use of the Garvaghy Road was a re-routing by the RUC, and in protest one of the lodges refused to walk the route and simply joined the district in Portadown town centre. The trouble was to come in the evening as the lodges returned to the centre of Portadown. Serious rioting took place as youths attempted to dismantle a barrier at Woodhouse Street. Such was the scale of the rioting that the Orange parade coming through the town was seriously disrupted. Trouble again occurred in Woodhouse Street the following evening as members of the Royal Black Institution returned from the 'Sham Fight' at Scarva.

In 1987 Portadown District held their Drumcree service at Obins Street in protest at not being allowed to walk the Tunnel. They did not go to Drumcree Parish Church that year and did not walk the Garvaghy Road. Subsequently the change of route agreed by Sir John Hermon, the Chief Constable, and Portadown District was adhered to. The district would walk to Drumcree Parish Church by way of the Corcrain Road, Charles Street and Dungannon Road and return by the Drumcree Road and the Garvaghy Road.

A stand-off situation between the two communities prevailed until 1995, when on 9 July Portadown District held their one hundred and eighty-eighth annual parade to Drumcree Parish Church. As we have seen, although the decision to change the route had caused great anger at the time and there were minor disturbances in the mid-1980s, it had since reluctantly been accepted and the heat had left the situation. The return route on 9 July 1995, as on previous occasions, was along the Garvaghy Road, the main thoroughfare into Portadown from the Dungannon side of the town. The road is bordered by industrial property and, at some distance from the road, three housing estates, two predominantly Roman Catholic and one predominantly Protestant. In a statement issued prior to the parade, Portadown District Lodge spoke of its desire not to cause offence to residents:

> Always conscious of the feelings of the local residents of the Garvaghy Road, the Orange Institution has been at pains to avoid confrontation and to conduct themselves with the utmost decorum as befitting a religious organisation parading to and from divine worship. Indeed impartial observers have commented favourably on this conduct.

The parade, which proceeded to the church, had the approval of the Royal Ulster Constabulary, the body which gave approval to parades prior to the establishment of the Parades Commission. During this period the Drumcree Faith and Justice Group had been agitating to have the return leg of the parade also re-routed. This had been rejected by the RUC, who had originally re-routed the Twelfth parade from Corcrain Orange Hall along the Garvaghy Road in 1986. However, early on the afternoon of Sunday 9 July, while the service of morning prayer was in progress, the RUC decided that to allow the parade to return along the Garvaghy Road would lead to public disorder, as protesters were staging a sit-down protest there.

The Portadown Orangemen were informed of this as they left the church, about two miles outside the town. Drumcree Road itself had been blocked by the RUC about two hundred yards from the church, while the protesters were blocking the Garvaghy Road a mile further along the route. This combination of events led Harold Gracey, District Master of Portadown, to announce that the Orangemen would remain in the

Drumcree area until the route was cleared of illegal protests and they were allowed to proceed. As the media carried the news of the situation during the day other Orangemen arrived from across Ireland to support Portadown District.

During the day it became apparent the parade would not pass, especially when the RUC informed the district officers that as the time for the parade as indicated on its notification had passed, it could not proceed, even after the Garvaghy Road was clear of protesters. The resolve of the Orangemen remained, however, and morale was high as the July evening progressed and plans were made for an evening service. Many Orangemen also attended evening prayer in Drumcree Parish Church. All the while more Orangemen arrived in regalia to lend support. After seven o'clock another parade was organised from the church down to the line of police Land Rovers where an open-air service was held. The Rev. Percy Patterson had been engaged to preach at the district's evening service in Seagoe Parish but his arrival at Drumcree was delayed because of the size of the crowd.

Although during the day negotiations had taken place between the police and the representatives of Portadown District Lodge, namely David Trimble MP and Harold Gracey, no agreement had been reached. That evening Ian Paisley arrived along with the Lord Mayor of Belfast and various supporters. Paisley spoke to the crowd and assured them he would do all he could, before driving off to Belfast to speak with Assistant Chief Constable Freddie Hall.

During the night the site of Drumcree had an almost surreal atmosphere, a mixture between a military camp and a Scout jamboree. Spirits were good as people met up with those they hadn't seen for some time, discussed past times and pondered future prospects. The graveyard was occupied by sleeping Orangemen in suits and collarettes; even a tent was pitched. The church hall was a hive of activity as local women made sandwiches and tea throughout the night, while the church provided a serene contrast as Orangemen slept or prayed throughout the dark hours. In the early hours of the morning the crowd at the Land Rovers dwindled away as the Orangemen returned to the hall to sleep. The RUC took this opportunity to advance their Land Rovers; news of this brought the crowds quickly back to the 'front' where they remained all night.

Next day the press arrived and the crowds continued to grow, although the Moderator of the General Assembly, Dr John Ross, had given an impromptu interview to the media suggesting that people would do better to stay away. In keeping with what the noted Ulster historian

A. T. Q. Stewart has described as 'that difficult and cantankerous disposition which is characteristic of a certain kind of political radicalism',[7] many thousands came to Drumcree in spite of, if not because of what he had said. In the evening a monster rally was addressed by politicians and leading Orangemen including the Assistant Grand Masters, Jeffrey Donaldson and Dr Warren Porter. The following resolution was passed:

> We the Orangemen assembled at Drumcree, loyal subjects of her Majesty Queen Elizabeth, do hereby resolve that we will maintain and defend our civil and religious liberty.
>
> We will not accept a ghetto system. As free-born Britons we demand equal treatment with every other British citizen.
>
> We repudiate the slander of those who accuse us of triumphalism and intimidation in the expression of our cultural and religious identity.
>
> We totally condemn the tyrannous and unnecessary interference with the peaceful procession returning from a Protestant place of worship on the Sabbath Day.
>
> We re-assert that the Queen's highway belongs to all law-abiding citizens. No faction, under any pretence whatever, can claim it as their own exclusive territory.
>
> We call upon the police to uphold this fundamental principle. That is their duty to the citizens of this land.

Towards nightfall sporadic violence erupted as youths became increasingly frustrated at the blocking of the parade. Calm was quickly restored by the leading Orangemen. Elsewhere in Northern Ireland roads were blocked and the port of Larne was brought to a standstill.

Word began to spread that the district was close to reaching a compromise and it was apparent that the RUC had realised that the resolve of the Orangemen and their supporters would not be broken. By this time the crowd's size was estimated at around thirty thousand, the majority of whom seemed intent on staying all night if need be. Finally Paisley returned to announce that a compromise had been reached that would allow those Orangemen who belonged to lodges in Portadown District to parade along the agreed route, although without bands. As a condition, the crowd was told, they must disperse and allow the local Orangemen to organise themselves.

In this volatile situation, speculation was rife all night as crowds gathered to greet the Orangemen, some of whom had been unable to wash or change their clothes since Sunday morning. William McCrea, the DUP

MP for Mid Ulster and an Orangeman, addressed the crowd gathered at Shillington Bridge to reassure them and prevent the spread of unhelpful rumours. No parade took place that night. Various explanations were offered for the delay, such as the RUC's slow progress in clearing the Garvaghy Road and securing it for the passage of the parade.

Finally, after 11 a.m. on 11 July, some forty-six hours after they were expected, Standard Bearer Alex Hyde and the district officers led the members of Portadown District along the Garvaghy Road and into Portadown. Once in town the hundreds of tearful Orangemen were greeted by cheering crowds. The Orangemen, certainly the most dishevelled parade in recent history, were joined by supporting brethren at the entrance to the town centre for the parade to Carleton Street. There Ian Paisley, David Trimble and Harold Gracey were afforded the enthusiastic applause and congratulations of the Portadown community.

Following the Drumcree stand-off in 1995, already being referred to as the 'Siege of Drumcree', the local Orange lodges decided to use another route into town. The logic offered for this was, firstly, that the Garvaghy Road was not their traditional route but one forced upon them in the mid-1980s by the RUC, and secondly, as Harold Gracey explained, so as 'not to cause any more hassle to our fellow citizens'.

Coming in the bicentenary year of the formation of the Institution, in a town in the heartland of Orangeism where there had been re-routing problems in the past, the Drumcree episode had great symbolic significance. It helped restore confidence to the wider Protestant community at a time of suspicion and uncertainty over the political situation. Commentators noticed how those who attended Drumcree were representative of all classes and shades of opinion, and included many who would not normally associate themselves with street politics of any kind. Regrettably, this confidence was not built upon in a positive way.

Several factors may be identified which combined to make Drumcree 1995 unique. One was the history of re-routing in the Portadown area, especially regarding this parade, to which the people of the town have perhaps more attachment than the July parade itself. The suspicion that the government of the Republic of Ireland was interfering in the issue was another. As the Orangemen had given at least seven days' notice of their intention to parade, thus allowing the Republicans the opportunity to organise a protest, the Republicans' actions were illegal; yet the police chose to take action against the legal parade but did not inform the Orangemen of their decision until the last possible minute. There was a sense of outrage and a feeling that Republicans were now tampering with Protestant religious worship with the backing of the government of the Republic of Ireland, and that a political decision had been taken to permit the protest and prevent the parade. The intervention of Cardinal Cahal Daly, speaking of the 'dignity' of the residents of Garvaghy Road, only added fuel to the fire.

It should not be assumed that all the residents of the estates near Garvaghy Road supported the illegal action of some. Most residents did not involve themselves in the protest. Portadown District was sensitive to this, and issued the following statement in the week prior to the 1995 parade: 'We feel sure that [the protesters'] confrontational approach is not welcomed by most people residing in the Garvaghy Road area. Orange Order parades in the Obins Street–Garvaghy Road area have a history and tradition dating back to a time when nationalists raised no objections to the parades.'

The impact of this issue on the Protestant community could be clearly seen in the way the protest snowballed, with thousands of Orangemen coming to lend support while others held parades and blocked roads in Larne and elsewhere. This snowball effect was evidence of the frustration among a community which believed it was being increasingly disenfranchised in matters concerning its own future, while terrorists and those who acted as their spokespeople were courted publicly.

The influence the siege had on the policing of parades is even more interesting. Immediately following Drumcree two parades were permitted to pass along the Lower Ormeau Road in Belfast. The Apprentice Boys of Derry Parent Clubs were also permitted to parade around the walls of Derry on 12 August in spite of Republican opposition and illegal protests. It could be argued that the police allowed these to proceed not on their merits as peaceful parades for which proper notice had been submitted and which followed traditional routes, but because an attempt to stop them might have resulted in another Drumcree-style rally. This would suggest that on the weekend of 9 and 10 July Protestants unwittingly started playing the numbers game which Republicans had been playing all year. This did not go unnoticed by some in the Orange Institution who attempted to use the same numbers game in later years, to no effect. The Institution failed to learn that tactics must not remain static, at risk of being outmanoeuvred.

In a prophetic article in the *Orange Standard* of April 1996, following the Ulster Hall Rally of the Spirit of Drumcree group, the unnamed author said: 'At Drumcree our strength was our unity. These rebel brethren have smashed that unity and we will therefore lack the strength for another Drumcree.'

While some adopted the philosophy of leaving next year's problems until next year, County Grand Master Denis Watson was all too aware of the need to resolve the matter. At the Bicentenary Parade he was heard telling Harold Gracey to 'sort this out before next year'. Others too were not prepared to stand idly by. The Education Committee addressed a meeting of the Irish Association in Dublin in March 1996 on subjects including Drumcree. The *Irish Times* reported it under the headline 'Orange Order set to repeat Drumcree siege', but Ruth Dudley Edwards commented the following week in the *Irish Independent*:

> This was the first foray south by representatives of that element of the Orange Order that likes to get on with its neighbours. The quartet came to explain that most Orangemen are decent human beings and that the brilliant Sinn Féin propaganda machine and the sensation-hungry media had misrepresented what happened last year at Drumcree.

As a result of this meeting we had made many friends. One of these, Father John Brady, Southern Secretary of the Irish Association, arranged and chaired a meeting in Tandragee on 3 May 1996 between Father Eamon Stack, Sister Laura Boyle and Eileen McNally, members of the Drumcree Faith and Justice Group, and Graham Montgomery, Richard Whitten and myself. The Executive Officer, George Patton, knew about this meeting in advance, as did Jeffrey Donaldson. The purpose of the meeting was purely exploratory; we were in no position to 'negotiate' or agree on anything. What became evident at the meeting was that a lot of work was needed if a permanent resolution of this problem was to be achieved.

As a spin-off from the events at Drumcree in 1995 the Education Committee produced a booklet, *The Order on Parade*, to present the case for the Institution. Because the immediate newsworthiness of parading had passed, it did not receive the media cover it deserved, though the *Irish Times* highlighted some of its salient points in an article on 15 September. Press speculation began again in 1996, and many articles appeared in support of the right to parade the Garvaghy Road.

As Sunday 7 July 1996, the date of the Drumcree church parade, approached, Chief Constable of the RUC Sir Hugh Annesley announced that the parade would have to return from the church the way it had come, that is, by the Dungannon Road and the Corcrain Road, because of the risk of public disorder. The 'Garvaghy Road Residents' Coalition' had threatened all sorts of obstructions, including a carnival. This appeared to the average Orangeman to be sanctioning the principle of 'might is right'. The natural human reaction prevailed: 'We too will show strength and might.' As Ruth Dudley Edwards put it in the *Daily Mirror* on 12 July, 'When last Saturday the Chief Constable banned them from walking down the Garvaghy Road, in Ulster Protestant eyes he succumbed to threats of violence from those who wanted to overthrow the state and turned the forces of the Crown on its most loyal citizens.'

The parade and service on 7 July followed a similar pattern to that of the previous year. Some fifteen hundred men of Portadown District Lodge walked along the Corcrain and Dungannon Roads to Drumcree Parish Church for morning prayer. After the service they declared their intention to remain in the area until they should be allowed to walk down the Garvaghy Road. RUC Land Rovers were blocking the Drumcree Road.

The media were there in force, including the BBC's top 'trouble-spot' reporter, Kate Adie. Unfortunately Orangemen generally had not learned the importance of cultivating a relationship with the media. Many of the reporters there would only write sympathetically if they understood the dilemma in which the men of Portadown had been placed, and they would not understand that unless someone articulated it to them. Portadown District, in order to overcome some of the problems of the previous year, had asked Graham Montgomery to act as press officer, but his genuine efforts to deal with the media were often hampered by the 'thick' attitude of some examples of the Ulster Protestant.

The Dublin-born Roman Catholic scholar and journalist Ruth Dudley Edwards is an exception to the rule of 'soundbite' journalism. In recent years she has made a sincere effort to understand Ulster Protestants. In the *Daily Telegraph* on 8 July she wrote:

> The lodge has already reduced its bands and cut its parades down the road from seven to one; it asks only to be allowed to make the fifteen-minute walk in silence. Its members know that should the Protestants be faced down, the Sinn Féin strategists will pick on another route, another march and in due course will resist marches by the British Legion or the Girls' Brigade, or any other public events that can be represented as 'hurtful' to nationalist feelings.

(The statement about the British Legion turned out to be prophetic, for in

November 1997 some of the residents in Bellaghy, County Londonderry, objected to the Remembrance Day parade because of the band which led it.)

News of the death of a member of the Roman Catholic community, Michael McGoldrick, broke early on the morning of 8 July. The general feeling of disgust throughout the Protestant community was expressed in the *Belfast News Letter* the next day: 'The murder of Lurgan taxi-driver Michael McGoldrick was a dastardly act which must be denounced by all right-thinking people everywhere.' The McGoldrick family were remembered in prayer in at least one Twelfth demonstration, at Kesh in County Fermanagh.

Monday on Drumcree Hill was spent establishing communications between the district's 'Control Room' and the outside world, as well as establishing an area of 'dead ground' between the protesters in the fields and the RUC. Incidents had been reported and some of the marshals controlling the crowds had been injured. Concrete bollards were erected in front of the Land Rovers during an advance by the RUC into the graveyard. The press were there all day but many felt uncomfortable at staying on the Orange side of the barricades, having been badly treated by some of the Orangemen who had evidently not learned the basics of public relations.

Elsewhere in Northern Ireland public protests were taking place, with the security forces in a much more active role than the previous year. Belfast International Airport was blockaded until the early hours of Tuesday morning, when the police, in Divisional Mobile Support Units, moved in and 'cracked a few heads'. The picket was to have been lifted at 10 p.m., and the general instruction from Orange headquarters had been for a 'flying picket' in order not to 'alienate our natural supporters'. Yet the behaviour of some Orangemen at the airport left a lot to be desired. Instructions from the County Grand Master were challenged. There was an unfortunate incident in relation to a funeral; when arrangements were made by the county chaplain for the cortege to go through, some of the blockaders refused and the bereaved family said they were intimidated. The media reported only one side of the story and the blockade as a whole was another public-relations disaster.

The blocking of roads also exposed the inherent hypocrisy of such actions. Those who lived in the rural communities affected saw individuals publicly participating in the blockading of roads in protest at Orangemen not being allowed to parade home from church, yet many of these same protesters had seldom if ever availed themselves of the opportunity to walk to their own church! This did nothing for the credibility of the Institution.

Tuesday saw David Trimble MP going to see the prime minister, and visits to Drumcree Hill from the Archbishop of Armagh, Dr Eames, and the Moderator of the General Assembly, Dr Harry Allen, himself a Portadown man. The arrival of Orangemen at Drumcree that evening brought some ugly incidents with the police. The marshalling of the protest was shown to be completely ineffective. Meanwhile there was disquiet in the Control Room that David Trimble had not contacted the county officers after his meeting with the prime minister. (He was attending a dinner in London in honour of Nelson Mandela.) It became evident however that a compromise had been suggested: the Orangemen would raise no objections to a parade in Portadown by Roman Catholics on St Patrick's Day, if the Garvaghy Road residents would offer no resistance to the Orangemen returning home by the Garvaghy Road. District Master Harold Gracey would not agree to this.

On the morning of 10 July District Officers Denis Watson and Stephen McLaughlin, along with David Burrows, the Deputy District Master, and myself, went to Belfast to meet with Assistant Chief Constable Ronnie Flanagan. Grand Secretary John McCrea and the Executive Officer George Patton joined us. Afterwards I made my way to Fermanagh, confident that the return leg of the Drumcree church parade would be concluded by noon on Thursday. While nothing had been spelt out in detail, this was my reading of the situation.

Events continued to raise the temperature throughout Northern Ireland, but particularly on the hill at Drumcree. The arrival of a JCB-type digger, of which Harold Gracey appeared to have some knowledge, caused a general stir and some physical attacks on members of the press who enquired as to its purpose. It was becoming clear to many at this stage that there was some paramilitary involvement. The name of Billy Wright, often dubbed 'King Rat', was brought to the fore at this time.

The same day, a young mother attempting to visit her dying grandmother in hospital was stopped and turned back at one roadblock after another by men wearing Orange collarettes. On each occasion she and her companions explained the purpose of their journey, but received little understanding, in one case being met with a torrent of abuse from an Orangeman: 'We don't care about your f****** granny – you're not getting through!' The young woman, whose grandmother later died, was the daughter of the Rev. Denis Bannerman, then a Deputy Grand Chaplain in the Orange Order. The Rev. Bannerman resigned from the

Institution in November 2003, affirming that as a Christian his conscience would no longer allow him to remain in membership in the face of such evident lack of respect for the law of God and the laws of the land.

The general stress and tension was only matched by that in the two small rooms behind the main hall at Drumcree Parish Church. At one stage those present discussed the possibility of suspending Portadown District Lodge as a means of resolving the situation. The Grand Secretary, John McCrea, advised that this would be possible. A strong contingent of members of the DUP were there as well as senior Orange officers, but the two groups appeared to be working from different documents. The five-point plan suggested by Dr Eames and the other church leaders was decided upon as a basis for discussion. Harold Gracey accepted this but later tried to repudiate it. Some senior Orange officers left for proximity talks at the Ulster Carpet Mills premises in Portadown.

The morning of Thursday 11 July broke with an air of unreality. The *Belfast News Letter* carried the headline 'They Hit the Road Today', and sure enough, word came through that the Chief Constable had changed his decision, on the same grounds upon which he had made his original decision – the risk of public disorder! The parade of Portadown District Lodge left for the return leg of their journey shortly after noon. The protesters on the Garvaghy Road greeted them with a silent protest. Chief Constable Sir Hugh Annesley, in a BBC Radio Ulster interview with Barry Cowan on Sunday 14 July, said in defence of his U-turn that 'that patch of road is not worth one human life'.

The Taoiseach, John Bruton, said he had told the Prime Minister, John Major, that a democratic state could not yield to force, nor could it afford to be inconsistent or partial in the way it applied the law. He said that all canons of democracy had been breached in the Garvaghy Road events. These injudicious remarks only worsened the tension.

On 11 July Eilis O'Hanlon wrote in *The Times*: 'Republicans have now embarked on a crusade to suppress all the symbols of a Protestant state whose days, they believe, are numbered. That the Orange Order is only asking the nationalist residents of the Garvaghy Road for fifteen minutes of tolerance cut little ice.' But she also criticised the Institution's inability to recognise how it was being used:

> In their protests about Orange marches, the republicans have found a way to reactivate sectarian conflict in Ulster without being seen as the sole instigators. The murder of a Catholic taxi driver in Armagh on

> Monday, the nightly eviction of Catholic families in Belfast and the chilling scenes of potentially uncontainable street violence all suggest that loyalists have ignored repeated warnings that they were sleep-walking into a trap, and have blundered into it anyway.

This was perceptive given Eilis O'Hanlon's background. Her uncle was the veteran Republican Joe Cahill and her sister Siobhan, according to David Sharrock and Mark Devenport in *Man of War, Man of Peace?*, was the 'one that got away' from the attempted IRA bombing in Gibraltar.[8]

Ruth Dudley Edwards, writing in the *Irish Independent* a week after the event, revealed something of the anomalies of Ulster thinking when she quoted Harold Gracey speaking before the commencement of the parade to Drumcree Parish Church: 'Hugh Annesley said last night on television that this was Custer's last stand. Well, friends, let me tell you that it was an Ulsterman at the Alamo – Davy Crockett – and we will be like Davy Crockett at the Alamo.' Dr Dudley Edwards commented, 'I don't think Gracey – a simple man – realised that Davy Crockett and the rest of the Alamo defenders were wiped out.'

As the parade prepared to leave Drumcree Hill, the Mediation Network negotiators Brendan McAllister and Joe Campbell, who had been deeply involved in 1995, issued a press statement 'as a matter of professional integrity'. They outlined the process of mediation in which they had been engaged since first invited to help by the Garvaghy Road residents' group in June 1995. Their crisis mediation in July 1996 had involved meetings with representatives of the Orange Order, the Garvaghy Road Residents' Coalition and the RUC, as well as prominent politicians like Trimble and Paisley. Deputy Chief Constable Flanagan had briefed them on the worsening situation on the morning of 11 July, and they took the view that Garvaghy Road residents should 'voluntarily remove themselves from the road without being constrained by the police'. Their statement went on to describe the 1995 discussions.:

> Subsequently Mr Flanagan repeated his views to Mr McKenna and Fr Eamon Stack in our presence. Mr McKenna agreed to request the protesters to remove themselves from the road on sight of the oncoming parade.
>
> As Mr McKenna left to speak to the crowd, we observed to Mr Flanagan that the mood of the crowd was such that Mr McKenna would have difficulty persuading the protesters to accede to his request. Brendan McAllister observed that Mr McKenna would have more

> chances of success if protesters knew there would be no march on Garvaghy Road in 1996.
>
> Mr Flanagan replied that there was no question of marches going where there was no consent from the community. We now believed that there would be no further marches on Garvaghy Road without the residents' consent. This statement was witnessed by Mr Campbell.
>
> We then moved to hear Mr McKenna address the crowd. When he asked them to clear the road, numbers of protesters heckled him and refused his request. Mindful of the Deputy Chief Constable's assessment of the possible consequences for the wider situation in N. Ireland, Brendan McAllister spoke to the crowd, advising them to trust Mr McKenna's leadership and encouraging them to engage in a dignified silent protest.
>
> As the parade drew near, the protesters complied with these requests with a discipline which is a matter of public record.
>
> In the autumn of 1995, after the marching season, we approached the Garvaghy Road residents to obtain their agreement to co-operate with our efforts to build a process which would lead to a consensus with the Orange Order. We agreed that if our efforts to establish dialogue were unsuccessful and a parade was forced down the road in 1996, we would bear public witness to the point of understanding which we had reached with Mr Flanagan.

The mediators described how their efforts at promoting dialogue in 1996 had been hampered by misinformation. They had been able to rectify this, but wariness on both sides continued to preclude the conditions necessary for credible mediation. Their statement continued:

> During the past year our efforts have been hindered by the inability of the Orange Order to recognise the bona fides of residents' groups such as the Garvaghy Road Residents' Coalition and the Lower Ormeau Concerned Community.
>
> We believe that both residents' groups are an authentic representation of the feelings of large numbers of their respective neighbourhoods.
>
> We acknowledge that both residents' groups have made strenuous efforts to address the marching conflict. We also acknowledge that a significant number of Orangemen at all levels of the Orange Order have made sincere efforts to address the problem and have fully co-operated with us.
>
> However, the Orange Order is a cultural expression of Unionism and

> consequently Orangemen will not engage in dialogue with those whom they view as republican while unionist politicians refuse to do so. This has had tragic effects on our whole community and our response will be a litmus test of our maturity as a people who have suffered years of fruitless violence.

Ruth Dudley Edwards analysed the events at Drumcree as follows:

> To local Orangemen this was the final unacceptable IRA assault on their rights; to Sinn Féin/IRA, this was an excellent trap into which they could confidently expect the Prods to fall. Trimble and peaceable Orangemen with brains could do nothing except pray that the Chief Constable would not give in to threats of republican thuggery. But he did.[9]

She went on to reveal the involvement of Billy Wright and alleged a power struggle between 'UVF HQ and the local rogue elements', as well as describing 'the desperate efforts of County and Grand Lodge Officers as well as Trimble to get Gracey to see sense'. She concluded:

> The Secretary of the Grand Lodge of the Orange Order is preparing a detailed report of what happened, for senior Orangemen are determined that they will never again let themselves fall into this double-paramilitary trap. But they must make their findings public and make the necessary organisational changes to ensure that in future someone like Harold Gracey, completely out of his depth, will not have to make decisions that unwittingly could start a war.

No detailed report was ever made, in spite of my pleas in the days following the Twelfth for the Grand Secretary to organise a de-brief. No organisational changes were made. Harold Gracey was still in power, and history was to repeat itself, increasingly tragically.

The events of the summer of 1996 were to cost the Institution dearly in terms of public relations. While there was quite a lot of damage to property and many Roman Catholics were intimidated from their homes, the greatest suffering was on the part of the members of the RUC. Many police families were attacked and intimidated out of their homes in County Armagh, especially in the Portadown area, and some who were members of the Orange Institution felt they could no longer remain in membership, particularly after their brethren abused them or their colleagues.

A highly damaging and sinister spin-off from the 1996 Drumcree confrontation was the Roman Catholic boycott of Protestant-owned and run businesses, which left those in majority Roman Catholic areas very vulnerable. While most Roman Catholic people did not wish to take part in this boycott, some were forced to join in because they were not willing to be seen doing business in Protestant-owned shops. Others who might have given a helpful lead to defuse the situation allowed sectarian bigotry and political bias to triumph over Christian charity. Father Hugh Quinn of Pomeroy revealed on 12 January 1997, on the BBC Ulster Radio programme 'Sunday Sequence', that he had joined the boycott. He was quoted in the *Irish News* on 13 January 1997 as saying: 'Boycotts are a matter of individual personal choice and it's not up to the Church to condemn them – I certainly don't believe it's my responsibility.' A joint statement by church leaders including the Roman Catholic Archbishop Seán Brady, however, condemned boycotts.

The Independent Review of Parades and Marches (the North Report) was announced in the House of Commons by Secretary of State Patrick Mayhew on 24 July 1996 and led to the formation in 1997 of the Parades Commission, which had limited powers until the spring of 1998 when it received its statutory role to make legal determinations. The Orange Institution had made representations to the Review, but, as will be seen later, they procrastinated at the crucial time.

The year 1997 saw some important PR work. On 13 January the *Irish News* revealed that 'Confidential negotiations between Archbishop Robin Eames and the Orangemen and residents of Garvaghy Road are raising hopes that a third Drumcree stand-off can be averted.' Officers of Armagh County Grand Lodge had made contact with senior politicians and civil servants in the Republic. Some of these contacts were facilitated by the Education Committee of the Grand Lodge. The visit of Robert Saulters and others to Harryville on 11 January to show support to those who were being picketed while attending Mass, based as it was on the principle of civil and religious liberty, did more to enhance the public image of the Institution than anything else in the recent past and prepared the way for a good year in terms of public relations.

On 4 March the Radio Telefís Éireann (RTE) investigative programme 'Prime Time' confirmed what the Orange Institution had long known: that Sinn Féin/IRA were 'behind the residents' groups'. The programme revealed the content of a speech Gerry Adams had made at a Sinn Féin conference in Athboy, County Meath, in November 1996:

> Ask any activist in the north 'Did Drumcree happen by accident?' They will tell you 'No'. Three years of work in Lower Ormeau, Portadown, and parts of Fermanagh, Newry, Armagh, Bellaghy and up in Derry. Three years work into creating that situation and fair play to those people who put the work in . . . they are the type of scene changes that we have to focus in on and develop and exploit.

In March 1997 there was a surprise resolution to another potential flashpoint, in the village of Dromore in County Tyrone, where there had been some confrontation in 1996 involving people from outside the village. The local lodges were determined that there should not be a repetition of that kind of incident. A representative meeting was convened by the parish priest, Father Thomas Breen, and the Church of Ireland rector, the Rev. Don Gamble, at which an 'agreement' was reached. This did not go down well with a few members of one of the local lodges, who interpreted this as 'asking' for the right to parade. The hardline Spirit of Drumcree faction attempted to have the decision overthrown by the district lodge, Fintona District LOL No 8. When they failed in this they attempted, quite irregularly, to have it overturned at county level, where it also failed.

The Kenwell family, members of the Orange Order who have a major business in the village, were to play a crucial part in this successful outcome. Charles Kenwell took the lead and faced down his critics, presenting his case in a letter in the *Belfast Telegraph* in April. He set out four conditions for a meeting:

> 1. The people invited to attend would have to be a near exact representation of all the views in the locality.
> 2. Those invited to come must all turn up in order that the views should be truly representative.
> 3. The meeting would have to be free of political interference.
> 4. It would also have to be free from outside influences.

Kenwell went on:

> I take this opportunity to assert the following to anyone thinking of embarking on a similar path: If rhetoric and entrenched positions are forgotten, then I can almost guarantee that, with the four conditions having been adhered to, goodwill will finally prevail. It must prevail and everyone at such discussions should be aware of their obligation to

> act responsibly and not take up a bullish stance. After an understanding has been reached, stand up vigorously for the understanding to be honoured and do not bow to external pressure from any quarter.

While Grand Master Robert Saulters and I were among the first to telephone Kenwell to encourage him, there was a 'stony silence' from many senior officers of the Institution.

Gerald Marshall, Deputy Master of one of the local lodges, refused to accept the democratic decision of his lodge and, according to the *Belfast Telegraph*, called for a boycott of the parade. The *Telegraph* reported that he expected 'hundreds of Orangemen to join the protest action'. Hundreds did not. The Twelfth parade passed off peacefully in Dromore, except for one nasty incident which involved Gerald Marshall himself. He subsequently resigned from the Institution.

The peaceful resolution of these local difficulties demonstrated what could be done when a spirit of goodwill prevailed, accompanied by a willingness to talk through any difficulties. The Parades Policy Statement agreed by Grand Lodge the following June embraced the approach of the Dromore Orangemen:

> With the possibility of more reasonable situations obtaining in other areas there is a need to educate and inform people of good-will in many communities. Such people require a clear understanding that though we are unapologetically committed to the Reformed Faith and Loyal to the Constitution, our processions are not 'triumphalist' nor are they intended to be offensive to any person, whatever their faith. Such a process of information will require meeting and talking with people who are committed to the principles of democracy and peace. This will not be to 'ask permission' to walk, as it is sometimes incorrectly alleged. It will be to ascertain what the local problems are, and seek to allay the fears of the community. There must be no betrayal of our principles in discussions taking place under these circumstances.

The Rev. Dr Warren Porter, Grand Chaplain and Assistant Grand Master, wrote an article for the *Irish Times* on 22 April 1997 articulating the case for Orange parades, which appeared under the headline 'Consensus, not consent, welcomed by Orangemen as the way forward'.

In a major interview with Brendan Anderson of the *Irish News*, published on 22 March 1997, the Spirit of Drumcree leader Joel Patton had alleged that a 'secret deal' had been agreed over the Drumcree parade: 'They are not telling the ordinary Orangeman exactly what they are doing. They are doing it in a most devious way.' At no time did he identify who 'they' were, and he did not specify the nature of these deals or what was being 'traded off' for what. This was all the more interesting in that on 14 December 1997 the *Sunday Times* revealed that Joel Patton had held secret meetings in June of that year with Northern Ireland Office officials, in which it was alleged he proposed a 'voluntary moratorium on all marches' in return for money for 'Orange culture'. Patton confirmed the contents of the discussions but said that they were 'hypothetical situations'.

On 5 May 1997, as convenor of the Education Committee, I sent an analysis of the situation to each of the County Masters of the County Grand Lodges. In this analysis, which was warmly commended for serious consideration and action by Grand Master Robert Saulters, Assistant Grand Master Dr Porter, Assistant Grand Master Jeffrey Donaldson and Sir James H. Molyneaux, I pointed out the following:

> Why should Sinn Féin/IRA want to destroy us?
>
> 1. We are the *only* organisation at present holding together all the strands of Protestant opinion.
> 2. We are still a mass membership organisation unlike the Unionist political parties.
> 3. We are the manifestation of the Protestant/British tradition on this Island. A tradition which Sinn Féin/IRA wants to drive into the sea!
>
> How can Sinn Féin/IRA destroy us?
>
> 1. By driving us into confrontation with OUR OWN forces of law and order in OUR OWN State.
> 2. Cause us to lose the 'middle ground' – moderate Protestant mainstream opinion – thereby no longer remaining a mass membership organisation.
> 3. Force us into a position where we will no longer be respected, but will be perceived to be only speaking for the 'rump' of extreme Protestant opinion.
> 4. Push us into a position where we are perceived to *cause* or *facilitate* public disorder. This will weaken the fabric of Northern Ireland – something Sinn Féin/IRA lives for and which we must NEVER permit!
>
> I believe we have reached a *defining moment* in the history of the Loyal

> Orange Institution of Ireland. The choice which faces us at this defining moment in our history is a choice between **conflict** and **consensus**. ***To do nothing is to give consent to conflict.***
>
> On the other hand we can choose the path of **consensus.** This may mean attempting to reach an agreement with the RUC and *bona fide* representatives of local communities. This is the difficult choice, which requires cool heads, and the systematic thought which our forefathers employed in the early days of this century. We ought to remember that they did NOT opt for violence, but expressed their determination to defend the Union with force of arms *only* if necessary. Failure to take this path of **consensus** will ultimately lead to disaster for our Order.
>
> There are certain obvious results from choosing the path of **consensus**, like reaffirming our commitment to Biblical principles, and the exposure of militants. Those within the Institution will have to be dealt with to preserve the credibility of the Order. We will maintain our credibility by providing real and imaginative leadership. We will hold the middle ground of the Institution, which consists of the silent majority.

I presented these ideas again at the Annual Dinner of Eldon LOL No. 7, on 5 November 1998, under the title 'A Vision for the Institution'. Members and friends expressed appreciation, and William Logan, the Imperial Grand Registrar of the Black Institution, took a similar line. Copies of the address were given to anyone who wished to have it, and sections of it appeared under the headline 'Reformation plea by top Orangemen' in the *Belfast Telegraph* of 7 November 1998. However, there was no positive response from the leadership.

The issue continued to be debated in the run-up to July 1997. On 27 May Eamon Stack, the Jesuit priest and secretary of the Garvaghy Road Residents' Coalition, wrote a very sectarian article in the *Irish Times* which, as Dr Garret Fitzgerald later observed to me, 'had to be answered'. One of Fr Stack's reasons why, he said, no one on the Garvaghy Road wanted the parade was that 'it expresses a permanent socio-economic imbalance' because the Orangemen wore suits! My reply, published on 10 June, posed the ultimate question which to date has never been answered: 'In what circumstances will you *not* object to the valid expression of a religion, culture and identity, held by the majority of the population of Northern Ireland, and not obstruct that expression by blocking the return route of the parade along the Garvaghy Road from Morning Prayer at Drumcree Parish Church?'

In June I accompanied a group of Orangemen from County Armagh who went to London for two days to communicate the simple message of Portadown District: that all they wanted to do was to walk in an inoffensive way from morning prayer to Portadown town centre, as their forefathers had done for nigh on two hundred years. Meanwhile the following letter was sent from the County Armagh Grand Lodge, signed by Denis Watson, the County Grand Master, and the Rev. William Bingham, the County Grand Chaplain, to each of the residents on the Garvaghy Road:

> We are writing to all the residents of the Garvaghy Road area to explain our position about the annual walk by members of Portadown District Orangemen from the service of worship at Drumcree Parish Church in July.
>
> This is a sincere and genuine attempt to deal with the many misconceptions concerning the walk and there are a number of points we would like to make for your information:
>
> 1. The service on the first Sunday in July is partly to remember those who died at the Battle of the Somme in 1916. We pay tribute to all those of both communities who died for the cause of peace and justice.
> 2. The Orange Order is traditionally a parading organisation. We see our parade as an outward witness to our sincere belief in the Reformed Faith. For that reason, we see attacks on our parades as both a denial of civil liberties and an attack on our religion. For us, this is as distressing as the disgraceful protest – which we unreservedly condemn – outside Harryville chapel.
> 3. In the interests of harmony, mutual respect and reconciliation the Orange Order has acknowledged objections raised by the Nationalist community and has already implemented the following principles for the Drumcree Church parade:
>   a. The number of parades in the area has been reduced from ten to one in the past ten years.
>   b. Only members of Portadown District parade.
>   c. No bands take part which could be perceived as antagonistic to our Nationalist neighbours.
>   Accordion bands lead the parade playing hymn music that is common to both traditions.
>   d. The Orangemen walk four abreast so that the walk will pass any one given point in less than five minutes.

e. The Order marshals and disciplines its own members to ensure there will be no confrontation on our part. If this was reciprocated, then there would only be a need for a minimal police presence.
f. The right to walk peacefully and in a dignified manner and the right to protest in a peaceful and dignified manner should not be denied to anyone.

It is the sincere hope of the Orange Order that the vast majority of the people of Portadown will work together in a new spirit of tolerance to defeat extremists who want confrontation this summer. As a matter of principle, we cannot be involved in talks with convicted terrorists because of what they have inflicted on our community. But we do want to listen to all those within the community who want to promote harmony and mutual respect among the people of Portadown.

The letter asked for constructive comments and ended by looking forward to 'a more peaceful and tolerant era for all the people of our land.' Several letters of various shades of opinion were sent by residents in response.

As the date of the service approached, hastily arranged proximity talks at Hillsborough Castle between representatives of the Garvaghy Road Residents' Coalition and the Orangemen achieved no resolution. On the evening of Friday 4 July Portadown District and Armagh County Grand Lodge held an event for the media in Craigavon Civic Centre in order to take the initiative with the press. Sadly the lessons of this exercise were soon forgotten.

Later that evening, the Secretary of State, Dr Mo Mowlam, met with members of Portadown District and Armagh County Lodge to hear their views on the situation and to encourage them to act in the best interests of the whole community. Facing a torrent of criticism, she acknowledged that no concessions had come from the residents to match those of Portadown District. Even the offer of financial aid to promote the Orange Order as a major cultural organisation could not buy off the Orangemen of Portadown.

The police and army moved into the Garvaghy Road area on the evening of 5 July, removed protesters and kept the road clear for the 'walk' the following day. On Sunday 6 July the members of Portadown District took their traditional route to morning prayer at Drumcree Parish Church, returning by the Drumcree and Garvaghy Roads to Carleton Street Orange Hall. This peaceful parade was followed by outbursts of violence in many nationalist areas of Northern Ireland.

On the evening of 10 July, at a specially convened meeting of County Masters at 65 Dublin Road, Chief Constable Ronnie Flanagan gave security advice with reference to the parades scheduled for the Twelfth. He told of his conviction that gunmen would attack Orangemen on Belfast's Ormeau Road, the 'shambles' area of Armagh, through which the Armagh County Grand Lodge had planned to walk, as well as in Newry and Londonderry City. In the light of this advice the Orange officers for each individual area decided to make alterations. In Newry and in Armagh the routes were changed. In Londonderry City the parade was quickly moved to Limavady and Belfast No. 10 District cancelled its parade completely. These were decisions taken separately by each area concerned, not by the Grand Lodge or its senior officers.

However wise and commendable these decisions were, and the media were the first to recognise their wisdom, some within the Institution misunderstood them to be a 'trade-off' for the Drumcree parade, and were determined that such 'concessions' should not occur again. Pressure was therefore on the leadership to project a tough line.

The *Irish News* editorial of 29 June 1998 stated:

> Disappointment faces anyone looking for a sign of movement on either side. The residents have a strong sense of victimhood. The Orangemen are as obdurate as ever. But the context has changed. The peace settlement, the referendum, and last week's assembly elections all show that the people of Northern Ireland want a society built on consensus not conflict.

This was an echo of my words in my analysis of 5 May 1997: 'The choice which faces us at this defining moment in our history is a choice between conflict and consensus.' But the die was cast, and the Institution walked headlong into confrontation in the summer of 1998.

Chapter Five

The Drumcree Debacle

'In the words of one of my more sympathetic correspondents, it has turned out to be an annus horribilis.'

Queen Elizabeth II

On 24 November 1992, in a speech at the Guildhall in London, the Queen described the year which was coming to a close as an '*annus horribilis*' for her family. For the Orange Institution, 1998 was its *annus horribilis*. Unfortunately, the consequences of that year of horrors are still very much to the fore.

The events of 1998 at Drumcree were to be very different from those of any of the previous years. The election in May 1997 had returned a new Labour government with a large majority. They were now firmly established in Westminster and the bipartisan policy in relation to Northern Ireland remained intact. The Parades Commission now had full legal powers to make determinations. Alistair Graham, its chairman, and members of the commission had witnessed for themselves the parade to and from Drumcree Parish Church in 1997. They attended many other parades, both contentious and non-contentious, including the Glenavy District Parade and church service on 8 June 1997.

The previous December, at the Grand Lodge meeting, the Grand Master had announced the 'establishment of a Parades Strategy Committee comprising one representative from each of the County Parades Committees, the Principal Grand Lodge Officers with Brethren of particular expertise being co-opted'. The remit of the Parades Strategy Committee was to help districts and counties wherever there was difficulty over parades. This committee met regularly in the early months of 1998, while public attention centred on the Stormont talks which eventually led to the Belfast Agreement.

The parades issue broke again in the media as a result of a television programme at the end of March, in which a group of schoolchildren were presented with three views on the conflict by Alistair Graham for the

Parades Commission, Brendan McKenna for the Garvaghy Road residents and David McNarry for the Orange Order. Graham Montgomery was asked by the Central Committee to represent the interests of the Institution in this programme, but he declined. He saw clearly at this early stage the mess the Orange Order was getting itself into.

This programme was followed by a statement from the 'House of Orange', the headquarters in Belfast, projected in the media as 'We Will Walk Our Traditional Routes'. Under the headline 'Orangemen Stand Firm on Parades', the *Belfast Telegraph*'s political correspondent reported: 'Mr [George] Patton confirmed the institution intends to parade its traditional routes this year – and said "positive" meetings had been held with the Spirit of Drumcree group, whose members have held a series of protests demanding a harder line on parades.' The Executive Officer had issued this statement after a meeting of the Parades Strategy Committee. For many in the Institution this raised two fundamental questions: who speaks for the Institution, and who benefits from this hardline approach? The answer to the first was clear. The Parades Strategy Committee was now the voice of the Institution. The answer to the second question was evident even to Brid Rodgers, the SDLP Councillor in Portadown, who was quoted as saying, 'I would ask the Orange Order to ask themselves in whose interest it is that there should be conflict on the streets of Northern Ireland.' Her perceptions would have been shared by the majority of Orangemen, who could see clearly the direction in which the Institution was being taken, and by whom. The same newspaper article reported Alistair Graham as saying: 'I do not think they will be hitting the right note with everyone in Northern Ireland if they seek to cause major confrontation in 1998.'

Most thinking people within and without the Institution knew very well that to say that we would 'walk our traditional routes' was simply nonsense. With demographic changes over the years many routes had been either changed or abandoned. The Orange Order in County Londonderry had not walked in Dungiven since the 1960s after the then Minister of Home Affairs, Walter William Buchanan Topping, had banned it. Incidentally, Topping was a member of the Orange Institution. The Belfast Orangemen had not walked past Holy Cross Roman Catholic Church in Ardoyne since the early 1970s. Belfast District No. 5, Sandy Row, had not walked down their 'traditional' route of the Grosvenor Road since the early 1970s, when the police told them that they could no longer guarantee their protection. Parades in Coalisland had been long since abandoned. Apart from the megalomania of some

Portadown Orange leaders, what was so special about the Garvaghy Road, itself a re-routing?

Events could have been different had it not been for the bitterness, expressed and unexpressed, over the disputed Belfast Agreement. To make matters worse, the most senior Orangeman in County Armagh, Denis Watson, was elected to the new Northern Ireland Assembly on an anti-Agreement ticket on 25 June 1998, ten days before the Drumcree church parade.

As the deadline approached for the Parades Commission to make its legal determination, a most perceptive article appeared in an unlikely source, the *Irish News*. On 29 June Roy Garland, a former member of the Orange Institution, wrote:

> On the face of it, it seems indefensible that Orangemen should wish to proceed down the Garvaghy Road against the wishes of Catholic inhabitants. This is particularly so when they apparently refuse to entertain dialogue. Not only does this seem wrong, it is self-defeating, whatever the violent backgrounds of some spokesmen for residents. They must know that there is little prospect of Orangeism emerging from these confrontations with an enhanced public image.

It was a view shared by all except those who seemed to be the blind leading the blind. The Irish writer Eoghan Harris wrote at the same time that the Institution 'is led by straw men and my best bet is that Tony Blair will blow them away if they stand in his path this summer'.

On 29 June the Parades Commission issued their legal determination that the parade could proceed to Drumcree Parish Church and that there was to be no assembly after the service. The members of Portadown District Lodge were to return to Carleton Street Orange Hall, by the route of the outward journey. This was met by defiance from many including Denis Watson, the County Grand Master of Armagh, who said that the Orangemen would stay for 365 days 'if necessary'. Given the events of the past, especially in 1996, and particularly the experience of Denis Watson himself in relation to all this, it is difficult to understand the enthusiasm with which he threw himself into the 1998 parade, particularly in calling for support from others to attend. This contrasted with the position he had taken up previously, along with others including myself, in arguing with members of parliament in London and with Garvaghy Road residents that this was a local district parade, with members of the district only taking part.

Prior to the Sunday of the parade there was an air of unreality throughout Northern Ireland. History surely could not be repeating itself? It revived in the minds of many Karl Marx's dictum that 'history repeats itself the first time as tragedy, the second time as farce'. In the week preceding the parade there were the usual panic measures, involving meetings, meetings and more meetings, but no meetings between the only two parties who could resolve the situation. The most alarming aspect of the events of those days was the arson attacks. Ten Roman Catholic churches were burned or otherwise seriously damaged, as were several Orange Halls and Protestant church buildings, apparently in retaliation. In the area around Drumcree Parish Church the security forces dug a six-foot-wide trench and laid miles of razor wire across the fields. A fifteen-foot-high reinforced barrier was positioned on the Drumcree Road. To even a casual observer, it was evident that the parade was not going to be allowed to go down the Garvaghy Road.

On the morning of Sunday 5 July the members of Portadown District left Carleton Street Orange Hall, reinforced by up to five thousand fellow Orangemen, for their traditional 'walk' to Drumcree Parish Church. To many the very fact that between five and six thousand Orangemen were walking to a church which could only accommodate at most eight hundred people turned this parade into a political statement. This was evidently going to be a showdown, and it would be a showdown, which, as observed by every serious political commentator, the Orangemen could not win.

After the service of morning prayer the Grand Master, Robert Saulters, and Denis Watson addressed those who assembled outside the church. The content of their addresses appeared to many to be political and out of place on the Lord's Day. This concern was later communicated to the Grand Master by representatives of the Orange chaplains who met on 13 July.

Violence erupted in many areas throughout Northern Ireland on the evening of 5 July. Though not to be on the same scale as in 1996, it was none the less disgraceful. Portadown District Master Harold Gracey had reminded everyone prior to leaving Carleton Street that 'We don't want trouble here today. Remember this is the Sabbath.' This fell on deaf ears as 'loyalists' used the events as the occasion for violence in the Sandy Row area of Belfast and in Lisburn, Carrickfergus, Newtownabbey, Ballyclare and Coleraine. Chief Constable Ronnie Flanagan made his position abundantly clear when he stated: 'The march will not be forced down. It is our responsibility to uphold the law and it is our responsibility to enforce the lawfully binding decision of the Parades Commission.'

On 24 July the *Belfast Telegraph* revealed that Archbishop Robin Eames had written to Portadown District on 5 July, 'stressing the importance of linking Christian worship to behaviour outside and after the service . . . I did not receive a reply – I was told my letter had been noted.'

On Monday evening a 'Freedom Camp' was set up in the Square in Hillsborough. Violence continued with the now customary ritual condemnations from those 'on the hill' at Drumcree and at the 'House of Orange'. By Tuesday evening the gunmen had come out in Belfast and the first of many cases of intimidation of RUC families and Roman Catholic families occurred in the Carrickfergus area. The local Presbyterian minister, Rev. Richard Graham, resigned from the Orange Order. Again there were the usual condemnations. The first minister designate David Trimble said: 'Orangemen must realise that if this violence continues, it will only be a matter of time before we are, once again, following coffins.'

Ugly scenes followed Seamus Mallon's visit to the Garvaghy Road, and David Trimble visited the officers of Portadown District, all to no avail. On Wednesday 8 July the violence continued with large-scale intimidation and petrol-bombing by loyalists. Nationalists also took to the streets in several areas, and Republican bombs disrupted rail services between Dublin and Belfast. That evening the largest crowd of the present stand-off turned up at Drumcree, and again it was evident that the marshals were unable to keep protesters from attacking the security forces. A very violent incident occurred in Newbuildings, near Londonderry, when an off-duty policeman and two others including an eleven-year-old boy were dragged from a car and beaten. At the meeting of Orange chaplains on 13 July the Rev. Stephen Dickinson claimed that this story was untrue, and that it had been 'planted' by the Northern Ireland Office. However, two men were later charged and appeared in court over the incident.

On Thursday 9 July a four-man delegation consisting of Denis Watson, George Patton, Stephen McLaughlin and the Rev. William Bingham met the prime minister in London. Tony Blair assured them that the government must be seen to uphold the rule of law, and that he was not in a position to overturn the ruling of the Parades Commission. That evening blast bombs were thrown at the police lines, injuring Chief Inspector John Barr. The crowd, many in Orange regalia, cheered this 'success'. It was later claimed by apologists for Portadown District that the detonator had been found to be one of the type used by the INLA. One hardly knew whether to laugh or cry at such idiocy.

On 10 July the RUC revealed the statistical extent of the violence to date: 548 petrol-bombings, 166 hijackings and more than six hundred attacks on homes, buildings and vehicles. Fifty-three RUC officers had been injured. It may well be argued that not all of these could be attributed to Orangemen, but the fact remains that many were the work of so-called supporters of Drumcree, and had the stand-off not taken place the likelihood of violence on this scale would have been very small. On Friday evening, though numbers were considerably reduced, a gunman used the cover of the crowd to fire at the security forces. Later that year District Master Harold Gracey was to claim that this was an INLA gunman. What a picture! An 'INLA gunman' cheered on the hill at Drumcree by Orangemen!

In spite of condemnations and pleas, the violence continued. Attempts to distance the Institution proved difficult because of the arrests of a number of Orangemen on 10 July. Among those arrested, charged and subsequently found guilty of offences were the Portadown solicitor Richard Monteith and Philip Black, who had been Denis Watson's election agent the previous June. They did not 'walk' on the Twelfth for they spent that day in Maghaberry Prison, where Denis Watson visited them. Those who had knowledge of Orange discipline knew that they need not hold their breath for any disciplinary proceedings.

Many decent Orangemen were finding it difficult to accept that the Orange Institution, pledged to 'the maintenance of the public peace', could have any part in the events now taking place. The Institution thirty years ago had condemned the Northern Ireland Civil Rights Association for bringing people on to the streets and not accepting responsibility for the violence which resulted. Now, to many thinking people, the Orange Order was doing exactly the same thing, and was just as guilty. Had the Institution had the courage to make use of the opportunity, they could and should have reacted to the frightening events of Thursday and Friday nights by 'going home with dignity'. Portadown District thus lost two opportunities to 'get off the hook'.

At a meeting in the office of the first minister at Stormont, attended by Seamus Mallon, Jonathan Powell, Denis Watson and the Rev. William Bingham, a genuine way of resolving the issue was torpedoed. It was suggested that as the Parades Commission's ruling could not be overturned, a solution might be for the parade to be brought down by Obins Street, the old 'traditional' way. This would have allowed the district to save face and perhaps weakened the residents' opposition by opening up the possibility of coming down alternately via Obins Street and the Garvaghy Road. When this was put to the leadership 'on the hill' they refused on the grounds that 'there are not enough Roman Catholic houses in Obins Street any more'!

Some began to suspect that the leadership were working to a different agenda, as when the district were asked what their 'exit strategy' was. The reply – 'body bags' – may have been a joke. It certainly disclosed the unthinking bombast controlling Portadown's reactions.

Saturday 11 July saw further developments in crisis management. Proximity talks between the two sides aimed at resolving the dispute began in Armagh Council offices. The prime minister's chief of staff, Jonathan Powell, oversaw these talks, and the Rev. Roy Magee, though not an Orangeman, acted as mediator for the Orange delegation. It was, as often in the past, too little too late.

Numbers were greatly reduced 'on the hill' throughout Saturday, as the full significance of what was happening throughout the Province began to sink in. To many Protestants, Orange or otherwise, this was beginning to seem 'a walk too far'. In spite of the assurances those in leadership had given in 1996 that this 'would never happen again', it had happened. The Orange Institution was fast losing any public sympathy it still had.

The three Protestant churches united in condemnation of the violence. The most damning of all came from the President of the Methodist Conference, the Rev. David Kerr, who pointed out: 'The Reformation was all about getting away from tradition to the Biblical basis again and it seems as if those who are representing themselves as defenders of the Protestant Reformation are in fact going categorically against it.'

The stand on the hill at Drumcree was now being presented by a hardline element as a struggle for the very existence of the Protestant way of life, as Ian Paisley expressed it in 1995: 'If we do not get down this road all is lost'. One Portadown District officer was so out of touch with reality that he actually vocalised the belief that England would support Ulster as they had done at the beginning of the century. He believed that England would be 'brought to a standstill' once the people realised that the British in Ulster were on the ropes.

In a further twist, Portadown District submitted another application to the Parades Commission for the parade to proceed down the Drumcree and Garvaghy roads. The district press officer, David Jones, commented, 'If this application is turned down the Parades Commission must take full responsibility for any violence.' The logic of this statement beggared belief.

As Sunday 12 July dawned, the world awoke to the news of the arson attack which had killed ten-year-old Richard, nine-year-old Mark and seven-year-old Jason Quinn at their home on a predominantly Protestant estate in Ballymoney, County Antrim. Crissie Quinn, their mother, described herself as Catholic, but the children attended a state school, not a Roman Catholic-controlled school. Her explanation was often quoted in the press: 'I brought them up as Protestants because their fathers were Protestant and because we were living on a Protestant estate. I didn't want them to feel different from the other kids around them. I thought it was the right thing to do.'

Grand Lodge officers hurriedly convened a meeting of county officers and the members of the Parades Strategy Committee, which apparently was now making the decisions for the Institution. There was huge media interest. The only adequate description of those in the House of Orange that morning is 'headless chickens'. It was one round of meetings after another, none of which – all too typically – produced any result. Members of the Confederation of British Industry (CBI) came to the House of Orange at the request of the leadership and spoke to senior officers. A meeting was held with David Trimble and Seamus Mallon, after which the Grand Secretary, the Grand Master and other senior officers travelled to Portadown where they met with officers of Portadown District. They had left those whom they spoke to at Stormont with the impression that they were going to tell Portadown District to 'call it off', but Harold Gracey told the *Belfast News Letter* of the following day, 'Robert Saulters did not try to influence us in any way.'

In his sermon in the morning service at Pomeroy Presbyterian Church, County Tyrone, attended by members of Pomeroy District Lodge as their pre-Twelfth service, the Rev. William Bingham called for the protest to be ended, repeating that 'no road is worth a life, let alone the lives of three innocent little boys'. He subsequently received over a thousand letters of support from a wide spectrum of people. Paul Connolly commented in the *Belfast Telegraph*: 'Reverend William Bingham's pulpit plea to his bewildered brethren was a million moral miles from the howls of the mob as RUC officers came under attack from blast bombs.' An unprecedented seventeen minutes of his sermon was shown around the world by the news media, to the delight of all right-thinking Orangemen. At no time did he blame the Orange Institution for the deaths in Ballymoney, but of course he was wise enough to know that in the modern world perception is often more important than reality. In the *Belfast Morning Telegraph* of 19 December 1998, Larry White awarded the Rev. William Bingham 'Man of the Year . . . for proving to a sceptical world that the words "decent" and "Orangemen" do belong in the same sentence'.

On the morning of 12 July the telephone at the House of Orange was transferred to and manned by Burnside Orange Hall outside Antrim to handle the many calls attacking the Institution, condemning the Portadown District and praising the Rev. William Bingham for his courageous stand. Such was the concern at Dublin Road that Mervyn Gibson, a member of the Parades Strategy Committee and a student for the ministry of the Presbyterian Church who had been helping with the office work, telephoned Bingham to find out exactly what he had said. He admitted that they were being inundated with calls of support for his stand. In contrast, only one of the senior officers, Colin Shilliday, the Assistant Grand Treasurer, took the opportunity of telephoning him to offer support. It was over a week later before William Bingham's own County Master, Denis Watson, and County Secretary, Stephen McLaughlin, made their way to Pomeroy. They were later to apologise to him.

In County Down the response of the 'freedom camp' at Hillsborough, a protest intended to support the Portadown Orangemen, was more rational and honourable. The camp was quickly demolished and replaced by three wreaths on the gates of Hillsborough Castle.

The officers of Grand Lodge apparently assumed that there was a relationship between the deaths of the Quinn boys and the Drumcree stand-off, and immediately sought to distance the Institution from this horrific event. Political people on the ground around Ballymoney suggested during the day that the arson attack had been drugs-related and had no connection with the Drumcree stand-off; some in the leadership quickly bought into this as a way of escape. The Chief Constable made it quite clear that, on the evidence to hand, it was sectarian. He said, 'This is not protest, this is not principle. This is not statistics. It is three wee boys . . . burned to death in their beds.'

As usual on these occasions, other rumours spread quickly, such as that the petrol bombs had been inside the house, not thrown in. The true nature of these events surrounding the deaths of the three children may never come to the light of day this side of eternity. However, the perceived association with the protest at Drumcree placed Portadown District on the horns of the proverbial dilemma. Rather than take this opportunity to leave the hill with dignity, again they chose to stay and did not even have the sense to keep silent. The *Belfast Telegraph* of 15 July reported: 'Portadown Orange Order spokesman David Jones claimed that security forces and paramilitaries colluded to launch the attack.' Jones was quoted as saying, 'I will be very interested to see the outcome of the investigation . . . I can only go on the information which we have received and it would point in that direction.' Such statements horrified decent and respectable Orangemen. They certainly did not win any friends, and only dug the Institution into a deeper hole.

A lengthy statement from the House of Orange condemned the 'tragic events' and offered 'our sincere sympathy and deepest condolences to the Quinn family', but displayed a number of contradictions. It recognised that 'there are those who are not prepared to let us have the kind of peaceful protest which is intended', yet there was no decisive leadership to call a halt to the events which were quite clearly giving rise to these acts of violence. It said that 'our country should be encouraged toward a more reflective mode', and yet the leadership would not provide the peaceful facilities for such reflection. The statement went on to talk about 'cultural apartheid' and needing 'to find a way to trust each other's identity'. The most objectionable phrase to many was 'the beleaguered brethren of Portadown District', when it was clear that the Portadown leaders had beleaguered themselves. It was this phrase which captured the headlines and communicated the idea to the watching world that all that Orangemen were interested in was a 'walk down a road', regardless of the human cost.

The first minister designate, David Trimble, demonstrated a much more courageous kind of leadership when, according to the *Belfast News Letter* of 13 July, he said: 'The only way they [the Portadown Orangemen] can clearly distance themselves from these murders and show the world that they repudiate those who murder young children, the only way to repudiate that, is to come down off the hill.'

On the day of the Twelfth (Monday 13 July) as many chaplains as possible were contacted. Meeting in the House of Orange that evening, they concluded: 'It was difficult to defend the Institution in the light of the political speeches on the Lord's Day and the presence of "Kick the Pope" bands from Scotland playing party tunes. The protest being hijacked by gunmen meant that we were culpable.' Central Committee 'had apparently been bypassed' and the Strategy Committee 'appeared to be running the Institution'. The chaplains noted that what was happening 'appears to be a continuation of the bitterness of the YES/NO campaign'.

These areas of concern were to be passed on to the Grand Master by a representative group of three chaplains, the Rev. Dr Warren Porter, the Rev. Ian McClean and myself. The chaplains agreed a resolution to be released to the press, subject to the approval of the Grand Master:

> As a representative group of Orange Order Chaplains we were greatly heartened by the courage of Brother Rev. William Bingham, Grand Chaplain of County Armagh, in defending the sacredness of human life. As far back as Thursday 9th July, Bro. Bingham rightly emphasised that no road is worth a life and we entirely support this sentiment. Those who vilify him are rejecting the clear teaching of the Word of God.

The resolution expressed 'utter revulsion' at the murders in Ballymoney and deep sorrow at the attacks on and intimidation of Roman Catholics. It continued:

> Our bitter shame at all this, allegedly carried out in the name of Protestantism, is not in any way lessened by the fact that many of our own people are the victims of terrorism.
>
> The spectacle of people attempting to injure or murder policemen and soldiers in Portadown, and the intimidation of police families, has brought shame on the Protestant community, and all the more since it has been done under the guise of supporting the Portadown District's protest against the determination of the Parades Commission.
>
> We pray that the day may quickly come when all the people of Northern Ireland will be enabled to live in mutual respect and neighbourly harmony, each fulfilling the Redeemer's command to 'love your neighbour as yourself'.

Our delegation met the Grand Master and the Grand Secretary the following morning. We discussed these areas of concern and pointed out that there was the perception abroad that the Institution was against the Belfast Agreement. The Grand Secretary said that indeed it was.

The Roman Catholic Archbishop Dr Seán Brady called the chaplains' statement 'courageous and generous' and hoped it would be 'a significant step on the road to building a new relationship . . . The blame does not all lic on one side. Our only future lies in working together.'

Immediately before the statement was issued, death threats were issued against three individual chaplains, the Rev. William Bingham, the Rev. Robert Coulter and the Rev. Dr Warren Porter. The police contacted these three to inform them in the early hours of Tuesday morning. The Grand Lodge Office issued the usual condemnatory statement, expressing 'deep shock'. The shock must not have been deep enough, because the chaplains concerned were never personally contacted by any of the Orange leadership about the death threats or offered any support.

The following press release was issued from the Grand Lodge Office on 15 July:

> We reiterate the importance of our position statement released July 12. We believe people have not fully considered this. It is therefore regrettable that selective quotes have only been used to satisfy media sound bites.
>
> We contend that the government and the security forces know who were behind the violence obviously orchestrated at Drumcree. We ask who has the capabilities to make and use blast bombs, it is certainly not the Orange Order!
>
> We repudiate the government for introducing into the House of Commons today a spurious element of conflict where none exists on the Agreement.
>
> Outrageous statements such as made today by Adam Ingram connecting the horrific and tragic murder of the young Quinn brothers to the peaceful protests involving Drumcree are contemptible and hostile towards the Institution. We condemn this type of cheap remark as both distasteful and dangerous. Such careless remarks can encourage further attacks on both our members and their property.
>
> We will not stand by and hear our principles demonised by anyone. We appeal to people to listen to us thereby opening up avenues of understanding.

As the reader will note, there was no mention of the attacks on the Rev. William Bingham at the Twelfth in Pomeroy two days before. No statement was ever issued in condemnation. Even the above 'Position Statement Update' reveals the world inhabited by senior officers of the Institution in the reference to 'peaceful protests involving Drumcree'. It was the *violent* protests which had imprinted themselves on the minds of the world.

The *Belfast Telegraph* of 20 July quoted County Armagh Chaplain the Rev. Tom Taylor's rebuke to William Bingham and others who spoke out in relation to the Quinn murders:

> The younger men should think twice before they make statements to the media. Where there is division there is always damage. I would have preferred he said what he said in private. There is a feeling that the Orangemen in Portadown have been let down by these chaplains. They are trying to be television stars. Publicity is doing no one any good.

Dr Warren Porter wrote to Taylor pointing out that he was doing what he condemned others for doing – speaking publicly. There was another fundamental problem with this behaviour. As a Christian brotherhood Orangemen are supposed to be following Scripture. The Lord Jesus Christ laid down principles governing relationships in Matthew 18:15: 'If your brother sins against you, go and show him his fault, just between the two of you.' When Taylor met Bingham at a subsequent meeting of the County Armagh Grand Orange Lodge, of which they are both members, he never raised this issue. In fact he supported Bingham in his efforts to resolve the situation.

Lord Molyneaux, at the Royal Black Institution demonstration at Scarva on 14 July, to his credit called for 'a period of silence and reflection'. But in the mean time all the press releases in the world could not undo the damage. The press savaged the Institution for its lack of vision, sensitivity and leadership. Andy Pollak, in the *Irish Times* of 15 July, wrote:

> The leadership is in a shambles. Last weekend the Prime Minister's chief negotiator, Jonathan Powell, said that it was clear that the Order's leaders should come out in support of the Armagh chaplain's call in the wake of the Ballymoney killings, but 'they haven't got the ***** [asterisks mine] to do it'.

On 29 October 1999 Thomas Robert Garfield Gilmore was sentenced to three life terms for his part in the murder of the Quinn children. This sentence was overturned on appeal on 5 June 2000, and Gilmore was sentenced to fourteen years for the manslaughter of the three boys. Two others who were named in court as having thrown the petrol bombs at the instigation of Gilmore, who was settling a long-running dispute, have never been convicted.

No one had accused the Institution of direct involvement in this wicked deed, and Lord Justice McCollum's judgement made no such implication. Those within the Institution who saw that the events at Drumcree had contributed to the atmosphere of violence in which such a horrendous crime could be committed were simply asking that this reality should be recognised. But such was the fear that an admission of this nature would be tantamount to a confession of direct guilt that the whole matter was dropped like a hot potato. Grand Lodge issued a press statement which asserted that the judgement:

> . . . confirms exactly where the blame for this terrible atrocity lies . . . Sections of the press and media both locally and at international level disgracefully sought to demonise the Orange Institution and members of the Orange family over the incident. The court conviction now compels these people to . . . issue an apology for the very obvious misrepresentation of the facts in the lead-up to, and the actual attack on the Quinn home.

The Rev. William Bingham also issued a statement asking the RUC to confirm that they had no evidence of any link between the Orange Order and the protest at Drumcree and the murder of the Quinn children. He said:

> The time has come for the full truth to be made known over these dreadful killings so that the good name of Orangeism is restored. I would once again put on record my continued support for the right of Portadown District Lodge to exercise their civil liberties. I unreservedly continue to condemn the violence at Drumcree in previous years from whatever source it came from, which in no way advanced the cause of Christ or true Orangeism.

The Grand Lodge officers indicated their intention to hold a press conference when the trial had finished, but like so many decisions taken at Grand Lodge, this was not implemented. Instead it was nearly two years before the next press release on the subject on 18 March 2000, calling for a social services report and condemning 'superficial and irresponsible reporting by the media which inferred [*sic*] that the Orange Institution was involved and ignored the clear involvement of terrorists and drug dealing'.

Those who shared the principles and aspirations of the Ulsterman, including the Scots with whom the majority population have the closest affinity, could only express their horror at the expressions of bitterness and hatred witnessed almost daily on television screens and in the press. The *Scottish Sunday Mail* of 26 July 1998 and the West Lothian edition of the *Evening News* on 27 July carried photographs of two Broxburn Orangemen dancing naked at Drumcree. The *Sunday Mail* quoted the Grand Master of the Grand Orange Lodge of Scotland, Ian Wilson: 'If they are members then it is a matter for the individual lodges to bring disciplinary action against them. I would be surprised if they weren't expelled for bringing the Order into disrepute.' Whether or not he still has cause for surprise remains unknown.

The Broxburn Loyalist Flute Band, from West Lothian, played party tunes at the barricades at Drumcree on the evening of Sunday 12 July, after the announcement of the deaths of the Quinn children. The band had received a £350 grant from West Lothian Council. The Council Provost, Joe Thomas, was reported to have said, 'It is sad West Lothian should be portrayed in this way by this band . . . We will not support any band involved in civil disorder and the matter will be brought to the council's attention.'

In the days following more very sad news was to break. On 14 July the Rev. Gordon McCracken, minister of Whitburn South Parish Church (Church of Scotland) in West Lothian, gave in his resignation from the Orange Institution in Scotland, in which he had held the second most senior post, that of Deputy Grand Master. The *Scotsman* on 22 July reported: 'Mr McCracken said he decided to quit on 12th July, on the Anniversary of the Battle of the Boyne. He believes the march along the Garvaghy Road, which lies in a nationalist area, should have been abandoned before the situation descended into violence.' He is quoted as saying: 'I do not lay the blame for the violence at the door of the Orange Order, but they created a situation where paramilitary groups, with their own interests, were going to take advantage – and that has come to pass.' The Rev. McCracken said his resignation 'did not arise out of the presence of Scottish bands in Ireland, nor from the regrettable and heartbreaking, but not directly related, deaths of the Quinn brothers, whose family have my deepest sympathy', but that 'the scenes of attacks on the security forces, and in particular the indentation on a police riot helmet caused by gunfire, was the last straw'.

Various columnists in the national press attempted to analyse the situation. In a perceptive article in the Scottish *Herald* on 24 July, Ron Ferguson wrote:

> Instead of supporting William Bingham, the hardline leadership pilloried him. Instead of making a dignified and respectful withdrawal, the Orange leadership decided to carry on regardless. It was the kind of judgement, which makes the commanders of the Light Brigade look like models of wise restraint. The cold-eyed Gerry Adams must have thought it was Christmas.

All this could not have come at a worse time for the RUC. The Patten Commission on Policing was taking evidence for its restructuring. The Sinn Féin/IRA standpoint was that the RUC was not an acceptable police force and never would be. Here we had the spectacle of those who made the most vocal claim to be Her Majesty's loyal subjects confronting the police and subjecting them and their families to horrific and vile abuse. All this played into the hands of Sinn Féin/IRA and reduced the credibility of anything that the Orange Institution might have had to say about policing. Unwittingly or otherwise, the Institution was contributing to the demise of the RUC.

Throughout Northern Ireland, relations between those members of the RUC who were also Orangemen and the wider Orange membership became very strained. This was particularly true in County Armagh where a number of RUC members were forced to leave the Order because their 'brethren' no longer regarded them as acceptable. Individuals were refused admission to their Orange Hall and generally given the cold shoulder. This was all the more repugnant to many genuine Orangemen, who took very seriously the professed 'brotherly' nature of the Institution.

The numbers of the RUC who were also members of the Institution were therefore further reduced during this debacle. In an article in the *Belfast Telegraph* on 8 July 1997, Father Denis Faul asked, 'Why are there over 3,000 of them in the Orange Order?' This figure was rather puzzling as there are no such records kept. In the subsequent Report of the Independent Commission on Policing for Northern Ireland (the Patten Report), it was noted that a 'cultural audit' had revealed that less than one per cent of police officers said they were members of the Order. A more accurate guess would therefore allow for something in the region of three hundred Orangemen in the RUC, although even this number was decreasing along with the general membership in the light of the confrontational nature of the Institution.

Rather than observing 'a period of silence and reflection' as called for by Lord Molyneaux, the County Antrim Grand Orange Lodge held an 'Affirmation Service of Unity and Faith' in Ballymena Showgrounds on the afternoon of Sunday 26 July. While the purpose of the rally was said to be to 'affirm the principles of the Reformation', in the popular mind of Orangemen and non-Orangemen alike it was viewed as a rally in support of Drumcree, coming as it did in the midst of the crisis.

This popular view of a 'Drumcree Rally' was not lessened by the contributions of the participants. The Rev. Stephen Dickinson was reported by the Guardian group of newspapers as saying, 'Drumcree has been blamed for everything . . . IRA terrorists could blow this place asunder, murder, maim, destroy and cost the government an absolute fortune . . . And yet there was not the same propaganda used against them.' The Rev. Martin Smyth, the past Grand Master, called for a public inquiry into the deaths of the Quinn children in Ballymoney, while the Grand Master, Robert Saulters, said:

> We are behind their [Portadown District's] stand for civil rights, a stand that if the Orange Institution did not make, then all our parades, all our liberties, would be targeted one by one, by those who oppose us . . . Some even tried to associate us with the horrific murders in Ballymoney. There is no place or support for such deeds in an Institution committed to upholding Christian principles and values.

To the discerning eye even the title given to this rally – 'The Affirmation Service of Unity and Faith' – was a strange one. For an organisation pledged to uphold the principles of the Reformation this was placing those principles in reverse. The Reformers did not put unity before faith, but faith before unity!

Proceedings at the Showgrounds were conducted behind a lectern bearing the text of Romans 14:12, 'Every one of us shall give account of himself to God.' One can only pray that the truth of that text may have taken root in the lives of some of those at the rally and be demonstrated in their lifestyle in the days and years to come.

The Antrim and Ballymena *Guardian*s estimated attendance at the rally at five thousand and reported that 'Robert Saulters has distanced himself from comments he made in Ballymena at the weekend. Prior to the start of Sunday's Affirmation Service [he] told reporters that it was probable that there would be talks with Residents' Groups.' Their front-page report quotes him as having said the previous Sunday, 'I would suggest, perhaps, that we have to look to the future, and it is probably inevitable that we will have to make contact.'

The *Irish News* on 27 July estimated attendance at three thousand and quoted the words of the Grand Master:

> At the moment, talking to Breandan MacCionnaith [*sic*] is out of the question but, because of the changing political situation, and the assembly at Stormont, I think it will be possible in the future. Looking at it from the long term of the new assembly being set up where Sinn Féin could be in positions of being ministers . . . through time we will have to talk to them. I think that talks with these groups are inevitable. The Grand Lodge will meet on Saturday to discuss the Drumcree situation and I will be suggesting that we change our policy.

Portadown's spokesman David Jones, however, was quoted as saying: 'To talk directly to MacCionnaith would be an insult to our many members who are ex-servicemen and are members of the Royal British Legion.' David NcNarry's response was likewise predictable: 'I think that it is highly unlikely that the institution will change course.'

It is questionable whether or not the Ballymena Showgrounds on a Sunday afternoon was the right place to present an apparent change of policy. It was supposed to be a 'religious' rally, but, as previously was witnessed following the service of morning prayer outside Drumcree Parish Church on 5 July, the politics of the day can be brought in all too easily.

The *Belfast Telegraph* on 27 July covered Saulters' 'U-turn' in a front-page article by Martina Purdy under the heading 'Portadown Marchers Plan Rally'. She commented, 'The Sovereign Grand Master of the Royal Black Perceptory, the most senior of the three loyal orders, refused to criticise a call by the Grand Master of the Orange Order, Robert Saulters, for Orangemen to talk to residents' groups about parades.' The editorial of the same day remarked:

> Robert Saulters, the Orange Grand Master, has shown commendable courage in recommending that the Order's refusal to talk to the Garvaghy Road residents should be rescinded and offering himself to act as a go-between. Presumably this new spirit could apply also to talks with the Parades Commission. More and more people, in the Order, the Church of Ireland and politics are prepared to put their heads above the parapet. With strong, brave leadership, backed up by the rank and file, the coming trials of the Apprentice Boys march and republican demonstrations can be overcome.

Jim Cusack wrote in the *Irish Times* the same day:

> The deaths of the three Quinn children and the violence at Drumcree appear to have persuaded the Orange Order leadership finally to talk to Catholic residents about its parades . . . The statement yesterday from the Grand Master of the Orange Order that 'we will have to talk to them' is the most important signal yet that the organisation is prepared to seek a compromise over the enduring crisis of Drumcree. Mr Robert Saulters will face strong opposition from militants in his organisation, led by the Spirit of Drumcree ginger group, but in recent years the Orange leadership has shown itself capable of taking on internal opposition over marching.

As subsequent events were to prove, what may have 'appeared' to Jim Cusack was not reality. The truth of the matter would be evidenced by first an 'amnesty' and then a 'deal' with the Spirit of Drumcree.

At a meeting of the Parades Strategy Committee on the evening of 27 July the mind of the Grand Master was changed and the fog of confusion once again descended on the Institution and the Province. This change of mind was revealed in the press, presumably as a result of a press release by the House of Orange. The *Belfast Telegraph* carried the news in disbelief on 29 July. Dr Philip McGarry, president of the Alliance Party, accused the Institution of having 'limited credibility' and attacked the integrity of the Order:

> The Orange Order gives the impression that it refuses to talk to local residents as a matter of principle . . . The fact that the protest at Drumcree was used as a base for a gunman to shoot at the security forces, for a nail bomber to cause injuries, and for other violent acts prevents any reasonable person from understanding the Order's self-proclaimed opposition to people because of alleged involvement in violence.

Dr McGarry drew attention to the fact that the violence at Drumcree had weakened the Order's position, as had its willingness to talk to convicted killer Kenny McClinton, a self-styled 'Pastor' who was not amenable to the jurisdiction of any denomination.

Martina Purdy reported in the *Belfast Telegraph* that 'senior Orange sources continue to deny that Mr Saulters was put under any pressure to clarify his remarks'. A Portadown Orangeman was reported as saying, 'As to why he [Saulters] took that U-turn, I don't know. I don't think any pressure was put on him. It just might have been a change of mind.' It was no coincidence that the 'child' of the Grand Master, the Parades Strategy Committee, had met on the evening of 27 July. When faced with a revolt from his own creation he caved in. In this instance infanticide would have been acceptable.

The editorial of the *Belfast Telegraph* on 29 July was less than complimentary, but reflected the thinking of many:

> The Orange Order which should be showing leadership is, frankly, in turmoil. It has a much wider community to represent than the Orangemen at Portadown, yet it lent its weight to a campaign at Drumcree against a legal ruling that was always likely to end in chaos

> and tears, damaging its long-term interests. The world could see how the Order was being cynically used by anti-agreement politicians to confront the government, but no one, until some brave chaplains, shouted 'Stop!'
>
> The Grand Master, Robert Saulters, provided evidence of fresh thinking at the weekend, when he indicated that he would be recommending direct talks with the Garvaghy Road residents at the special meeting of the Grand Lodge on Saturday. Sighs of relief were breathed in the community at large, only to be followed with exasperation when he side-tracked yesterday. The possibility of direct talks, he said, could only be considered when Sinn Féin and the IRA made it clear that terrorism had ended for good, that weapons had been decommissioned and that remorse had been publicly expressed.
>
> Small wonder that rank-and-file Orangemen are just as confused as anyone else about the Order's future policy. From the outside it seems obvious that if the proximity talks are stalled, sooner or later, with or without pre-conditions, there must be direct talks.

The editorial was reflecting and expressing the exasperation of the community at large. It was immeasurably more difficult for those close to Grand Lodge to give vent to their sadness and frustration.

A special meeting of the Grand Orange Lodge of Ireland was called for Saturday 1 August 1998 in Ballymacarrett Orange Hall, Belfast, to 'consider the current situation and the way forward'. Members of Grand Lodge arrived to be greeted with three 'Information Sheets'. The versions released to the press are reproduced here:

> INFORMATION SHEET No. 1 – DRUMCREE SITUATION
>
> There has been much talk and advice as people tell the Institution what they should do about the Portadown Orangemen's continued presence at Drumcree Parish Church. There has also been much speculation as to the reasons why they have not completed their parade. However, what is important, is that we concentrate on assisting the Portadown brethren to return to Carleton Street Orange Hall. There will be a full assessment of the events surrounding the initial phase of the stand-off in due course. But even at this stage it is clear the terrorism and violence carried out during this period, had a serious negative effect on our peaceful strategy.
>
> The focus moved from our peaceful protests and the reasons for the stand-off, to that of the inexcusable violence. The story unfortunately

became the trouble and not the injustice and infringement of civil rights. Thus it is worth re-focusing on why the situation arose in the first place.

Portadown Orangemen were refused permission to walk along the Garvaghy Road, a main arterial route from their annual church service at Drumcree Parish Church. This decision was taken by an unelected government quango, the Parades Commission, which is perceived to be neither independent nor impartial. The reason the Commission gave for re-routing the parade was, that they wanted to 'break the cycle' of Orange parades along the road, even though they recognised the parade would be peaceful, orderly and dignified.

The campaign against parades is organised by Sinn Féin/IRA as a tactic in their campaign to remove the British presence from Northern Ireland. Gerry Adams confirmed this at Athboy in 1997 when he spoke of the republican anti-parades strategy being three years in preparation. The Garvaghy Road Residents Association have no logical reason for objecting to the parade. Their opposition involves a broader equality agenda of matters relating to social economic issues, over which the Institution has no control. Many believe their agenda includes having a levy paid by government so others can enjoy the right of free assembly and movement. No talk – No walk – No money – No march. Blackmail by any other name.

The Orange Institution will continue to support the Portadown brethren, but it must be realised phase two will be a long-term strategy and thus different in nature and character.

However, this only increases our determination and commitment to see civil rights upheld. There will be opportunities over the coming weeks to support the campaign in many ways. Please ensure all who join us in this campaign understand they will only be made welcome if they are committed to peaceful protest. Violence is the weapon of terrorists and thugs, there is no place for it in any event organised by the Orange Institution.

Contact district and county officers to hear what is happening in your area. Stop rumours and do not be drawn into any public debate which is stage-managed to split the unity and purpose of the Institution.

INFORMATION SHEET No. 2 – DRUMCREE & GOOD FRIDAY AGREEMENT

One of the great misconceptions that abounded in some quarters in Northern Ireland and beyond over the Drumcree protest by Orangemen was that the issue was part of the political opposition articulated against the Good Friday Agreement.

Such an assessment is far removed from the truth and it can be instantly dismissed by the fact that the members of Portadown District and their friends and supporters in the wider Orange and Unionist families have been campaigning vigorously over the past decade to have their civil liberties upheld in their traditional march along the Garvaghy Road.

The great concerns and apprehensions raised in relation to the hijacking of the parades issue by extreme Irish republican elements, in Portadown and other places, were expressed years before the Stormont deal was brokered and the new Northern Ireland Assembly spawned.

The Orange standpoint at Drumcree is quite simply in defence of civil liberties for all; the right to walk the Queen's Highway unhindered from the threat of intimidation and violence, from whatever quarter. This principle – an accepted part of normal democracy throughout the world – has been supported by unionists of the widest spectrum of opinion and the question of whether one voted 'Yes' or 'No' in the recent Referendum is totally irrelevant.

Indeed, Portadown District Lodge in their stand-off received the wholehearted backing of many public representatives and ordinary citizens, who, although they favoured the Good Friday Agreement in the Referendum, nevertheless felt the need to raise their voices against the denial of freedom of assembly and the obvious erosion of democracy in decisions reached by the unelected quango the Parades Commission. It is interesting to note that of the 33 members of the Assembly who are in the Orange Institution, half were broadly in support of the Good Friday Agreement and, all of these persons, expressed sympathy for the action taken by the Portadown lodges.

The democratic decision taken by the people of Northern Ireland by the 'Yes' vote in the referendum is recognised by the Orange Institution and we intend to play our part in proposed civic structures. The allegations continually made by members of government, political parties and regrettably some leading church figures, linking the Drumcree situation to the referendum 'No' campaign are reprehensible. The Northern Ireland Office tame opinion formers, negated by exposure prior to the referendum, appear to be crawling out of the woodwork. They seek to invent divisions were none exist, rather than building trust between and within communities.

The Grand Orange Lodge of Ireland fully supports the work of the new Northern Ireland Assembly in its task of underpinning the future peace and stability of this Province within the United Kingdom for the benefit of all its citizens. Part of our political agenda is, to safeguard the Union and, in upholding this constitutional imperative, we make absolutely no apology to anyone for doing so. The referendum is over; let us all deal with the realities of the present.

INFORMATION SHEET No. 3 – QUINN MURDERS

The Orange Institution along with all in society condemned the horrific murder of the Quinn brothers unequivocally and unreservedly, and expressed our sympathy to the family circle. We, unlike others, do not believe in exploiting the deaths for propaganda purposes. However because of the hostile press linking the murders to the protests in support of Drumcree we believe it is important to clarify some issues.

Why were the Quinn Brothers murdered?

We are told it was simply because of sectarian hatred. A hatred bred out of intolerance, misconceptions, and a lack of respect. Violence spawned by such hatred is not new in society; we have all experienced it particularly over this past 30 years. It has been evidenced by the ethnic cleansing of Protestants from certain areas by Sinn Féin/IRA, and the indiscriminate murder of Roman Catholics by loyalist terrorists. Segregation breeds a society where hate is fuelled and violence results. We live in such a society and we must play our part to reconstruct communities free from injustice and inequality. A society where accommodation becomes the stepping stone to normality.

Was the Orange Institution to blame for the murders?

No – the ultimate blame rests with whoever started the fire. However society as a whole must accept the role all sections have played in creating the conditions whereby negative sectarianism flourishes. Whether that is the intransigence of the residents' groups, the legalised segregation of the Parades Commission or the determination of the Orange Order to see that civil liberties are upheld. Whether that be the stand of the churches, the silence of the business community or the positioning of politicians, society is a product of all of its constituent parts. If sectarian hatred was the reason for the murders then society must shoulder the responsibility. The Orange Order is not the scapegoat for society's shortcomings. Murder and violence are most definitely not the stock and trade [*sic*] of the Orange Institution.

> *Is the price of walking a road worth any life, let alone that of three innocents?*
> The answer of course is No. But it must be stressed no one ever said that it was. Lives are lost because there are those who would turn to violence to further their twisted logic and hatred. Unfortunately in Northern Ireland this is endorsed by government policy which rewards terrorism and those who threaten violence. The Orange Order repeatedly condemned the violence and asked for it to be stopped, but our pleas were just as ineffective as those of the church leaders and politicians. The price of not walking the Queen's Highway is a further segregated society. A society where potentially more tragedies would occur. Working for and supporting civil rights for all will assist in reducing segregation and sectarian hatred.
>
> The Orangemen at Drumcree or those supporting them cannot be held to account for the murder of the three Quinn brothers, any more or any less than any other section of society. The continued demonisation of ordinary decent people who engage in peaceful protest and were sickened by all the violence is a despicable manipulation for political purposes of this tragic event.

These 'Information Sheets' were not debated and the Grand Lodge took no decision on their contents. No indication was given as to who was responsible for their production and the Grand Lodge was not informed that they were to be presented to the media. There was of course little time to read and digest their contents. But one statement in the final paragraph of sheet No. 2 did stand out as perhaps a true reflection of the political motivation of the writers: 'Our primary agenda is, at all costs to safeguard the Union.' It was pointed out that this was not our 'primary agenda', and this was changed before its release to the media to read 'Part of our political agenda is, to safeguard the Union.' Perhaps the original version was closer to the truth than we realised. Another interesting change prior to public release, in the same paragraph, was the deletion of the words 'nationalists as well as unionists' after 'citizens'.

While the substantive content of the 'Information Sheets' was in keeping with the professed standards of Orangeism, basically all that they did was to remind the world that 'The Orange Institution will continue to support the Portadown brethren.' The world of course was not very interested in this reminder. It was more interested in the spectacle of two middle-aged Orangemen running naked in a field at Drumcree, and it was certainly interested in the cheering from Orangemen as a police officer was wounded by someone firing lethal weapons from among the supporters of the stand-off.

But aside from the world's reaction, even the Institution at large did not 'support the Portadown brethren'. In fact, very many Portadown brethren did not support the protests at Drumcree, as shown by the fact that only a minority of the fifteen hundred members of Portadown District were on the hill there.

The *Belfast Telegraph* responded to the 'Information Sheets' in an editorial on 14 August:

> After a dreadful summer, in every sense of the word, the Orange Order is trying to redeem its tarnished image . . . but it will take more than fine words to win the high moral ground . . . The Orange Order's 'full support' for the Northern Ireland Assembly is also somewhat mystifying when set against the Institution's original opposition to the Good Friday Agreement. To make matters worse, the Drumcree protest was hijacked by the No campaign, and once again the Orange leadership failed to assert itself . . . An organisation which purportedly embraces the concept of civil and religious liberty for all should indeed be at the forefront of the crusade to create a pluralist society. But this summer, once again, Orangeism has come to stand for 'not an inch' politics . . . The longer the Drumcree protest is allowed to fester, the greater will be the damage to the Order's reputation. A resolution of that dispute would do more to help the Order's image than any amount of fancy information sheets.

At the Grand Lodge meeting on 1 August 1998, the Grand Secretary gave a lengthy verbal report from the Parades Strategy Committee. Because this was not in writing, it was difficult to address the issues raised, or point out inconsistencies and contradictions. If this was part of a strategy of confusion by inducing a general 'fog' of discussions and debates within the Institution, it succeeded only too well. No clear indication or direction was given as to how the Institution could get itself 'off the hook'.

Both the Grand Master and Grand Secretary had received numerous letters from individuals and lodges expressing concerns, but none of these were read at the meeting. One that came into my hands read as follows:

> Why could you talk to some ex-terrorists while refusing to talk to other elected representatives?

> Why did you stop the proximity talks before the Lord's Day, but expected the Parades Commission to have to meet and work today?
>
> I would ask you to note what the religious leaders including William Bingham have said. It is time to go home.
>
> I appreciate that the Order has been officially committed to non violence this week. I also know that many individual members have ignored this. I would stress that your strategy has played into the hands of the men of violence, and undermined the standing of the Orange Order in the eyes of many who would previously have supported it.
>
> Sincerely,
>
> Rev. Richard Hill BSc BD
> Minister of Cairncastle Presbyterian Church

Present at this Special Grand Lodge meeting was the Rev. W. J. Watson, a well-known North Antrim Presbyterian minister and District Chaplain of Ballymoney District LOL, previously a very infrequent attender at Grand Lodge. His contribution, like that of many others, was quite alarming. They appeared to reject the idea that the Institution could be faulted in any way, and refused to admit to any need for repentance. They appeared to have forgotten that history has not judged Pontius Pilate well.

However, to use the phrase of the Irish journalist Eoghan Harris, 'good authority' was given in this crucial situation by a member of fifty-four years' standing, the past Assistant Grand Master the Rev. Dr Warren Porter, who proposed the following resolution:

> That this Grand Orange Lodge of Ireland, met in special session on 1st August 1998, in a spirit of deep penitence before Almighty God, declare that every effort must be made to uphold the Christian principles of our Order; to implement the explicit requirements of our Rules, which make the observance of the Laws of the Land mandatory at all our Public Demonstrations (See Rule 28); and for the future, to adopt such positive and peaceable measures as shall uphold the principles laid down in the Basis of the Institution and in the Qualifications of an Orangeman.

Lord Molyneaux seconded this resolution. In the subsequent debate there was little acceptance of the responsibility placed on those who organise mass protests. Neither was there any realisation of the implications of 'obedience to the Laws'. There was the realisation by some that the Biblical principle of Matthew 10:14, 'If anyone will not welcome you or listen to your words, shake the dust off your feet when you leave that home or town,' was of more significance than that of Matthew 5:13–16:

> You are the salt of the earth. But if the salt loses its saltiness, how can it be made salty again? It is no longer good for anything, except to be thrown out and trampled by men. You are the light of the world. A city on a hill cannot be hidden. Neither do people light a lamp and put it under a bowl. Instead they put it on its stand, and it gives light to everyone in the house. In the same way, let your light shine before men, that they may see your good deeds and praise your Father in heaven.

This resolution was defeated by way of an amendment 'that no resolution be passed today'. Few if any of those who supported that amendment realised that they were not only closing the debate but also effectively closing the meeting. None of those who supported Dr Porter's resolution was prepared to enlighten them!

This was for many the crossing of the Rubicon, not only on the part of the senior officers who had made a 'deal' with the Spirit of Drumcree group, but by the Institution itself, in the form of the Grand Orange Lodge of Ireland. It was the estimation of one member from County Tyrone that when they rejected Dr Porter's resolution, 'they threw God out of the Institution'. On leaving the Lodge Room, Lord Molyneaux commented to me, 'They are committing suicide', a phrase he repeated at the funeral of the Treasurer of his lodge on 6 April 1999. Suicide it may well have been, but there are easier ways to commit suicide than the death of a thousand cuts. The Grand Orange Lodge of Ireland undoubtedly lost much respect, even among those who by loyalty and tradition had always been foremost in its defence.

At the next regular meeting of the Grand Lodge on 9 December 1998 bitterness overtook brotherhood and reason was replaced with rhetoric. The recommendation of the Central Committee that a delegation meet with the Parades Commission to put the case for Portadown District was defeated by fifty-two votes to four, with four abstentions. The Grand Lodge meeting began at 11 a.m., but, true to form, the Secretariat saw to it that this proposal was put after 5 p.m. By that time those who had other business to attend to had gone. The outcome may well have been unchanged in any case, but the fact remains that a mere fifty-two votes committed a forty-thousand-strong Orange Institution to the continuance of a sterile and stupid policy of 'non-recognition' of a body which had the authority of parliament behind it. No one argued that the Parades

Commission was infallible, but no one could maintain either that the decision to adopt an Orange version of Sinn Féin abstentionism had resulted in any positive achievements.

There was no report from the Strategy Committee, but the Grand Master paid tribute to their work, saying that he could not have survived without them. Subsequently the position of the Grand Master and the Strategy Committee was reaffirmed on the proposal of Thomas Ross and seconded by William Leathem.

The hypocrisy was not to end there, as is seen in the press release which was approved:

> The Orange Institution is a Christian organisation! It has clear and precise attitudes to the Christian faith and the practice of it.
>
> In its Annual Twelfth of July Resolution on Faith it reiterates the Orangeman's priorities in life – personal faith in Jesus Christ.
>
> It is an axiom of Orangeism – 'A good Orangeman is a good Christian'. The Orange Institution is Protestant! It stands positively for the Reformed Faith.
>
> The Institution's thinking on politics and social questions is governed by its Christian basis.

One wonders at the use of the exclamation marks at the end of the two statements, 'The Orange Institution is a Christian organisation!' and 'The Orange Institution is Protestant!' Was there perhaps some doubt in the mind of the writer as to the authenticity of these statements?

Canon S. E. Long had been asked to prepare this press release two days before the meeting of Grand Lodge. Although no one would wish to criticise Canon Long for acceding to the request, it normally would have been the practice for Central Committee to have prior sight of any such statement. This was not done. To some, it seemed that the good Dr Long was being used to put a religious veneer on an Order which was moving further and further away from its basis. In the words of William Brown, an Ulster Christian with a lifelong interest in the Order, 'It seems incredible that an Order that sometimes claims to be Christian should be so interested in its own alleged rights as to be impervious to its responsibilities and to the obvious moral argument here.'[1]

While 1998 could well be considered the *annus horribilis* of the Orange Institution, it was also to be something of a watershed with respect to both the Institution's direction and its public image. The leadership had capitulated to its hardline element. Parading was now the *raison d'être*. No concerted attempt was made to create a better public image. The result of all this was a greater unwillingness on the part of an ever-increasing section of the respectable Protestant community to be identified with the Orange Order. Many from the professional classes reduced their profile within the Institution. Others resigned completely.

Chapter Six

'Wheels and Deals': the Spirit of Drumcree

> *'We love peace, as we abhor pusillanimity; but not peace at any price. There is a peace more destructive of the manhood of living man than war is destructive of his material body. Chains are worse than bayonets.'*
>
> Douglas Jerrold (1803–57), English playwright and journalist[1]

There have at various times throughout the history of the Orange Institution been 'ginger groups' urging it to more decided action. One such in the 1960s was Cell, under the chairmanship of the Rev. S. E. Long. This group started as a private group of concerned Orangemen who met to discuss the implications for the Institution within the current environment of Northern Ireland.

The group met in Wellington Park, Belfast, at the home of William McGrath, who fifteen years later was to achieve notoriety as one of an active group of paedophiles associated with the 'Kincora scandal'. According to the journalist Chris Moore:

> McGrath found himself at odds with the Chairman of 'Cell', the clergyman who clearly was not adopting a hard enough line. McGrath contrived to have the clergyman removed from office in November [1966] . . . He changed its name to 'Tara' and took over as chairman.[2]

One essential difference between Cell and the Spirit of Drumcree was that the former was a private group, the latter a very public affair. Publicity was to be the life-blood of this hardline ginger group.

The Spirit of Drumcree came into existence following the problems surrounding the 1995 Portadown District Lodge church parade. Prior to the launch of the group at a meeting in the Ulster Hall on 14 November 1995 its Steering Committee, consisting of William Bigger, David Dowey, John McGrath, Joel Patton and Harold Price, had carefully cultivated a relationship with the press and continually fed them information, so that an air of expectancy surrounded the meeting. The spokespersons to the press at that stage were David Dowey and Joel Patton, but only Patton's name came to public attention prior to 14 November.

The group said of its origin:

> After a successful Siege of Drumcree in July 1995, some of the Brethren got together to find ways of building on the new sense of Pride and Achievement felt by ordinary Orange Brethren from all over the Province, who had stood at Drumcree. For the first time in years grass roots Protestants, as well as Orangemen, felt that the Orange Order had done something positive at last.[3]

This group was described in the press as 'A radical new faction within the Orange Order' (*Belfast Telegraph*, 27 October 1995), 'A gaggle of hot-heads parading their prejudices under the title of the Spirit of Drumcree (which for the sake of brevity I shall call SOD)' (*Sunday Times*, 10 December 1995), 'Rebel Orangemen' (*Sunday Life*, 14 January 1996), 'militant' (*Irish News*, 22 March 1997) and 'belligerent bigots' (*Irish Independent*, 24 March 1996).

The Education Committee produced a news sheet on 3 November 1995 to address some of the issues this group had raised in the press. Once preparation of this news sheet was well advanced its content was shared with the Executive Officer, George Patton, who revealed similar work of his own which he had circulated among the County Lodges. The news sheet pointed out that the Institution had a representative democracy, that the formal link to the Unionist Party was being examined and that the Grand Lodge could not be held responsible for parades, since it was counties, districts and private lodges who organised them. The Committee drew attention to the fact that not only was the Institution primarily a religious organisation based on the principles of the Reformation, but the bi-annual Report Book which contained all this information was sent to every private lodge.

The *Belfast Telegraph* of 11 November 1995 reported that the Spirit of Drumcree responded to the news sheet by saying, 'The leaflet said we already have representative democracy within the Order – well, what we want is direct democracy.' It was strange indeed that a group which maintained its opposition to republicanism should espouse the fundamentally republican principle of direct democracy.

At the launch of the Spirit of Drumcree the Ulster Hall was filled to its capacity of twelve hundred people, including several who had gone with the intention of making a report. The Education Committee's news sheet was distributed on the street to those entering the hall. Joel Patton and David Dowey addressed the meeting. All those present were wearing Orange regalia, in a clear breach of Law 23 of the Institution. Those who attended with the Education Committee had been given permission to wear their collarettes by the Grand Master, the Rev. Martin Smyth.

The content of the rally was reported to the Central Committee on 8 December, and the following resolution was issued:

> The Central Committee of the Grand Orange Lodge of Ireland does not accept that the meeting on 14 November 1995 in the Ulster Hall was 'representing' the Institution, since those who organised it were not democratically elected by their Brethren.
>
> We totally and unreservedly condemn the unchristian and republican remarks made by those involved and reported to us. Encouragement to violence is unchristian, and calls for 'direct democracy' are republican.
>
> The material content of the six resolutions adopted at the meeting on 14 November can only be addressed by *bona fide* Orangemen using the regular channels of the Institution.

The Central Committee asked me to present my report to Grand Lodge, and it was subsequently circulated, on the decision of the Grand Master, to every lodge within the jurisdiction.

David Dowey's speech at the Ulster Hall was not only personally offensive to many within the Institution but was in total contradiction of these words in the Basis of the Institution: 'It is exclusively an Association of those who are attached to the religion of the Reformation, and will not admit into its brotherhood persons whom an intolerant spirit leads to persecute, injure, or upbraid any man on account of his religious opinions.' His lengthy presentation included calls for the Grand Lodge to break the link with the Ulster Unionist Party and to take a hard line on parades, as well as for the reduction of the number of Deputy Grand Masters and Deputy Grand Chaplains.

Dr Clifford Smyth, who had been in attendance at the rally and whose leaflet *Reform the Orange Order* had been distributed outside the hall beforehand, described Dowey's speech:

> It was the content of what the brother had to say which betrayed the weakness at the heart of this reforming movement. While on the one

> hand he called on the Orange brethren to adopt a much more sophisticated approach to the media, he used intemperate language, which echoed of old-style Paisleyism, raising questions about his understanding of the whole issue. It was fortunate that the press had been excluded from this portion of the rally, because otherwise the movement would have found itself under sustained media assault, and it is debatable whether the answers provided by those promoting the 'Spirit of Drumcree' would have sounded credible.[4]

The media were in fact not excluded. The freelance journalist Alan Murray, who had a weekly column in *Sunday Life*, remained for the whole of the rally after others were excluded. His article in *Sunday Life* on 19 November, made no mention of 'intemperate language', nor indeed anything by way of substance of the content of the speeches.

Media reports at the time named only Joel Patton, not David Dowey. Clifford Smyth alluded to Dowey in the article quoted above only as 'the second speaker, from County Antrim'. Mark Simpson in the *Belfast Telegraph* of 15 November referred to the second speaker only as 'a greater Belfast Orangeman', although a large picture of the platform party, including Dowey, appeared above the article. It was not until 29 February 1996 that the name of the second speaker appeared in print, in *Republican News*. For some reason parts of the media appeared to be concealing the identities of the speakers.

Events caught up with David Dowey on 16 October 1998 when he was suspended from his job as technical officer with the Department of the Environment's planning service in Belfast. According to the *Sunday Times* of 18 October he was 'sent home on full pay . . . after senior officials including Ronnie Spence, the department's permanent secretary, viewed a video of a speech Dowey made at a rally in the Ulster Hall in November 1995'. After an investigation, as reported by Chris Ryder and Vincent Kearney in *Drumcree: The Orange Order's Last Stand*, Dowey 'received a formal written reprimand and a warning as to his future conduct after it was decided that he had breached his Conditions of Service Code'.[5]

Following the Ulster Hall meeting, on the morning of 15 November 1995 a Spirit of Drumcree deputation went to the Grand Lodge Office and handed in the following resolutions:

1. That the Grand Master, Worshipful Brother Martin Smyth, should immediately tender his resignation as he no longer has the

confidence of the rank and file members of the Institution.

2. That Grand Lodge immediately introduce open and free elections, on the basis of 'one Orangeman one vote' for the principal officers, namely, Grand Master, Deputy Grand Master, Grand Secretary, Grand Treasurer and Grand Chaplain.
3. That the Grand Lodge initiates, within three months, an Annual Congress of Orange Delegates, elected by their Private Lodges, to formulate policy, oversee the operation of Grand Lodge and to supervise the development and reorganisation of the institution.
4. That the Grand Lodge issues an immediate directive to the effect that there will be no voluntary re-routing of any traditional Orange Parade, and that no member of the Institution will negotiate with any community group or other nominated representative.
5. That the Grand Lodge gives an immediate commitment not to enter into or support any talks with IRA/Sinn Féin or their surrogate groups.
6. That the Grand Lodge announces immediately its disaffiliation from the Ulster Unionist Party, and undertakes that in future this Institution will not be formally linked to any political party.

The group said it was 'imperative' that Grand Lodge respond within ten days.

It amazed many members of the Orange Institution that those whose names appeared on these resolutions, William Bigger, David Dowey, John McGrath, Joel Patton and Harold Price, were long-serving members of the Institution. They evidently had not learned very much about its workings over the years of their service. The Grand Lodge Office is merely an accommodation address. It is in no position to make decisions about the future or policy of the Institution. Only the Grand Orange Lodge of Ireland at one of its regular meetings can make such decisions. The Grand Orange Lodge of Ireland then met on two occasions each year, traditionally on the second Wednesday of June and December. The Grand Lodge was therefore not in any position to 'immediately introduce open and free elections', issue any 'immediate directive' or 'immediate commitment' or 'announce immediately its disaffiliation from the Ulster Unionist Party', let alone respond within ten days.

Furthermore, any change in the voting method as suggested in the Spirit of Drumcree's second resolution would have required three readings and, as is common in most democratic organisations, a Notice of

Motion to change the rules. The Grand Lodge does not usually organise parades and was therefore not in any position to give any directive. In any case the issuing of directives is contrary to the very open, free and democratic procedures which the Spirit of Drumcree were professing to want introduced.

The connection with the Ulster Unionist Party also appeared to be misunderstood. The Grand Orange Lodge of Ireland was affiliated to the Ulster Unionist Council, not the Ulster Unionist Party. Furthermore, no organisation can bind future generations and restrict their decisions, as was suggested in the sixth resolution, 'that in future this Institution will not be formally linked to any political party'.

Had these resolutions been drawn up by inexperienced Orangemen one could have given them a 'fool's pardon', but all those whose names appeared had many years of experience in the Institution. One must therefore conclude that there was a certain malevolence in their practice.

It appeared that some people could not keep to their own resolutions. While two of the resolutions called for no negotiation or talking, Joel Patton was to appear on the 'Counterpoint' programme on 9 May 1996 with Brendan McKenna of the Garvaghy Road Residents' Coalition. At the subsequent meeting of Grand Lodge on 12 June in Newmills, County Tyrone, Patton defended himself by saying that 'at no time did he address the Sinn Féin representative on television and all his remarks were addressed to the programme's chairman', and that 'he had appeared on this programme as an individual'.

At the half-yearly meeting of the Grand Orange Lodge of Ireland on 13 December 1995, as a result of the debate which followed my report on the Ulster Hall meeting, a resolution was passed reaffirming that 'our Order's principal concern is for the maintenance of the Protestant and Reformed Religion and that any political action necessary to be taken must always be subservient to and supportive of its primary evangelical concern'. It is worth remembering this resolution bearing in mind events two and a half years later. On that occasion, at a meeting of the Grand Orange Lodge of Ireland on 1 August 1998, a similar resolution presented by Dr Warren Porter was defeated by a procedural amendment. It is also worthy of note for the record that Harold Gracey, at the meeting on 13 December 1995, 'appealed to any one with influence with the Spirit of Drumcree group to use that influence to get them to drop "Drumcree" from their title'.

However, no charges were preferred against anyone in the Spirit of Drumcree. The counsel given by Ruth Dudley Edwards in the *Sunday*

Times on 10 December 1995 – 'For the sake of their ordinary decent members, they need to trample on the SOD's and devise better ways of improving the image of the Orange Order' – was ignored.

Following the 13 December meeting I received a letter from David Dowey. He accused me of making 'several errors' in my report and asked for information. In my reply I drew attention to the fact that the report was the property of the Grand Orange Lodge of Ireland and that any further enquiries should be made to the Grand Secretary.

The Spirit of Drumcree distributed a 'contradiction' of the report around every private lodge in the Institution. This correspondence was under the seal of 'Holdfast' LOL 1620 and was signed by William Bigger, David Dowey, John McGrath, Joel Patton and Harold Price, as the 'Steering Committee'. It was of such a personal and serious nature that I contemplated taking legal action, and it was only when the Central Committee decided to send a 'strong letter' to LOL 1620, after examining their books, that I undertook not to proceed. The Executive Officer, George Patton, compared the report with the video of the event. His notes, in substance, endorsed my report.

According to *Sunday Life* of 14 January 1996 plans were afoot for a further rally in the Ulster Hall in the spring. This never took place, and neither did any subsequent rally.

Various attempts were made by the Central Committee to meet with the Spirit of Drumcree group but they pulled out of all these meetings until at last the five members of their Steering Committee, with Walter Millar, a member of the group and District Secretary of Killyman District LOL, met with the Central Committee on 28 May 1996 in the House of Orange. Eighteen or twenty supporters who were not admitted to the meeting accompanied them. The behaviour of the Spirit of Drumcree representatives on this occasion left a lot to be desired. David Dowey refused to be seated or to recognise the authority of the chair. The Grand Master, the Rev. Martin Smyth, who occupied the chair that evening, was surprisingly mild in his conduct of the meeting. Normally he was a very firm chairman, and on occasion was not averse to issuing stern remarks, but on this occasion he did not adopt a strong approach. With the benefit of hindsight one would wish that a much stronger line had been taken. Was it then that the first indication of capitulation was signalled? If so, it unfortunately did not register.

During the discussions of their six resolutions, the Steering Committee accepted responsibility for the leaflet *The Orange Banner* which had been put into circulation. One of their main complaints was that numbers in the

Institution were in decline. They alleged that there were only twelve thousand on parade in Loughgall the previous September. Walter Millar said, 'We counted them.' The police had estimated the numbers at fifty thousand.

The Spirit of Drumcree group continued to hold meetings throughout the country over this period under the name 'Loyal Orange Order Spirit Of Drumcree', inviting Orangemen to wear regalia, contrary to Law 23. On the recommendation of the Central Committee, Grand Lodge on 12 June 1996 adopted the following statement for inclusion in the Rule Book:

> The Grand Orange Lodge of Ireland affirms that membership of or involvement with any organisation or group, purporting to be of the Loyal Orange Institution of Ireland, working outside the structure of the Grand Orange Lodge of Ireland and/or operating without the authority of the Grand Orange Lodge of Ireland, for the purpose of changing the structure or effecting the policy of the Loyal Orange Institution, is incompatible with membership of that Institution.

On the evening of 27 March 1997 the half-yearly meeting of County Antrim Grand Orange Lodge at Carnlea Orange Hall was disrupted by the arrival of busloads of Spirit of Drumcree supporters and had to be abandoned amid scenes of violent disorder. The IRA in over thirty years of terrorism had not managed to achieve what the Spirit of Drumcree had achieved – the abandonment of a County Grand Lodge meeting. The resumed meeting, arranged for the afternoon of 9 April 1997 in Cloughmills, was also disrupted.

There were public statements of condemnation from the County Master, Robert McIlroy, and the Grand Master, Robert Saulters, but no discipline whatsoever was exercised in relation to this thuggery. In fact both McIlroy and Saulters caved in to this physical intimidation. Instead County Antrim Grand Lodge set up a 'Strategy Committee', drawing its membership largely from the Spirit of Drumcree and its supporters. There was now no need for them to overthrow the establishment. They were effectively in control.

In the early months of 1997 the Central Committee discussed how best to deal with the situation. There appeared to be the feeling among some that they would 'go away if left alone'. Others expressed the opinion that we should be standing united as the 'parading season', and perhaps the third Drumcree, confronted us. Obviously even at this stage there was not the will to take these issues on board and deal with those who had done so much to undermine the principles of the Institution. Accordingly an amnesty was agreed and suitable wording was presented to the meeting of Grand Lodge in Portadown on 11 June 1997. The following resolution was passed on recommendation of the Central Committee:

> The Grand Orange Lodge of Ireland is fully aware that in recent years, some Brethren have clearly acted outwith the Laws & Ordinances of the Institution.
>
> In the spirit of brotherhood and in the interest of maintaining harmonious relationships and unity within the Order, an amnesty will be declared on any previous misdemeanours which should have invoked any procedures under our Laws. This will not apply in cases where charges have already been preferred.
>
> Any breach of Laws, in particular Laws 10 & 23, will not be tolerated and disciplinary action will be stringently enforced by the next level, with the right of appeal to the next superior authority.
>
> Failure to enforce this discipline will also be recognised as defiance of superior lodge authority and will be dealt with, in accordance with the Laws and Ordinances of the Institution.

I can well remember Dr Porter saying on the way home from this meeting that there would be other opportunities to deal with the defaulters in the future. Opportunities there certainly were, but opportunities which were not grasped. Confrontation lay ahead.

Before the year was out two other episodes took place, neither of which enhanced the image of the Institution in the eyes of an already sceptical world. Both centred on the headquarters of the Grand Orange Lodge of Ireland at 65 Dublin Road, Belfast.

On the evening of 12 September 1997 the Education Committee met in Dublin Road prior to a meeting with the Parades Commission, only to discover that our exit was blocked by a group of protesters from the Spirit of Drumcree. For one and a half hours we were physically prevented from leaving the building. This was obviously the opportunity the extremists had been waiting for. The Education Committee had not been the flavour of the month since some of its members had been among those reporting on the Ulster Hall rally.

At the next meeting of the Central Committee on 3 October the behaviour of the Spirit of Drumcree was considered and advice sought about bringing charges. The seven members of the Education Committee concerned could only identify five of those who had taken part in the blockade. The Executive Officer, George Patton, the Grand Treasurer, Mervyn Bishop, and the Grand Secretary, John McCrea, all of whom on leaving the meeting of the Education Committee had walked through the protesters ahead of the committee, were asked to identify anyone they could. They all refused. The only logical reason for this refusal was a fear of the consequences they might suffer should they be seen to pursue the matter vigorously. Their silence did not go unnoticed by many members of Central Committee.

On receiving the advice of Central Committee at the 3 October meeting, the seven members of the Education Committee – Arnold Hatch, Cecil Kilpatrick, Warren B. Loane DL, Graham Montgomery, David Richardson, James Richard Whitten and I – preferred charges against those whom they could identify as having taken part in the obstruction. Charges were brought in accordance with Orange Law against Joel Patton, Walter Millar, William Smith, David Tweed and Alexander Newell, 'that on the evening of Friday 12 September 1997 they did appear, with others, in Orange Regalia, at the House of Orange, 65 Dublin Road, Belfast, contrary to Law 23 of the "Constitution, Laws and Ordinances of the Loyal Orange Institution of Ireland"'. They were further charged under Law 17 of the Constitution, Laws and Ordinances 'that their behaviour on the evening of Friday 12 September 1997 was of such an "aggravated character, endangering the honour and dignity of the Institution", as to be an offence against both religion and morality, in that they did on the same evening act contrary to the principles of the Institution, by obstructing the Education Committee in the performance of its duties', and under Law 18 that 'their behaviour on the evening of Friday 12 September, constituted "conduct unbecoming an Orangeman", in that they did behave contrary to the "Basis of the Institution" which demands of members that they should not display an "Intolerant spirit" and their behaviour was contrary to the "Particular Qualifications" which demand of members that they be "true and faithful to every Brother Orangeman".'

The technical preliminaries to these charges were processed at a meeting of the Central Committee on 31 October. The charges were sent to the counties which had jurisdiction over the alleged offenders, Armagh, Tyrone and Antrim, in letters signed by the Assistant Grand Secretary, Denis Watson, on 7 November.

The first hearing to be arranged was under the jurisdiction of County Armagh Grand Orange Lodge and took place on 2 December 1997 at

8 p.m. at Carleton Street Orange Hall, Portadown. Four members of the Education Committee attended to act as witnesses to the charges: Arnold Hatch as Chairman, Graham Montgomery, Richard Whitten, and myself as Convenor. We arrived in good time for the meeting and were conducted into a small ante-room to wait. The meeting began, but was quickly invaded by a mob including Alexander Newell, the person from County Armagh who was being charged, together with David Dowey, Joel Patton and Clifford Smith, a member of the Institution who had been suspended for refusing to meet with the Central Committee. Also in the mob was Gerald Marshall, who had previously resigned from his lodge and the Institution after disagreeing with his local brethren over a peaceful settlement of difficulties in the village of Dromore in County Tyrone. Also present was Mark Harbinson, a member of 'Stoneyford Temperance' LOL 1253 who was to come to prominence at Drumcree on 2 July 2000 when, from the vantage point of an army Saracen, he described Drumcree as 'Ulster's Alamo' and declared, 'The war begins today.'

As we remained in the ante-room throughout these proceedings, we could hear Denis Watson attempting to get the proceeding under way, to no avail. He received an injury to his wrist and another member of the County Committee was hurt in the scuffle. All this was later reported to Central Committee and Grand Lodge.

The circumstances which prevailed that evening in Portadown meant that the County Committee was unable to hear the charges. They reported back to Central Committee accordingly. Those who brought the charges never heard anything officially from County Armagh Grand Lodge. It was later reported to Grand Lodge that 'the Brother concerned [Alexander Newell] had resigned from the Institution and had gone to South Africa'. This was in clear breach of Law 11: 'A Member is entitled to resign upon paying all dues and discharging all liabilities, provided there is no charge pending against him.' No organisation can retain any credibility by applying its rules in a selective way, or to suit the agenda of some particular individuals.

The second hearing to be arranged was in Tyrone. All those concerned received a letter in which they were informed that 'you *may* [italics mine] attend this meeting in Newtownsaville Orange Hall on Thursday 4 December 1997 at 7.30 p.m.' On receiving this letter those who were seeking to bring the Spirit of Drumcree transgressors to justice took the advice of the legal adviser of the Grand Orange Lodge of Ireland, Mr David Brewster LL B. He advised us not to go, and gave his opinion that we were not legally obliged to go. However, since we had sent representation to Armagh on 2 December, we decided that we should also send representation to County Tyrone. Arnold Hatch, Warren Loane, David Richardson and I arrived in good time at the home of the County Master, Thomas Reid, who was to have taken us over to the Orange Hall at the appropriate time. As it turned out, no summons from the 'court' ever reached us. I related the strange circumstances in a letter to the County Grand Secretary dated 6 December 1997. I pointed out that we had been waiting in the custody of the County Master to be called to the hearing, but our personal security could not be guaranteed because of the presence of an unruly mob. I also pointed out we had been willing to attend although not obliged to do so.

The County Committee of Tyrone reported to a specially convened meeting of County Tyrone Grand Orange Lodge on 7 February 1998 that 'none of the Brethren bringing the charges attended to present the charges or be witness against the accused', and that Joel Patton and Walter Millar 'together with supporters forced their way into the Hall and demanded that the Committee rule on the case in the absence of witnesses'. Their report concluded: 'It was unanimously agreed that in the absence of evidence from witnesses that the charges be dismissed.'

At the Central Committee meeting of 21 March a verbal report was given concerning the behaviour of the mob which had invaded Newtownsaville Orange Hall on 4 December 1997. It was revealed that members of the County Committee had been physically abused to the extent that one of them, who was a member of the security forces, temporarily lost his legally held weapon in the fracas. This revelation shocked and disgusted many members of the Central Committee and once more showed that 'bully-boy' tactics were being used within the Order.

December meanwhile had brought a second episode of such tactics by the Spirit of Drumcree at the headquarters of the Grand Orange Lodge of Ireland. On the afternoon of 9 December some members of the Spirit of Drumcree entered 65 Dublin Road and refused to leave at the usual closing time of 5 p.m. They were joined later by other supporters. Those who entered and refused to leave are believed to have been David Dowey, William Smith and David Jordan.

The three brethren spoke to the Executive Officer, George Patton, and the Grand Secretary, John McCrea. According to Chris Ryder and Vincent Kearney they were given the keys of the building by Patton.[6] The strange thing about this is that at the subsequent meeting of Grand Lodge the following day the Grand Secretary, when asked for the names of those involved in the occupation, deliberately avoided answering. At a later date when he was asked in Central Committee specifically to name those three 'Brethren' who had entered the Dublin Road Headquarters and refused to leave, he again absolutely refused.

The Grand Orange Lodge of Ireland meeting on 10 December was hurriedly moved to West Belfast Orange Hall on the Shankill Road, a venue later described as 'obscure' by Joel Patton, who went on to say that he regarded the election as invalid: 'This is the headquarters of the Orange Order and this is where the meeting was convened. I don't see how they can reconvene a meeting and elect a Grand Master unless all members of Grand Lodge are notified. That decision will be null and void.'

The occupation of Dublin Road was described by the *Belfast News Letter* the following morning as 'A Black Day for House of Orange'. The editorial called for the Order to act against the bullies: 'The Grand Orange Lodge of Ireland would be signally failing in its duty to the overwhelming majority of its members if it did not act to severely discipline and even expel those who caused so much disruption and embarrassment to the Order yesterday.'

The same edition of the *Belfast News Letter* carried a photograph of some of those who had occupied the headquarters. As well as Joel Patton and Walter Miller, it showed Ivor Knox Young, Worshipful Master of 'The Earl of Beaconsfield Primrose League, Clounagh' LOL No. 9 in Portadown District. It was not until some two and a half years later that I realised the significance of his presence at the Spirit of Drumcree occupation. On the evening of 3 July 2000 Young, still Worshipful Master of LOL No. 9, appeared on Drumcree Hill in the company of some 'fifty loyalists'[7] including Johnny 'Mad Dog' Adair, as part of a paramilitary display. The fact that his photograph appeared widely in the media, and that no disciplinary action was taken, indicated the unwillingness of the leadership to take on their own hard men. Soft targets are much easier.

The *Belfast Telegraph*'s editorial of 10 December 1997 gave the following analysis:

> The row in Orangeism is essentially between those in the Spirit of Drumcree faction who think confrontation is the way to defend one's interests and those who prefer reasoned argument . . . It would be disastrous for community relations if the order was to turn militant at a time when the need is for the ensuring that all parades are disciplined

> and non-provocative in line with the policy of the new Parades Commission. The Orange Order – and Northern Ireland itself – could not afford a return to the confrontational approach of the past, whipping up emotions on either side and endangering the fragile peace.

Joel Patton was quoted in the *Belfast Telegraph* on 11 December as claiming that the premises were occupied by '400 of its members who represent many thousands of people'. Yet the front page of the same paper the previous day had estimated the number as 'perhaps as many as 100', while on page 4 Mark Simpson stated, 'In this reporter's brief visit inside the building only about 30 Orangemen were seen.'

The impact of this event cannot be underestimated. It was widely seen as damaging to the reputation of the Orange Institution and playing into the hands of those who would be opposed to its principles. Denis Watson recognised the situation as 'grave' and Jeffrey Donaldson said, 'Those who would profess to call themselves Orangemen have by their actions today clearly brought delight to IRA/Sinn Féin. They are doing the work of our enemies.' Donaldson expressed the fear that the Order was 'facing a very serious split'. This remark was quite understandable in the circumstances but history shows us that the Orange Order does not split – decent people just walk away, increasing the general haemorrhage which has plagued the Institution for generations.

The Grand Lodge passed the following statement for release to the press:

> The Grand Orange Lodge of Ireland meeting in West Belfast Orange Hall on Wednesday, 10 December 1997 abhors the conduct exhibited in the 'House of Orange' today by persons who call themselves Brethren. Such conduct and act of defiance is reprehensible.
>
> Grand Lodge categorically states that the only course for those persons to take is to resign forthwith from the Institution.
>
> Persons not prepared to accept the Rules of the Institution are unwelcome and are unworthy to be called Members of the Loyal Orange Institution.

The above statement may well be regarded as 'wise words and well spoken', but sadly, true to form, the history of the Grand Lodge hierarchy was to prove it to be mere words.

Not for the first or last time, the editorial of the *Belfast News Letter* captured the moment:

> The undignified protest at the Order's Dublin Road headquarters certainly did not advance the cause of Protestantism and loyalism and the people who will glean most satisfaction from the action were those in nationalist and republican circles who have been agitating for the re-routing of Orange parades.
>
> Joel Patton and his associates in the so-called 'Spirit of Drumcree' group can have no place in a libertarian and fraternal organisation like the Orange Institution if they resort to the kind of bully boy tactics that were in evidence yesterday.

After the meeting of the Grand Orange Lodge of Ireland in West Belfast Orange Hall, at which Robert Saulters was re-elected as Grand Master, he was quoted in the *Belfast Telegraph* of 11 December as saying, 'Unfortunately they are bringing the bad side to the fore. It's only a small element that are causing this.' He declared they would 'have to be dealt with'. The future revealed that 'dealt' was to become 'deal', for what was clear to the world was apparently not so clear to those in leadership, including the Grand Master in spite of his previous statements. No deals can be made with thugs and bully-boys in any society. They act as a cancer, which requires removal. For any respectable organisation to survive it must stand up to its recalcitrant minority. The Order shrank from such an operation.

At the Grand Lodge meeting on 10 December the officers were instructed to consult with the solicitors J. C. Taylor and Co. 'to ascertain the appropriate action to take' against those who occupied the building. At a subsequent meeting of the Central Committee on 16 January 1998, it was reported that the solicitors had arranged for counsel's opinion from Stephen Shaw (junior counsel) and Peter Smith (senior counsel). Their advice was that no action could be taken with reference to the occupation of Dublin Road on 10 December 1997, but that Grand Lodge could hear the charges which had not been proceeded with in County Armagh Grand Orange Lodge because of the invasion of Carleton Street Orange Hall.

This was the meeting at which the Grand Secretary refused to name the three 'brethren' whom he had spoken to on the occasion of the occupation. Presumably, even if the solicitors had recommended charges to be brought, it would not have been possible to prefer charges if no one was prepared to name names. The motive for John McCrea's silence still remains a mystery.

The press clearly had analysed the situation correctly and the 'peace moves' initiated by the leadership were not to bring peace but further confrontation. The lessons of history went unobserved. As Chamberlain's slogan of 'Peace in our time' pleased the visionless for a few months in 1938, so the thought of 'unity in the face of the enemy', and the avoidance of painful duty which this slogan seemed to justify, appealed to the unprincipled. Instead of discipline it was to be dialogue. The injunction of Martin Luther had clearly been abandoned: 'Peace if possible, but truth at any rate.'

The *Sunday Times* of 14 December 1997 revealed a new twist to the antics of Spirit of Drumcree leader Joel Patton. Under the heading 'Patton offered to halt marches', Liam Clarke revealed that during a secret meeting the previous June with Northern Ireland Office officials, Patton had 'told them that there could be a voluntary moratorium on all Orange marches, including the Drumcree march in Portadown, in return for a wide-ranging investigation into ways in which Protestant culture could be promoted'. This demonstrated, yet again, duplicity on the part of Joel Patton, who had affirmed the resolution at the Ulster Hall rally on 14 November 1995 that Grand Lodge should issue 'an immediate directive to the effect that there will be no voluntary re-routing of any traditional Orange Parade, and that no member of the Institution will negotiate with any community group or other nominated representative'. This incident was conveniently airbrushed out of the minds of the leadership.

Secret talks of a different kind between the leaders of the Grand Orange Lodge and the Spirit of Drumcree faction were initiated as a result of the suggestion of the Secretary of County Antrim, Drew Davison. He approached the Grand Secretary, John McCrea, who initially seems to have planned to proceed without the Grand Master, but was obliged to tell him. Saulters insisted on being involved. Davison had previously attempted to persuade the Rev. William Bingham to act as a reconciler with Joel Patton and the Spirit of Drumcree. Bingham refused on the grounds that he and the Spirit of Drumcree had two very different concepts of the Orange Order.

The first of the secret talks in Magheragall Orange Hall, facilitated by William Leathem who was sympathetic to such 'reconciliation', took place on 15 January 1998. The County Grand Master of Antrim, Robert McIlroy, within whose jurisdiction the talks took place, was unaware of the meeting until one o'clock that afternoon, and Central Committee, which has the power of Grand Lodge in between actual sittings of the larger body, was kept in the dark despite having a meeting the next day.

Robert Saulters, Grand Master of Belfast 1993–99 and Grand Master of the Grand Orange Lodge of Ireland 1996 to date

John McCrea, County Grand Master of Belfast 1984–93 and Grand Secretary of the Grand Orange Lodge of Ireland 1986–98.

Dr Patrick Duigenan, Grand Secretary of the Grand Orange Lodge of Ireland 1801–16. 'Paddy' was married to a practising Roman Catholic.

The Rev. William Martin Smyth, County Grand Master of Belfast 1969–73 and Grand Master of the Grand Orange Lodge of Ireland 1972–96.

RUC officers carry the coffin of Constable Frankie O'Reilly through the streets of Waringstown, Co Armagh. Constable O'Reilly died from injuries suffered when a blast bomb was thrown at him from a loyalist crowd in Portadown, during a protest against the Drumcree Orange Order parade being rerouted.

Whiterock Parade, 28 June 2003. The Robinson Bannerette of Old Boyne Heroes LOL 633 is regularly carried in this contentious annual parade. The Bannerette is being carried here by Eddie McIlwaine, who was sentenced to eight years for his part in the Shankill Butcher's campaign of terror.

William McCaughey (with beard), with Joe Anderson (far left) and Billy Houston (far right) all wearing Orange Regalia at the Harryville Protest in Ballymena.

William McCaughey walking at the Twelfth Parade in Ballymena in 2005.

Stoneyford Orange Hall. Searched by the security forces, who discovered copies of security files on over three hundred Republican suspects, on the evening of 1 November 1999.

Below: Alleged members of the Orange Volunteers parade with their own Colour Party in Crumlin, 6 July 2001.

Left: Senior Officers of County Antrim Grand Lodge lead the parade that included alleged members of the Orange Volunteers. The Officers (from left): William Thompson, Thomas Ross and William Leathem, the County Grand Secretary.

Two Scottish Orangemen dance naked at Drumcree on 13 July 1998, following the death of the Quinn children.

Ivor Knox Young (left, with moustache), Master of LOL 9, walks with Johnny 'Mad Dog' Adair at Drumcree on 3 July 2000.

Spirit of Drumcree Ulster Hall Rally, 14 November 1995. From left: Harold Price, Walter Millar, William Bigger, Joel Patton, David Dowey and William Brown.

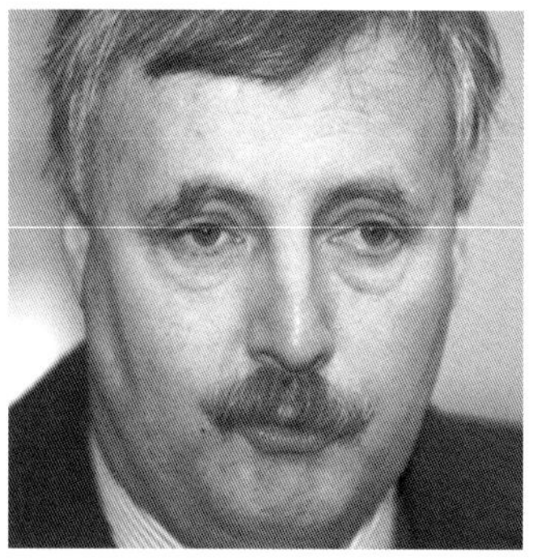

Joel Patton, spokesperson for the Spirit of Drumcree, later expelled along with Walter Millar for their behaviour at the Pomeroy Twelfth 1998.

Carnlea Orange Hall, where the Spirit of Drumcree broke up the County Grand Lodge meeting on 27 March 1997 in scenes of violent disorder.

Right: Magheragall Orange Hall, where John McCrea and Robert Saulters made a deal with the dissident Spirit of Drumcree.

Banner of 'Ireland's Heritage' LOL 1303, an Orange Lodge in the Belfast County. It had a brief existence from 1970 to 1982.

Ruth Dudley Edwards, who wrote sympathetically about the Orange Order until it lost the plot, listens on the Garvaghy Road to members of the residents' group.

Grand Master Robert Saulters supports Catholics' right to worship. From left: the Rev. Ian McClean, the Rev. Brian Kennaway, Colin Shilliday, Grand Master Robert Saulters, Graham Montgomery and the Rev. Dr. Warren Porter.

Joel Patton had previously called for an end to 'secrecy' and in an article in the *Belfast News Letter* on 7 January had stated, 'In contrast the small self-appointed clique who are currently running the Orange Order do so in what can only be described as a deceitful and secretive manner.'

News of the meeting was revealed in *Sunday Life* on 18 January, probably as a deliberate leak to prepare the membership for what was to follow.

On 26 January 1998 the Grand Master, Robert Saulters, travelled to a dinner in Dublin, accompanied by Denis Watson, Colin Shilliday and me. There was an evident change in the attitude of the Grand Master at this stage. During the dinner he said that he thought things could be 'worked out' between Grand Lodge and the dissidents. This was interesting in the light of the article by Joel Patton in the *Belfast Telegraph* on 15 December, following the occupation of 65 Dublin Road. Making reference to 'the old men of Grand Lodge', he said, 'Orangemen, like those in the Spirit of Drumcree, can never reconcile with these people. We are pledged to oppose and expose them.' In view of this, there was only one way things could be 'worked out'.

At the Central Committee meeting on 6 February 1998 members were given to understand that matters were 'too delicate' to discuss in detail. When the Central Committee met again on 21 March they were told that meetings were continuing in the absence of the Grand Master and that another would be held following his return from a visit to New Zealand. It was made clear to Central Committee that this meeting with the Spirit of Drumcree was to be the last, and that the group would have to pledge themselves to the authority of the Grand Orange Lodge of Ireland.

Sunday Life on 8 March carried the story of hopes of reconciliation, announcing that 'Grand Lodge Officers are close to producing an unexpected new accord, preventing a serious split in the ranks'. A source was quoted as saying, 'A small number may oppose them, but they will be in the minority. The unity of the institution is paramount, and if the Grand Lodge officers make recommendations, they will be overwhelmingly endorsed.' The report, by Alan Murray, also revealed that Joel Patton and John McCrea had 'refused to comment on what has been agreed'. This appeared very much like another deliberate leak. As to the substance of this alleged 'accord', ordinary members were still very much in the dark.

At the end of March, in an article in the *Belfast Telegraph* in relation to the 'hardline' statement issued by the House of Orange as a result of the meeting of the Parades Strategy Committee, political correspondent Paul Connolly quoted Joel Patton as saying: 'We had five meetings and they have been very good and very amicable. Our objectives are nearly the same and there is not that big a gap between ourselves and the Grand Lodge as there was before.' This raised the questions of who had narrowed the gap, and at what price. Was this capitulation? Future events were to answer these questions.

The next meeting of the Central Committee, on 11 April, was held in the absence of both the Grand Secretary and the Grand Treasurer. The members were told at the outset that 'Unity is paramount', particularly in the light of the forthcoming Referendum on the Belfast Agreement. A general report was given about the meeting with the Spirit of Drumcree, but when asked if there was 'remorse' or 'regret' expressed the Grand Master gave a rather vague answer. It was pointed out that the group was still making statements and appearing on television. The Grand Master was reminded of the public statement by Grand Lodge on 10 December 1997: 'Grand Lodge categorically states that the only course for those persons to take is to resign forthwith from the Institution.'

It became known that two envelopes were on the table during that meeting. These were letters of resignation, to be opened if the Central Committee decided that disciplinary action should be taken against the leaders of the Spirit of Drumcree faction. In the event the letters were not read to the meeting. Those whose signatures appeared on the letters were absent.

At the meeting of the Grand Lodge on 15 April 1998 a full and detailed report was given by the Grand Secretary. A statement of intent was included in the excessive detail of the lengthy report, and it was clear that some kind of concordat had been arrived at between the parties to the talks. Grand Lodge accepted that report and resolved that no action was to be taken.

Two significant actions followed this meeting. Joel Patton immediately broke the pledges which John McCrea's lengthy statement had led us to believe had been given. Patton ran true to form by speaking to the press and denigrating the Grand Lodge for what he considered to be a lack of leadership over the issue of the forthcoming Referendum. The second significant action was taken by the Rev. Dr Warren Porter, Grand Chaplain and past Assistant Grand Master, who placed his Grand Chaplain's collarette in the Grand Master's hands at the close of the meeting in protest at what he saw as a dishonest and dishonourable fudge and surrender to bully-boy tactics. He later wrote to the Grand Master tendering his resignation from the office of Grand Chaplain. This of course is not mentioned in the 'annals of Orangeism'. When the election of a successor came around in December 1998 the only verbal reference was that Dr Porter had 'stepped aside'.

Thus this opportunity for action passed. As C. S. Lewis said, 'We have the tendency to think but not to act, we have the tendency to feel but not to act. If we go on thinking and feeling without acting, we are soon unable to act.' This has been the situation in the recent history of the Orange Institution. We have issued statements, passed resolutions and spent long hours in discussion, all of which bore little fruit in action. If any multinational company spent as long in such fruitless occupation it would be bankrupt.

One was left wondering what 'deals' had been done behind the closed doors of Magheragall Orange Hall, what promises given by senior Grand Lodge officers, in the vain attempt to buy off the danger of further anarchy. A deal of some sort there obviously was. Robert Saulters stated on 9 June 2000, in reference to David Trimble and his sympathisers, 'These are the people who criticised me for talking to the Spirit of Drumcree and bringing them back.'

The third attempt to hear the charges brought by the seven members of the Education Committee against those involved in the blockade on 12 September 1997 was arranged for 2 April 1998 at Dunloy Orange Hall at 8 p.m., to be heard by the Antrim Grand Lodge's County Committee. A letter was sent to the seven Education Committee members stating that we were 'requested to present these charges'. I responded asking for a copy of the procedure used by the county for the hearing of charges, and to know what steps had been taken to protect the witnesses. The County Grand Secretary responded, in a letter dated 27 March 1998, that they would 'hear later from the two Brethren charged so as to avoid any confrontation'. We were therefore surprised to discover that those charged, David Tweed and William Smith, were also in attendance at the hearing. When the attention of the County Secretary and County Master was drawn to the contents of the letter of 27 March and in particular the words 'hear later from the two Brethren charged', the response was that 'later' meant 'later in the evening', not 'at a later date'.

Cecil Kilpatrick, Graham Montgomery, Richard Whitten and I each gave evidence and answered questions separately and in turn. One circumstance which caused us some concern was the presence of William Leathem as one of the secretaries throughout the proceedings. For someone who had been an active member of the Spirit of Drumcree group (he had been a steward at the Ulster Hall rally) to take part in judicial proceedings concerning members of that same group was, to put it at its mildest, highly inappropriate. Another member of the 'hearing committee' was David Dowey, one of the speakers at the Ulster Hall rally. Dowey had also been present as part of the mob which invaded Carleton Street Orange Hall when County Armagh Grand Orange Lodge had attempted to hear charges brought against Alexander Newell.

Not quite in the same category was a further member of the 'hearing committee', Thomas Ross, District Master of Glenavy and a member of the Education Committee appointed by the Junior Grand Lodge. Ross was strongly opposed to the Education Committee meeting the Parades Commission, as was recorded in the minutes read to the County Antrim Grand Lodge on 18 March 1998.

In view of the evident partiality of some members of the committee, it was no surprise when the verdict was pronounced. The committee found Tweed and Smith guilty on their own admission of the charge under Law 23 and 'repremanded [*sic*] the two Bro for wearing Regalia without permission'. On the charges under Laws 17 and 18 the committee found that no action should be taken 'due to the lack of evidence presented'. The fact of the determinations was reported to the Grand Orange Lodge of Ireland at the special meeting on 15 April 1998, but their specific contents were not made known to the meeting.

Appeals against the verdicts of the Tyrone and Antrim Grand Lodges were lodged on 20 April with the Grand Secretary by the seven members of the Education Committee, in accordance with the Constitution, Laws and Ordinances of the Loyal Orange Institution of Ireland. In the case of County Tyrone the appeal was on the grounds that the charges had been neither put nor heard as determined by the Central Committee. In the case of County Antrim the grounds for appeal were that the sentence imposed for the charge under Law 23 was not in accordance with the Constitution, Laws and Ordinances, and that there was in fact 'more than sufficient evidence' for the charges under Laws 17 and 18. We asked for the evidence to be reheard at a higher level. We also contended:

> The fairness of the hearing has been brought into question. Those hearing the charges should be impartial. The impartiality of the Committee may have been compromised by its previous discussion of the case to the extent of receiving a report from Wor. Bro Thomas Ross, at a previous County Committee meeting.

The Central Committee considered the appeals on 5 June and recommended them to the Grand Orange Lodge of Ireland, which at its meeting in Banbridge on 10 June instructed the Grand Committee (the appeals committee of the Institution) to hear and determine them. The letter sent out to members of the Grand Committee called them to a meeting on 20 October 'to carry out a preliminary investigation into, and set up the mechanism whereby Appeals against the County Grand Lodges of Antrim and Tyrone by W. Bros. Rev. B. Kennaway, A. Hatch, C. Kilpatrick, G. Montgomery, W. Loane, and R. Whitten can be heard'. The name of David Richardson was omitted. This was another example of a 'breakdown in communication'.

Eight members of the Grand Committee, out of a total of sixty-one, met to deal with the stated business on 20 October. The Antrim and Tyrone County Grand Lodge representation of five each had not been notified. This at least was correct procedure. The appeals technically involved the entire lodges and therefore they were 'parties at the bar'. (However, this had not prevented Spirit of Drumcree personnel being directly involved in the Antrim 'hearing'.) Those therefore present at this meeting were the Grand Master, Robert Saulters, the Grand Secretary, John McCrea, Samuel Gardiner who was to chair the proceedings, Blaney Cartright, James Clark, Jim Heyburn, Henry Latimer and David McNarry.

The Grand Secretary later told both the Central Committee and the Grand Lodge that he had advised the Grand Committee that he was only there to give guidance, because he had previously voted against taking the charges to appeal. This declaration of prejudice to the Grand Committee badly served the cause of impartial justice.

Those of us who had brought the initial charges and presented the appeals waited patiently to receive an invitation to a hearing to present our case. Instead we received a letter, dated 30 October 1998, communicating the decision of the Grand Committee. The appeal against County Antrim Grand Lodge was dismissed. County Tyrone Grand Lodge was instructed to 're-hear' the charges.

This came as quite a shock. We had assumed that the Grand Committee could only do what the circular summonsing them had stated, i.e. 'carry out a preliminary investigation into, and set up the mechanism whereby' the appeals could be heard. The convenor of the Rules Revision Committee, Jack Ashenhurst, was informed and a copy of the correspondence from the Grand Secretary was made available to him with a request that the committee consider the matter. I wrote to him on 17

November that 'It should be stated somewhere that for an appeal to be heard, all parties should be required to give their evidence in person, unless for medical or security reasons,' and that 'It should be made clear that the ONLY penalties under discipline are EXPULSIONS and SUSPENSION. (There is no provision for a reprimand).' The Rules Revision Committee considered this matter when it met on 18 November. They were unhappy with the proceedings and with the fact that a 'reprimand' had been given in connection with one of the cases, a penalty which is not provided for in the Laws. They expressed the opinion that I should raise these points with the Central Committee. We therefore, as appellants, submitted a letter for the attention of Central Committee dated 2 December, pointing out the following:

> The Grand Committee was to 'hear and determine' the Appeals, yet the circular convening the meeting of the Grand Committee called the meeting 'to carry out a preliminary investigation'.
>
> Natural Justice was not adhered to as all parties in an Appeal should have the opportunity to give their evidence in person.
>
> The letter of 30 October 1998 stated that 'after careful consideration of the relevant documents . . .' The appellants were not asked for any documentation. The 'documents' referred to must therefore have been from the defendants. This certainly is not in accordance with the general principles of natural justice.
>
> Regarding the APPEAL AGAINST COUNTY ANTRIM GRAND LODGE, the letter of 30 October 1998 stated that there was 'conflicting evidence presented at the original hearing'. No indication is given as to the nature of the alleged 'conflicting evidence', and no opportunity was given to comment on or clarify this evidence. It also stated 'the fact that some Brethren claimed they didn't even know one of the Brethren they had charged, [so] a "prosecution" would not be safe'. Yet they were 'found guilty on their own admission' (County Antrim Grand Orange Lodge, letter of 6th April 1998).
>
> [As to] The Charge under Law 23, 'that a serious reprimand was sufficient', we pointed out that 'The Constitution, Laws and Ordinances of the Loyal Orange Institution of Ireland' makes NO provision for a reprimand; this was the very point of the Appeal and was submitted as grounds for Appeal.
>
> Regarding the APPEAL AGAINST COUNTY TYRONE GRAND LODGE, it was pointed out that the decision of the Grand Committee was that 'there should be a re-hearing by County Tyrone Grand Orange

> Lodge'. The Grand Committee were instructed to 'hear and determine'. This was not done.

The Central Committee met on 4 December. Because of the length of the business and the lunch break, as often happens, some of the most important business was left to the end of the meeting. In this case the meeting was guillotined at 5 p.m. and the remainder of the business was taken up on Saturday morning. A 'small house' heard the letter on Saturday morning, read very reluctantly by the Grand Secretary. No discussion on the merits of the case was allowed and no decision on the contents of our letter was taken. To date no reply has been forthcoming.

The Grand Orange Lodge of Ireland met on 9 December 1998 in Belfast, where the final phase of the charges was dealt with. In spite of the abundant evidence presented, the Grand Lodge accepted by a majority the decision of the Grand Committee, thereby refusing to apply the basic principle of civil liberty so often boasted about by the Institution. One of the most heartbreaking aspects of this was to witness two of the most senior members of the Institution, the former Grand Master the Rev. Martin Smyth and Lord Molyneaux, listening in silence and making no attempt to save the Institution from itself.

To deny us the right of presenting our case was not only a denial of natural justice but a break with precedent. The previous case heard by the Grand Committee, on 26 February 1997, had been an appeal by Ballymacarrett No. 6 District against the County Grand Lodge of Belfast. In that instance James Heyburn, the District Master of No. 6 District, presented the appeal on behalf of his district. This was the same James Heyburn who sat in judgement on the members from the Education Committee and denied them the rights of appeal which he himself had previously enjoyed.

Thus ended a genuine attempt to apply the Constitution, Laws and Ordinances of the Loyal Orange Institution of Ireland and promote the true principles of what could once be described as an honourable and respected Order. Readers can judge for themselves as to the merits of the case and the whole proceedings.

This refusal to deal decisively with the rebellious activity of the Spirit of Drumcree placed the Institution in the position where it could no longer, with any consistency, morally condemn the government for not dealing with terrorism. It seemed to escape the notice of those who voted for a blatant act of injustice that if any organisation fails to deal with its own factious rebels it is in no position to give instructions to anyone else.

On 13 July 1998 Joel Patton and Walter Miller made an abusive verbal attack on the Rev. William Bingham as he conducted worship at the Orange Demonstration in Pomeroy. To the Orangemen of Pomeroy District this behaviour was totally unacceptable, and, in spite of pressure not to do so, they courageously brought charges. They recognised that by not taking action they would be crying 'peace, peace, when there is no peace'. Patton and Millar were expelled from the Loyal Orange Institution as a result. Such courageous action was missing from the highest level of the Institution.

On 10 October the same year the Scriptural prefix to the Constitution, Laws and Ordinances of the Loyal Orange Institution of Ireland, 'Let all things be done decently and in order' (1 Corinthians 14:40), was sacrificed on the altar of expediency as a sop to the demands of the Spirit of Drumcree faction. The principle of representative democracy, established at the foundation of the Institution in 1798, was overturned by the decision to draw representation directly from the districts.

When the Law concerning the make-up of Grand Lodge was being considered, and the previously noticed amendments of the Rules Revision Committee were tabled, a new amendment was proposed to allow one representative from each district to be members of Grand Lodge. The Grand Master did not rule this out of order, and it was carried even though one of the most senior and hitherto greatly influential members, Lord Molyneaux, spoke against it.

Other changes were made at this late stage, including the reduction in the number of Deputy Grand Chaplains and denial of voting rights to the fifty Deputy Grand Masters as demanded by the Spirit of Drumcree faction, in spite of the fact that the Convenor and most members of the Rules Revision Committee were unable to be present. This was known to the senior officers. These changes remained in spite of the procedure being challenged by legal opinion on 9 December 1998. The die was indeed cast.

Chapter Seven

Parades and Strategy

> *'Like most of those who study history, he learned from the mistakes of the past how to make new ones.'*
>
> A. J. P. Taylor on Napoleon III

Ian Paisley, who is not a member of the Orange Order, said at the Drumcree protest on the evening of 10 July 1995, 'If we cannot parade we might as well give up everything.' That statement suggests that parading is essential to Orange Order and its ideals. This is not true. Even if the Loyal Orange Institution of Ireland never held another parade it would still be the Loyal Orange Institution of Ireland. Granted, for some, parading is their reason for being in the Orange Order. Indeed, the conflict over parading in recent years has been the reason why *some* have joined the Institution, as well as being the reason for *many* leaving.

While there is much more to the Loyal Orange Institution than parading, this public display has now become one of its major functions. The reasons for this are obvious to any observer of Northern Ireland affairs. The genuine sense of disaffection among Protestants after enduring thirty years of terrorism, the political vacuum since the withdrawal of local power from the Northern Ireland government and the contents of the 'Framework Documents' suggesting plans for a power-sharing assembly left the majority population in Northern Ireland with a sense of powerlessness. A public display of unity such as a parade, in the words of the Centre for the Study of Conflict in its publication *Loyalist Parades in Portadown*, 'gives the impression of stasis, of lack of change, even timelessness; and thus a security of identity to those taking part'.

It is therefore important to understand the relationship of the Institution to the Parades Commission, or indeed to any established body whose function is to regulate this public expression of 'security and identity'. The Parades Commission came into existence as a result of the government's acceptance of the Independent Review of Parades and Marches (the North report), published on 30 January 1997. The very fact that the government should set up a 'review' of the parading issue was anathema to many within the Institution, yet it was the failure of the Institution to deal with the confrontation over parading, particularly at Drumcree in 1996, which had set in motion the train of events which resulted in the establishment of a Parades Commission.

One County Grand Lodge, Tyrone, which called for the Grand Lodge not to make any representation to the review body, typified the traditional negative response. However, Tyrone was the only County Lodge to make such a call. The Grand Orange Lodge of Ireland made a substantial representation. The Royal Black Institution declared early in the proceedings that it would meet the review body and subsequently did so, as did the Apprentice Boys and representatives of the loyalist bands.

The fundamental flaw of the North Report was that it did not address a central fault in the Public Order (NI) Order 1987, according to which conditions may be imposed on a parade if there is a threat of serious public disorder, serious damage to property or serious disruption to the life of the community, or if the intention of those holding the parade is the intimidation of others. This encouraged people to make parades contentious by threatening violence, thereby provoking restrictions. Failure to address this issue would be a sticking point in the years to come.

One of the first actions of the Parades Commission was to write on 9 April 1997 asking all interested parties to make representations. One such letter was sent to the Grand Orange Lodge of Ireland, and was read at the next meeting of the Central Committee on 9 May, but in the midst of the usual 'fog' the issue of whether or not the Institution should make representation to the commission was never discussed. The following evening the *Belfast Telegraph* reported that Alistair Graham, the chairman of the Parades Commission, was 'frustrated' that he had not heard from the Institution: 'A month after the new five-strong commission contacted the Order, it is still awaiting a "yes or no" response.' The following Monday the *Belfast Telegraph* quoted Graham as saying, 'I have been disappointed at the slow response of the Orange Order to have formal discussions,' although he 'had managed informal contact with some Orangemen'. Still the matter was not discussed at the next meeting of the Central Committee, on 6 June. It was only revived on 10 December 1997 when the Grand Lodge decided 'there should be no contact with the Parades Commission until the Parades Strategy Committee has deliberated'. The only correspondence between the Grand Orange Lodge of Ireland and the Parades Commission was the letter of acknowledgement of the original request and a subsequent submission of two names to assist with the drawing up of a Code of Conduct.

The report of the meeting of Grand Lodge on 11 June 1997 simply states: 'No action was taken on the other [letter] which requested that Grand Lodge Representatives meet the Commission.' The letter from the Parades Commission of 9 April was therefore not replied to with reference to its contents. This was confirmed on 3 July 2000 in the determination on the Drumcree parade for Sunday 9 July, in which the Commission rebuked both Portadown District for their 'implicit threats of violence' and the Grand Lodge, from whom they were 'still waiting for a reply or acknowledgement'. This was bad manners if nothing else.

In its comments on the North Report, the Institution stated that it was 'grateful to those bodies already in existence which seek to play a helpful role in mediation and the quiet building up of possible accommodations in a limited number of problem areas'. Yet the same Institution frequently refused to *encourage* the use of local mediation. This was seen in the Grand Secretary's refusal to include words suggested by me, 'In situations of difficulty local lodges may wish to make use of third parties as they seek accommodation without the surrender of principle', in the policy statement of 11 June 1997. A previous press release, issued from the House of Orange in the absence of the Grand Secretary on 19 May 1997, had included that exact wording, and had stipulated that 'any protest in the face of a decision to prohibit or re-route a parade should be carried out in a peaceful and lawful way', a claim which the commission's chairman said he was sure 'reflected the attitude of the vast majority of Orangemen who do not seek confrontation'. The Institution's publication *The Order on Parade* uses the language of accommodation: 'Negotiations prior to parades between Orange Order officials and local residents are to be welcomed and indeed are not unknown in some areas. However Orangemen must not be given the feeling that the community groups are just fronts for the IRA.'[1]

The use of language in relation to the question of parades was of paramount importance to members of the Orange Order. The use of words like 'mediation', 'consensus', 'third parties', 'compromise' and even 'negotiate' did not come easily to some in senior office. There was not the wisdom to see that as long as the Institution said 'No' and presented a constantly negative image to the world it would lose friends and not influence people. The use of narrow and exclusive language was communicating an image to the wider world which was unacceptable at the end of the twentieth century. It also failed to reflect important Christian values set out in the Order's Basis and Qualifications.

Another confrontation, in the County Antrim village of Dunloy, fell foul of the 'mediation process'. The Dunloy parade was banned not by the Parades Commission but by the Royal Ulster Constabulary. There had been a long history of problems in the largely Roman Catholic village, going back to the 1950s. John Wylie, one of Ian Paisley's Free Presbyterian ministers, often conducted open-air meetings at which he denounced 'Popery' under the guise of preaching the Gospel, and provoked a sometimes violent response from villagers.

There has not been any Orange parade in Dunloy since September 1995, when the return parade from the Presbyterian church coincided with the return of supporters of the Gaelic hurling team to the village, resulting in an attack on the Orangemen. The Rev. Dr Warren Porter and I joined with County Antrim officers, on their invitation, on the evening of 13 December 1996, and met with members of Dunloy Lodge to offer guidance and help. In spite of encouragements to negotiate through Mediation Network, and the indicated willingness of local residents to accommodate three parades a year, which the lodge would have accepted, the whole agreement was betrayed by local politics and pressure from the Spirit of Drumcree group, as when the meeting of the County Antrim Grand Orange Lodge in Carnlea Orange Hall on 27 March 1997, which would have endorsed the settlement, had to be abandoned amidst scenes of violent disorder. Martina Purdy reported in the *Belfast Telegraph* of 27 March that a protest was planned and that 'Dissident Orangemen are angry at what they see as an attempt by the County Grand Lodge to impose a deal on the Dunloy Lodge following mediation with village residents.' By any standards an imposed deal resulting in a parade would have been preferable to no parade at all. But the County Grand Lodge was not 'imposing' anything. It was the Dunloy Lodge members who had met on 13 December 1996 and agreed mediation as the way forward.

The outworking of this hardline Spirit of Drumcree element within the Orange Order has, in spite of all their protests to the contrary, been to reduce the number of parades. The same could equally be argued as the result of the Grand Lodge's policy of not talking to the Parades Commission. They have not achieved a parade in Dunloy. It is unlikely that there will ever again be a parade by any of the loyal orders in the village of Dunloy, particularly since it was completely blocked off by 'flying pickets' of Orangemen on the evening of 2 July 1998. The spokesperson, Thomas Ross, the District Master of Glenavy District

Lodge, declared in a television interview that this action was in support of Drumcree.

Over the years there has developed a 'conspiracy' mindset within the Protestant and Unionist community. This is particularly noticeable in the Orange Order. Everyone is said, and seen, to be 'against us'. The government is often portrayed as having no interest in Northern Ireland and as 'wanting rid of us'. The Northern Ireland Office is perceived as the agent of the government, and is therefore demonised as 'the enemy'. Individuals are often referred to as 'no friend of this Institution'. Government officials are suspect, as are all the agencies of government including the police. However, the greatest venom is reserved for the media, collectively described as 'no friends of ours'. This unfortunate relationship has a long history. Alvin Jackson, in *Colonel Edward Saunderson: Land and Loyalty in Victorian Ireland*, says that at the Rosslea demonstration against the Land League on 16 October 1883, 'Two journalists were assaulted by an Orange mob.' With reference to events at Drumcree in 1996, Chris Ryder and Vincent Kearney write in *Drumcree: The Orange Order's Last Stand*:

> Although the confrontation had started on a positive note between the Order and the media, who were offered tea and scones in the church hall, the relationship speedily deteriorated and camera teams and journalists were soon told it would be 'inadvisable' to venture into Orange ranks. Two foreign photographers who ignored the warnings were attacked and ended up in the ditch in front of the police lines.[2]

Too many in the Order have failed to understand that the media, in any liberal democracy, have an important role to fulfil. They may not always get it right; after all, they are like the rest of us – human. They may at times put their own 'spin' on things, but they can hardly be condemned for reporting the violent events over subsequent Drumcree parades, when the Institution facilitated that violence by its failure to reach an accommodation with local residents.

In the run-up to the Twelfth of July 2000, Robert Saulters, writing in *The Twelfth Millennium Year 2000*, a booklet published by the County Grand Orange Lodge of Belfast, stated, 'I would suggest that the time has come for everyone to make himself heard through the media.' I for one took this instruction very seriously and sought to implement it!

*

At the 10 December 1997 Grand Lodge meeting, the Grand Master established the Parades Strategy Committee, comprising 'one representative from each of the County Parades Committees, the Principal Grand Lodge Officers with Brethren of particular expertise being co-opted'. Without any in-depth discussion or consideration of the pros or cons of such a development, it was decided by Grand Lodge that there should be no further contact with the Parades Commission until this committee had deliberated. This was reminiscent of the attitude of Pope Pius IX decreeing that the faithful should not recognise Victor Emmanuel's decree of 1870 seizing Rome and incorporating it into a united Italy. The Grand Orange Lodge of Ireland, like Pius IX, thought that if they did not 'recognise' the Parades Commission, it would go away. United Italy did not go away; neither has the Parades Commission.

The Parades Strategy Committee deliberated on eight occasions and a report was presented to a meeting of the Grand Orange Lodge of Ireland on 15 April 1998. So paranoid were some of the senior officers who control the business of Grand Lodge that the members were not given the opportunity to consider the contents of the report prior to the meeting. The report was circulated during the meeting; members were given a few minutes to read it, and the copies were then collected following the acceptance of the report.

While this document posed many questions and contained many contradictions, two statements stand out and deserve to be highlighted, in view of what followed: 'As a Christian organisation our actions must be underpinned by Christian values,' and, 'It is important that we do not alienate our natural supporters.'

The Parades Strategy Committee continued to meet in the months leading up to the Twelfth of July 1998. Those of a perceived 'moderate' opinion were ignored and some were verbally attacked within the Strategy Committee. On one occasion a chaplain was accused in his absence of having had contact with the Parades Commission. The accusation came from a district master who had himself encouraged members of his district to make representation to the commission. Such hypocrisy went unchallenged within the Strategy Committee, but even had this been drawn to their attention, it would have made little difference.

These meetings of the Strategy Committee resulted in a press conference, held on 30 June, and the issue of a press release. The Central Committee discussed neither the contents of this press release nor the intentions articulated at the press conference. In fact, the Central Committee, which ought to have been controlling matters, was not even called to meet. The Parades Strategy Committee was running the Institution.

The press release ran to over a thousand words – much too long for the media to deal with seriously. Its main statements were that the Institution welcomed the Assembly, was 'unified and determined under attack' and would continue to engage in dialogue with interested parties but not with 'residents' groups influenced by terrorist organisations nor with the Parades Commission'. It also deplored 'sectarian ghettoisation'. The use of words like 'consultation' and 'united' was very far off the mark in the real world of the Orange Order.

In July a poster campaign was launched with such anti-Parades Commission slogans as 'Alistair Graham's the one to blame', which the Parades Strategy Committee later explained to Grand Lodge was the result of a decision 'to highlight the Parades Commission as a body which had been totally discredited'.

As things began to fall apart over Drumcree, the Strategy Committee met twelve times during July but evidently failed to achieve its objective as set on 15 March 1998 – 'To formulate a strategy which will ensure all parades are afforded full civil liberties and maintain the unity and integrity of the Institution'. The Central Committee, the body with the authority to act between meetings of Grand Lodge, was never called to meet throughout this crucial period, much to the displeasure of some senior members. It was becoming increasingly evident that some individuals were working to their own agenda.

At a special meeting of Grand Lodge called to discuss the situation on 1 August, the Grand Secretary read a 'comprehensive report' from the Parades Strategy Committee. The Committee's remit had been 'to help different Districts and Counties or anywhere where there was difficulty over particular parades'. This was now amended, without the approval of the Grand Lodge, to read: 'to assist in ensuring all parades proceed along their traditional routes'. This report from the Strategy Committee was never presented to the meeting for approval. One can only speculate why!

The Grand Secretary presented a second report from the Strategy Committee on the 'way forward'. Following subsequent discussion, the decision was made not to pass any resolution.* Because of this decision it was not possible to deal with the Strategy Committee's 'Phase 2' document, and this was sent to County Grand Lodges for comment.

* See Chapter Five, pp. 122–4.

The document was concerned primarily with Drumcree, though the Strategy Committee's remit was to be concerned with 'all parades'. It consisted of Paper A, setting out the proposals for 'Phase 2' of ongoing support for the continued presence at Drumcree, laying down principles and giving guidelines for the conduct of the protests, and Paper B, a discussion document as to how the Order could proceed in broadening the parades issue and making contact with

> . . . groups in civic society with whom it would be beneficial to talk. This includes political parties, all religious leaders, businessmen, pressure groups, etc. We have nothing to fear by talking and presenting our case to anyone, our cause is just. It must be stressed however, we will not negotiate on the issue of parades, as no one should be required to barter or grovel for their civil rights.

Paper B went on to list topics for further discussion such as discrimination against members and against RUC officers who are members; the need for Orange Halls to be free from rates; funding from government or European sources; and the statement: 'In any display or information events Orange culture should be fully recognised and receive equal treatment with that of Nationalist culture.' The possibility of 'local civic forums or similar bodies being used as a possible conduit to resolve the parading issue' was identified, but with the caveat, 'No forum should be entered into which solely deals with parades.' The document concluded:

> The overall objective of broadening the parades issue into a wider arena, can only help our cause and ensure those who oppose us are no longer free to focus all their resources on one issue. They will also be exposed as the intolerant opportunist bigots that they are, whose agenda on parades is only another tactic in their terrorist campaign.

The 'Phase 2' document displayed many of the typical contradictions and misapprehensions in the leadership's thinking. It was in fact not a strategy for resolution but a wish list. It was a strategy of confrontation which contained many contradictions, such as, 'Indeed any protest where there appears to be a potential for violence must be abandoned or cancelled.' Does this imply that the Drumcree church parade should be 'abandoned or cancelled'? An example of self-delusion on the part of the Parades Strategy Committee is displayed in the statement, 'Confrontation with the security forces must be avoided – This tactic worked successfully for Brethren during Phase 1.'

The document begs the question of what defines 'legitimate protest' and makes unrealistic demands such as 'Organising bodies must ensure they have the required support and ability to marshal any protest to prevent it from being hijacked by others as happened at Drumcree on several evenings.' This cannot be done. Once you bring crowds on to the street you must accept responsibility for their behaviour. This was the argument of the Institution in the past against the Civil Rights movement.

The document's proposed 'strategy' confirmed the Institution's confrontational image. Even if that image had been amended, no amount of good PR and presentation could substitute for correct behaviour. The Institution had managed to 'alienate our natural supporters' and had failed to ensure that its practice was a reflection of its principles.

The Parades Strategy Committee had evidently failed in its remit 'to assist in ensuring all parades proceed along their traditional route'. At no time was this acknowledged. Neither was it revealed that the failed publicity strategy of the summer of 1998 had cost the Institution in the region of £15,000.

Reports were received from the County Grand Lodges on the contents of this document, but at the next meeting of the Grand Orange Lodge of Ireland on 9 December there was no report from the Parades Strategy Committee and therefore no feedback on the counties' responses. Again, one can only speculate why.

A petition pledging support for the right to walk the parade route, as called for by the 'Phase 2' document, was widely distributed but it was not 'delivered to Downing Street and/or new Assembly' as promised. Like the 'Ulster Day Folk & Music Festival and Pageant' scheduled by Portadown District for 26 September 1998, it entered the organisation's 'big black hole' without any further explanation. The membership was never informed of the result of the petition. The truth of the matter was that there were not sufficient signatures on the petition, any presentation of which would have revealed the true level of support for the Institution.

On 16 November 1998 the Executive Officer wrote to all district secretaries enclosing a copy of 'The Case Against the Parades Commission'. Some time later a fuller version was posted on the Grand Lodge website. The sheer length of this document, at over three thousand words, gave the impression that the Institution's case was weak. While the document contained many valid points, it was damaged by the reference to the appointment of two representatives to meet the commission 'to provide expert advice on a Code of Conduct', when it stated that 'our representatives were never invited to a meeting with the Parades Commission'. The same document referred to the commission as an 'unelected quango' and 'not representative.'

'The Case Against the Parades Commission' emphasised the 'civil liberties' aspect of the parading issue, as enshrined in legislation in many countries, but with a particular appeal to the European Convention on Human Rights. It also gave examples from the courts where the right to parade had been upheld. It listed the reasons why the Institution opposed the Parades Commission, including that it 'in our opinion fundamentally undermines basic human rights' and 'legitimises the concept of apartheid'. It went on to state forthrightly, 'In the determinations to date the Parades Commission have: issued contradictory statements, been inaccurate, shown little evidence of research, have taken decisions on parades because of perceived threats from others and determinations have not been consistent.' This inconsistency was demonstrated with reference to the Ormeau Road, and the document quoted the Parades Commission's recognition that 'there is now a clear emerging sense of deep hurt amongst loyalists which arise from our decisions to re-route'. It went on to emphasise the way forward:

> As an organisation committed to civil liberty we would obviously favour a model based on the freedoms in the American Constitution and on the European Convention on Human Rights.
>
> All roads should be open to all law-abiding citizens. No community owns any road, particularly if that road is the most direct route to a town or city centre. No group has any right to impede or harass any other group in the peaceful exercise of their civil rights.
>
> If the state would exercise its lawful power to maintain such basic principles then no party need pretend to any feeling of alienation and all citizens would have equal rights.
>
> The police however must be given clear and unambiguous guidelines and these should also be made clear to the general public.
>
> The police however, are ultimately responsible for ensuring that good behaviour in general is maintained and this should remain so.

The document concluded by categorising parades as traditional, occasional, political and cross-community, and maintained that the RUC should be the body to give approval and guarantee free passage.

As with many of these documents, it is what is *not* said which is the problem. There is no reference to the fact that the Institution might have been responsible for some of the 'lack of research' by not communicating with the Parades Commission. Nor is the inconsistency noticed between opposing the commission as an 'unelected quango' and making representations to the Patten Commission, similarly an unelected quango.

Tremendous work had gone into the production of this long document, but one could not help but think that the matters might have been more easily resolved by talking directly to those concerned. The Institution had failed to realise that they had in effect created the Parades Commission by their inability to reach an accommodation.

One of the most despicable and offensive items of propaganda, which presumably came from the Parades Strategy Committee since no other body was meeting or making decisions at the time, was a card which parodied the famous words of Pastor Martin Niemöller to apply to Orangemen. The parody read:

> In Ulster in the Seventies, they
> came for the 'B' Specials and I
> didn't speak up because I wasn't
> in the 'B' Specials.
>
> In the Eighties they came for the
> Ulster Defence Regiment and I
> didn't speak up because I wasn't a
> member of the UDR.
>
> In the Nineties they came for the
> Orange Order and I wasn't an
> Orangeman so I didn't speak up.
>
> Then they came for me . . . but by
> that time there was no one left to
> speak up for anyone . . .

Apart from revealing alarming signs of both megalomania and paranoia, it was grossly stupid and deeply offensive to compare walking down a road with the fight against Nazism.

*

One glimmer of light in the darkness of the tunnel did appear in this period. A seminar was organised in September 1998, by Belfast's No. 10 District Lodge in Ballynafeigh Orange Hall. This was the Belfast district directly involved in the confrontation on the Ormeau Road. Their forward-thinking Worshipful Master, Noel Liggett, invited Alban Maginness, Belfast's first nationalist Lord Mayor, along with Eoghan Harris, the Rev. Roy Magee, David Ervine of the PUP and Monica McWilliams, leader of the Women's Coalition, to an open discussion forum. According to a report in the *Belfast Telegraph* on 21 September, there was a general endorsement of the principle of talking to resolve the conflict. Unfortunately, as with so many things in the Orange Institution, nothing further was done.

Sunday Life on 4 October carried the story that the Central Committee, which had met the previous Friday, had 'heavily rejected proposals to invite nationalist residents' associations representatives to conferences to debate the marching issue'. Alan Murray gave a full report of the events, stating:

> The decision calls into question the role of the Parades Strategy Committee set up by the Grand Lodge last December, and which is answerable to Mr Saulters. The Committee drew up proposals for two separate conferences to discuss the parades issue with nationalist opponents, which would have been backed by the Community Relations Council. One conference would have seen Orangemen addressed by leading residents' spokesmen, while at a separate venue a nationalist audience would have been addressed by leading Orangemen. But the idea was kicked into touch on Friday, calling into question the whole existence of the Parades Strategy Committee.

(The Central Committee may have rejected such proposals in October 1998, but six years later, on 18 October 2004, SDLP Assembly member Tommy Gallagher addressed such a meeting. The event was organised by Tyrone Orange Vision, an initiative aimed at building an understanding of Orangeism in County Tyrone.)

Numerous support parades took place in Portadown town centre and to Drumcree Parish Church throughout the autumn of 1998 and into the spring of 1999. Alistair Graham, chairman of the Parades Commission, was quoted in the *Belfast Telegraph* on 22 June 1999 as saying, 'If they had seen the very clear message that was spelled out in our decision last year, they would have seen if they had been prepared – no doubt very reluctantly

– to accept the decision for 1998, instead of pursuing what I think has been a very counter-productive strategy of trying to bring pressure to bear through large numbers of parades.' Many Orangemen admitted privately that Graham was right in his assessment. In spite of this Ian Paisley Jr, though not a member of the Orange Order himself, said in July that the only way they would get down the road was by force of numbers.

At the Grand Lodge meeting on 2 June 1999, once again there was no report from the Parades Strategy Committee. At the meeting of Central Committee on 21 May the Grand Master had made it clear that there had been an irregular meeting of the Strategy Committee, and declared, 'When a committee goes beyond its remit I call a halt.' Yet in the very recent past he had stated, 'They did a good job last Year'! The Strategy Committee continued to exist in a semi-moribund state. The Grand Master evidently did not have the courage to 'stand down' the committee of his own creation.

The most disappointing element of the 2 June meeting of Grand Lodge was the decision to seek 'clarification' of the three pledges issued by Archbishop Robin Eames at the Diocesan Synod of Armagh in October 1998, which had been accepted at that time by Denis Watson, County Grand Master of Armagh and subsequently Grand Secretary, although David McNarry went on record as rejecting them. The three pledges which the Archbishop sought from the Portadown lodges were perfectly reasonable. He simply asked for:

- The avoidance of any action before or after the service which diminishes the sanctity of that worship.
- Obedience to the law of the land before and after the service.
- Respect for the integrity of the Church of Ireland by word and action and the avoidance of the use of all church property or its environs in any civil protest following the service.

The Archbishop repeated these pledges in his address to the General Synod of the Church of Ireland on 18 May 1999. He disclosed that he had again conveyed the pledges to the Portadown lodges in a letter dated 16 February and had received a reply only the previous day – 17 May. In this response Portadown District said:

- The District Lodge would contend that it has at no time encouraged, sanctioned or condoned any action before or after the service which diminishes the sanctity of that worship.

- The District Lodge had always encouraged their membership and the wider community to obey the law of the land, while at the same time reserving the right to peaceful protest at the denial of our fundamental Civil Liberties, Rights and Freedoms which are universally enshrined in Human Rights Charters.
- Since its inception, this lodge has always shown respect for Church property.

The Archbishop acknowledged at the General Synod that he had had 'insufficient time to consider whether the response meets the full criteria of what I considered entirely reasonable requests regarding attendance at the service'. He later said on record that the response 'does not acknowledge acceptance of the three pledges'.

Many Orangemen found it difficult to understand how the acknowledged leader of one of the main Protestant churches could be treated with such contempt by an avowedly religious organisation which had made use of that denomination's property. Not replying to a letter, the content of which was crucial, for three months was unacceptable by any standards.

At the meeting of Grand Lodge on 2 June some members were delegated to seek a meeting with the Archbishop on this matter. This took place on 21 June, and the Primate and Church of Ireland representatives put forward the Church's perspective. A forum of the Central Committee, Strategy Committee and Advisory Committee then met the same day to respond to the Archbishop in the light of the clarification he had given. However, the prolonged wrangling left an impression of both 'fog' and 'fudge', and once again the matter was not resolved.

The evident unwillingness of the leadership to face up to the issues which confronted the Institution resulted in Colin Shilliday leaving this meeting and resigning from his office of Deputy Grand Treasurer. Dr Warren Porter also resigned, in the days which followed, from various offices and positions he held within the Grand Lodge. The following day the Rev. William Bingham wrote to the Grand Master resigning from the Strategy Committee because he was unwilling to be abused any further. His resignation was reported by the BBC on 29 June. A press release was issued giving his reasons as 'pressure of church and Orange commitments [*sic*]' and claiming that he was 'at one with Portadown District'. This bore little resemblance to his actual letter of resignation.

I also wrote to the Grand Master, at his home address to make sure there was no danger of the letter going astray at headquarters, to place on record 'my profound regret at both the conduct and content of the meeting':

> The manner in which the withdrawal of Bro. Colin Shilliday, and the letter from Bro. John Richardson was treated betrayed the obvious fact that there is little left in the Institution which could be regarded as anything of a brotherhood.
>
> The allegation that there was someone working for the NIO . . . should have been ruled firmly by the chair as it places everyone in the meeting under suspicion.
>
> The contemptuous way in which the Holy Scriptures were treated poses the question as to whether or not we can any longer legitimately defend the Institution as a Christian organisation.

No reply was received. As a result of a report in the *Belfast Telegraph* of 30 June, I again wrote to the Grand Master:

> The article written by Darwin Templeton reports an interview with you as saying – 'It seems to me that they are saying if you are a thief or a murderer or someone who is full of immorality, you are welcome in church, but if you are an Orangeman, then you have to abide by three stipulations.' I assume that the 'three stipulations' to which you make reference are the 'Three Pledges' of the Archbishop. As you must be aware the 'Three Pledges' are in keeping with the professed principles of the Order. This was acknowledged by Bro. Denis Watson, the Grand Secretary, when they were first issued in October 1998. Denis is on record at that time, as stating that he had no difficulties with the three pledges.
>
> However it is the personal 'naming' of the Moderator of my church, Bro. Rev. Dr Lockington, which has caused me the most personal grief. Can I assume that you were obedient to the Biblical injunction of Matthew 18:15–17 in this respect? You cannot claim to be ignorant of this as I have pointed it out to you in the past. Did you speak to him privately before mentioning him in public? Not only is this a Biblical principle but it is also enshrined in the Principles of the Institution. I refer you to the Particular Qualifications; 'that he will be true and faithful to every Brother Orangeman in all just actions . . .'
>
> Ministers are finding it difficult enough to defend the Institution at this present time and this report of your interview only makes the situation even more difficult.

> May I respectfully draw your attention to something you said at the meeting of 21 June with reference to the gunman on the hill at Drumcree in July 1998? It really does not matter who the gunman was, it was the fact that the *Loyal* Orange Institution had created the conditions for a gunman to fire on Her Majesty's Security Forces.
>
> May I also remind you of a document which you endorsed on 5 May 1997 and which I sent to all County Grand Masters? We are in confrontation with our own security forces. We have lost the 'middle ground'. We are perceived by an increasing number of people to be a 'rump', and since last year we are perceived to have been the facilitator of disorder. To make matters worse now we are seen to be on a collision course with the Protestant churches.

The Rev. Denis Bannerman also wrote to the Grand Master. We both received replies which did not address the issues raised in our letters. However, the Grand Master stated: 'I intend to call a Central Committee and the letter you have written together with similar type mail received will be read and fully discussed at an open meeting.' The next meeting of the Central Committee was held on 17 September but, as expected, neither the above letters nor any similar letters were read. The exception was the resignation letter of Colin Shilliday, which was read at the specific request of Dr Porter. Colin Shilliday stressed that he was resigning from the 'leadership team' to maintain his own personal integrity. The substance of the letter was, as expected, not addressed.

Though the Grand Master's Parades Strategy Committee was not meeting, David McNarry continued to adopt the role of spokesman and was represented in the press as a member of the committee. He made various unsuccessful attempts to resolve the situation. In the *Belfast Telegraph* on 19 August 1999 he was quoted as saying, 'We would be forced to cut connections with the government.' David Jones, the Portadown spokesman, had made a similar threat in April when he gave the government 'thirty days' to sort out Drumcree.

David McNarry had already entered the history books as the man who claimed that the Orange Order had the ability to 'paralyse the country in a number of hours' in the tense days prior to 12 July 1998. It seemed that repeating the mistakes of the past was the only strategy left. But McNarry was to develop a strategy entirely of his own. When the Parades Commission came to the end of its tenure in the early months of 2000, he applied unsuccessfully for chairmanship.[3] This action would appear to any reasonable person to have been in direct contravention of the decision of the Grand Orange Lodge of Ireland to have no contact, directly or indirectly, with the Parades Commission.

The Grand Master 'stood down' the Parades Strategy Committee on 26 November 1999. He did so because it was reported to him that David McNarry had used his position as a member of the committee to issue a call in support of David Trimble on the eve of the Ulster Unionist Council meeting. Such a stance was fast becoming the principal 'mortal sin' in Orangeism.

Chapter Eight

To Talk or not to Talk

'To jaw-jaw is always better than to war-war.'

Winston Churchill

As the Institution entered 1999, disillusionment was well and truly setting in for some in the leadership. Melvyn Hamilton, a former Assistant Grand Secretary of the Grand Orange Lodge of Ireland, had left the Institution a few months previously when RUC man Frankie O'Reilly was murdered by the Red Hand Defenders in a blast-bomb attack at Drumcree. The County Master of Tyrone, Tom Reid, did not stand again for office in 1999. In the *Sunday Times* of 28 February 1999 he said, 'I wouldn't offer the Portadown District any advice on how they should move forward . . . I have been so disillusioned with the Orange Order over the past year and a half that I am just an ordinary nominal member now.'

The newly constructed Grand Master's Advisory Committee took the initiative by having two 'Cultural Evenings' in the Waterfront Hall, on 29 and 30 March. Various individuals, including the Archivist, but not the Education Committee, were involved in presenting an exhibition of Orange artefacts and the delivery of an evening of entertainment. The following letter to me from a Presbyterian minister, who was an invited guest, gives an idea of what took place:

> Not being an Orangeman, but having an interest in the organisation, I was invited by a good friend to the recent celebrations and information evenings in the Waterfront Hall Belfast.
>
> My friend assured me that the cultural night would be of interest to me; which indeed it was. The Organisation had obviously gone to a lot of trouble to present themselves to the watching world in the best possible light. The displays were informative and well presented and the literature was concise and educational.
>
> On our entry we were heckled by a contingent from the Markets area who were protesting about the presence of Orangemen in their

immediate area. This was a new experience for me and my wife as we were jostled into the Foyer of the Waterfront Hall and stones began to be thrown at us. The hatred and bitterness expressed as we entered a 'cultural evening' was intense and very unsettling, indeed quite alarming. However the response inside the hall was even more disconcerting as huge numbers of people ran to the front windows and hurled abuse toward the people outside singing 'The Sash' intermittently along with other unquotable rhymes etc. After some minutes men whom I presume were marshals calmed the situation down and we were able to proceed to our seats for the performance.

Although already embarrassed and apologetic my friend continued to reassure me that this evening would really help me see how and why the Orange movement operated. Amid the pipe band displays and other items, introduced by Walter Love, the messages of unity, cultural heritage, and tolerance did shine through. In fact I was greatly impressed with the whole presentation, particularly the computer-generated history and rationale of the organisation.

Of course the key word was 'tolerance' in all the items presented especially the computer-generated one which ended with a great feeling of all being well with the world – which was probably more than I had expected!

Unfortunately, it was what happened next that made me go cold all over! For after such an excellent presentation the gathering was addressed by Mr Robert Saulters, the Grand Master, who began what I had expected to be a promotional talk to rally support with the following line of talk: 'Well brethren, we've pushed the scum down the road and across the bridge back to where they belong and the boys from Antrim are on their way to give us the protection we need to get out.'

The Hall erupted with cheers and other vitriolic cries – some of which are unrepeatable, and I think it was also at this point that the gathering rose to its feet and sang 'The Sash' again with great gusto! What, can I ask, happened to all the talk about tolerance and freedom of religion? I was not only horrified at what I was hearing but deeply disappointed.

I did not appreciate being hassled and stoned on entering the Hall but neither did I feel had anyone the right to call someone else scum with such venom and bravado, especially on an occasion which was trying to teach tolerance and freedom. Or more particularly, what grounds had they to tell me, as a non-Orangeman, that the organisation which had been getting some bad press was really very different on the inside?

> Sir, I consider myself a good Protestant. I have a sincere Christian faith. I love my Queen and country, and it would have not taken much to make me join the Order; but not now. The naked bigotry and sheer hatred I witnessed on this occasion was more than enough to turn me right off the idea of ever being an Orangeman!

At the meeting of the Grand Orange Lodge of Ireland on 2 June 1999, the Waterfront evenings were described as 'a success'.

The first meeting of what the media called a 'reconstructed' Grand Lodge had taken place on 27 March 1999 with the introduction of representatives from the districts. Among the new members of Grand Lodge were at least two leaders of the Spirit of Drumcree group, David Dowey and William Smith. In the minds of many this 'reconstructed' Grand Lodge was a consequence of the 'deal' which senior officers of Grand Lodge had worked out to appease the Spirit of Drumcree. In the *Sunday Times* of 11 April, Vincent Kearney reported the event under the headline 'Self-confessed bigot joins the Orange rulers', a reference to David Dowey's declaration at the Ulster Hall rally that he was proud to be 'a sectarian bigot'.

The meeting of 27 March achieved very little except to demonstrate the consistent intransigence of the mindset then evident in Grand Lodge. The media reported that Grand Lodge had decided to go to Drumcree on 12 July 1999 if the Drumcree stand-off was not resolved by that date. On 4 April *Sunday Life* reported: 'Delegates voted by 114 votes to 27 to set a 40-day resolution period for the Drumcree parade, and for a guarantee from the Prime Minister that all other Orange parades this year will take place without impediment – including this July's Drumcree parade.' The Institution was now, even at Grand Lodge level, behaving in a manner which many right-thinking people found reprehensible. This ultimatum to the prime minister of the United Kingdom, from an organisation pledged in loyalty to the United Kingdom, was megalomania on a startling scale.

The lack of any clear thought and direction was seen in the support given at the Grand Lodge meeting on 2 June 1999 to the 'Long March', initiated by a number of Orangemen and Bertie Campbell. This matter was not even on the agenda, although an A4 sheet of paper was placed on members' chairs before the meeting began, informing them that the objective of the Long March was 'To provide an effective VOICE for the REAL VICTIMS of Northern Ireland in the struggle to have their CIVIL AND RELIGIOUS LIBERTIES RESTORED'. The preceding meeting of Central Committee had not voiced any support for this whatever, and indeed there was much scepticism about both the motivation and the organisers. However, Grand Lodge at its 2 June meeting endorsed the Long March. The official record of the proceedings reads:

> W. Bro J. McGrath referred to the forthcoming 'Long March' from Londonderry to Portadown the purpose of which was to highlight injustices against the Protestant people and appealed for the support of Grand Lodge. The Grand Master reiterated this appeal and Grand Lodge endorsed this.

Scepticism was justified when on 24 September, on the eve of the Second Phase of the Long March which had originally been promoted as 'highlighting the plight of the victims', the *Belfast Telegraph* reported, 'Organisers of the loyalist Long March said today that a new walk will highlight that "the Belfast Agreement has failed".' On 25 September a few hundred walked behind the banner 'No Terrorists in Government', confirming that this was a *political* demonstration. The *Belfast News Letter* that day quoted one of the organisers, Fraser Agnew, a United Unionist Party Assembly member, saying: 'I have washed my hands of the whole thing . . . I believe innocent victims are being manipulated and exploited for political ends. It's almost like emotional blackmail.'

The *Belfast Telegraph* reported on 27 September 1999 that Mark Neale, an Ulster Unionist councillor from Portadown, had come out in support of Agnew, claiming that the organisers of the Long March were 'using the victims for their own narrow political purposes'. Neale called for the inclusion of 'innocent nationalist or Catholic victims'.

This change in the public purpose of the Long March, from highlighting 'injustices against the Protestant people' to a cynical use of victims' grief to make capital against the Belfast Agreement, placed the Institution, not for the first time, in a contradictory position. 'Information Sheet No. 2' on Drumcree and the Good Friday Agreement had stated: 'The Grand Orange Lodge of Ireland fully supports the work of the new Northern Ireland Assembly in its task of underpinning the future peace and stability of this Province within the United Kingdom for the benefit of all its citizens.'

The Long March captured headlines in the press over the summer of 1999, but support for its tactics was gradually lost, and the February 2000 'Phase Four' rally in Newtownards attracted little support. The initiative, however, was to be reinvented. On 22 January 2001, Chris Thornton reported in the *Belfast Telegraph*:

> A scheme for putting up an alternative to the Good Friday Agreement was unveiled today by the organisers of the Long March. Spokesman Bertie Campbell was quoted as saying that the purpose of the Long March Campaign is to build 'positive and far-reaching proposals for the production of a democratic alternative to the Belfast Agreement'.

The Drumcree debacle continued unresolved throughout 1999 though various attempts were made to resolve the situation. The Advisory Conciliation and Arbitration Service (ACAS) negotiator Frank Blair attempted further proximity talks on 4 June and a four-man delegation of Orangemen, with the 'knowledge and approval' of Portadown District,[1] met in face-to-face negotiations with the Garvaghy Road Residents' Coalition at Stormont on 26 June. This, according to a report in the *Belfast Telegraph* on 29 June, had the backing of Portadown District Lodge by seventy votes to five.

'Drumcree Sunday', as it had become known, was essentially trouble-free in 1999. Harold Gracey and the six district officers marched to the police line and handed over a letter of protest, while the main parade was led to the rector's field and dispersed. It was widely held, rightly or wrongly, that Tony Blair had given an undertaking that, provided things went off peacefully, they would get down the Garvaghy Road later in the year. 'Getting down the road' had become the preoccupation of the Portadown leadership.

As the day approached there had been the usual consternation and uncertainty throughout the community both in Portadown and the whole province. The Moderator, Dr John Lockington, had prayerfully considered what spiritually positive contribution he might make to the situation. On 23 June he issued a statement which urged people to make the issues a matter for prayer in the days up to the event. He particularly encouraged Orangemen who were Presbyterians to attend their usual places of worship that day. He called for a day of prayer and asked that Presbyterian churches might arrange for times of prayer to be set aside to seek God in a volatile situation, and he encouraged Presbyterians who were Orangemen to attend these. When 'Drumcree 1999' passed off peacefully Dr Lockington issued another statement commending those involved for their actions in ensuring a trouble-free Sunday.

In an interview in the *Belfast Telegraph* on 30 June Darwin Templeton quoted the Grand Master, Robert Saulters, as feeling 'betrayed' by the leaders of the main Protestant churches. On the 'intervention' by Dr Lockington, Saulters said, 'He's a moderator now and he must do as he sees it to keep his people on the straight and narrow. But I think there are some people in his Church who aren't too happy about it.'

Dr Lockington responded privately to this public criticism. He wrote to the Grand Master through the Executive Officer, George Patton, on 1 July, putting the following nine questions:

1. Did the Grand Master read the whole letter sent to all Presbyterian Ministers or at least the whole statement which I asked to be read before making his opinion known to the press?
2. Could the Grand Master identify which part of the statement he found to be objectionable and why?
3. Could the Grand Master explain why he did not approach me for an explanation of the letter before making a critical statement to the press?
4. Could I be provided with a resume of the remainder of the interview given to Darwin Templeton which was not printed in the article?
5. Does the Grand Master stand by the Particular Qualifications on Page 3 of the Constitution, Laws and Ordinances viz. 'that he will be true and faithful to every Brother Orangeman in all just actions; that he will not wrong him or know him to be wronged or injured without giving him due notice whereof, if in his power'?
6. Is the Grand Master expressing his own personal opinions, the opinions of any body within Grand Lodge or voicing the opinion of the Grand Orange Lodge of Ireland?
7. How can I be convinced that the organisation which I joined and of which I have been a member for the last 46 years is the same organisation still standing for Biblical principles ?
8. How can I be convinced that I personally have any place or can have any continuing part in the Orange Institution?
9. Are there any reasons why I should continue to encourage men to remain in the Institution?

The Grand Master did not reply until 20 August, and then through the Executive Officer. While his letter 'made specific responses to each of your 9 questions', it made little rational sense.

The *Belfast Telegraph* revealed, on 30 July, that Portadown District had submitted an eleven-page document to the Parades Commission through their legal representative, the solicitor Richard Monteith, one of those convicted of causing criminal damage in Lurgan in July 1998. Though the Parades Commission responded that the submission contained no new evidence, this was evidently a 'seismic shift' on the part of Portadown District, who up to now had maintained that they could not have any dealings at all with the Parades Commission because of a policy decision by the Grand Orange Lodge of Ireland.

In the eyes of most people all this was pure duplicity. But the Grand Orange Lodge of Ireland, stubborn to the last, refused to change its policy in relation to either the Parades Commission or the residents' groups. This was particularly interesting in the light of remarks made on Downtown Radio on 5 July 1999 by the Grand Master Robert Saulters, when he said with reference to residents' groups 'that he might ask Grand Lodge to drop their ban'. On UTV's 'Insight' programme on 6 July he said, 'If that's their only argument, call their bluff.' The next day he claimed that he had been 'misrepresented'.

The continuing confrontation over the Drumcree parade encouraged all sorts of religious extremists to attempt to get a foothold. The *Irish Times* of 6 July 1999 ran a photograph of a sign outside Drumcree Church which read: 'BEHOLD YE HAVE FILLED DRUMCREE WITH YOUR DOCTRINE Well Done Rev. Pickering'. The theological implications behind this statement are beyond comprehension!

Many Orangemen were simply 'drifting out' of the Institution. Some had the courage to write to the press, like 'VERITAS ET VICTORIA' of Springfarm, Antrim, in the *Belfast Telegraph* on 25 June 1999:

> As an Orangeman I support the fundamental right to march but I feel compelled to express an opinion which I know is more widespread in the Orange institution than is currently shown and one which the 'support-us-or-you're-a-traitor' brigade will find hard to accept: the long-standing dispute over Portadown District LOL No. 1's return along the Garvaghy Road is a cancer which is eating away at the heart of this Institution of which I and many are so proud. Few, if any, brethren have said this openly for fear of verbal castigation.

He had the courage to write, but it takes more than courage in this environment to put your name and address at the bottom of such a letter, particularly if you have a family to consider.

Another letter-writer in the same paper, signing himself 'A.J.C. Belfast

6', concluded: 'The Orange Order has been tricked into adopting the Provo plan for Drumcree.' This was what many of us had been preaching to those in leadership for the previous two years, to no avail. Even the cost, estimated at £30 million a year by a community audit commissioned by Craigavon Borough Council, would have no impact on a stubborn leadership.

The Twelfth of July demonstrations in 1999 presented as clear proof as possible of the direction in which the Institution was now going. Hardline anti-Agreement speakers addressed virtually all the demonstrations. This was particularly noticeable at the Belfast County demonstration where for the first time a Free Presbyterian minister, the Rev. Ronald Johnstone, addressed both the religious service and the Resolution on 'Faith'. DUP politician Nigel Dodds, a relatively new Orangeman, addressed the Resolution on 'State'.

In the spring of 2000 Portadown District Lodge received the support of Armagh County to forward a resolution to Grand Lodge in an attempt to change the policy of not talking to the Parades Commission. When the resolution came to Central Committee on 3 March 2000 it was evidently too cumbersome to be clearly understood. It was left to the senior officers to frame a resolution to test the mind of the subsequent meeting of Grand Lodge. Others in the Central Committee, including Franklin Kelly, Dawson Bailie, William Murdie and Tom Haire, supported the idea of talking to the Parades Commission. Yet when the resolution was proposed on 18 March 2000 in Grand Lodge, it did not receive a seconder.

This, if nothing else, highlighted a lack of courage and conviction within the Orange Institution. The same people who had supported this resolution at Armagh County sat silent in Grand Lodge, and some of those who two weeks previously had supported it at Central Committee now spoke against it!

At the next meeting of County Armagh Grand Lodge the Lurgan solicitor Richard Monteith verbally attacked the County Master, Denis Watson, as to why he could not support the decision of his own County. Watson replied that as Grand Secretary he had to remain impartial. It was suggested to him that he perhaps had a conflict of interest.

Portadown District and Armagh County were not prepared to let matters drop. They tenaciously presented another resolution to rescind the decision not to talk to the Parades Commission, for submission to the 14 June 2000 meeting of Grand Lodge. It came before the Central Committee on 9 June and Denis Watson was forced to speak on the issue, in reply to direct questions. He admitted that it had seventy-five per cent support in County Armagh.

At the meeting of the Grand Orange Lodge of Ireland in Limavady on 14 June the issue was discussed for over two hours. No positive leadership was given on the issue from the senior officers. Denis Watson again did not speak in support of his own County Grand Lodge's decision. Harold Gracey and those present from Portadown District spoke strongly in favour of changing the policy. When the resolution was presented, such were the personal convictions of members that a secret ballot was called for. This was unprecedented at a meeting of the Grand Orange Lodge of Ireland. Evidently many were not prepared to express their opinions to their brethren. None of the leadership expressed any opinion, let alone gave any leadership on the issue. When the question was put forty-seven voted yes and eighty-eight voted no. The issue therefore remained unresolved.

A few months after this Grand Lodge meeting, an Orange delegation made a submission to the Select Committee on Northern Ireland Affairs, as part of which Robert Saulters responded to a question about opinion within Grand Lodge in favour of talking to the Parades Commission:

> It was last discussed in June, and at that time they called for a secret ballot; normally, it was a show of hands, but they called for a secret ballot at that time within Grand Lodge, which is about 160 people, at present. So they were granted the secret ballot, and out of that, I think, there were about nine who would have talked to the Parades Commission.[2]

A memory lapse may have been responsible for this gross distortion of figures, from 88:47 to 151:9, but it was not corrected by any of the other Orange delegates, two of whom as, principal officers, must have been aware of the error.

The millennium year was again dominated by the Drumcree debacle and associated matters. The resignation of the majority of the Education Committee on 14 June, on the grounds that the Grand Lodge had behaved in an unbiblical and unbrotherly way,* was a clear indication to the outside world that all was not well. On 12 July there was an unprecedented castigation of the leadership on BBC Radio by two former County Masters of Down, William Brown and Gerry Douglas, as well as

*See Chapter Nine.

Henry Reid, a former member of the Education Committee. William Brown courageously stated: 'We need a complete change of leadership . . . just like any company, if they are turning out bad results they should have the honour to go, and I think they should go.' William Murdie, Assistant Grand Secretary, who was also interviewed, said he was 'concerned about the future of the Institution' but supportive of the leadership: 'Your views are listened to and I feel there is a ground swell where things will be changed.'

Drumcree Sunday, 2 July 2000, was again marked by scenes of violence which denied the religious principles of the Orange Institution. While the service of worship was taking place, Mark Harbinson mounted an army Saracen and declared that Drumcree was 'Ulster's Alamo' and that 'the war begins today'. The RUC were attacked at Drumcree that evening, after a speech in which District Master Harold Gracey verbally attacked a variety of people and blamed the situation on everyone else. He called for 'hundreds of thousands' to 'carry the protest right across the province'.

Every true Orangeman was stung by the sight of Johnny 'Mad Dog' Adair at Drumcree with 'a group of 50 loyalists'[3] on the evening of Monday 3 July, followed by a paramilitary display and the firing of shots in the nearby Corcrain Estate. The *Belfast Telegraph* later quoted Adair as saying that he was there 'in response to Harold Gracey's comments'. David Jones, the Portadown District spokesman, refused to condemn either this appearance of a well-known paramilitary figure or the paramilitary display, but was quoted in the *Belfast Telegraph* of 4 July welcoming 'all expressions of support'. Adair's presence may have come as a surprise to many, but Vincent Kearney had forecast it in the *Sunday Times* as far back as 30 April: 'Hardline Orangemen in Portadown have entered a secret alliance with Johnny Adair, a loyalist terrorist, to seize control of the Drumcree protest in July.'

In the week which followed, we witnessed the now usual widespread disruption, thuggery, intimidation and wanton destruction. Many businesses closed early in Belfast. By the end of the week the RUC revealed the 'vital statistics' of the debacle: 140 petrol-bomb incidents, fifty vehicles hijacked, nearly forty police officers and soldiers injured and forty-three houses and twenty-seven other buildings damaged. In an interview with BBC journalist Peter Hunt on 7 July Harold Gracey declared: 'I'm not going to condemn violence because Gerry Adams never condemns it.' Gracey was later to suggest that he had been caught on the hop by the media, yet he repeated this remark later on in the interview and further went on to refuse to condemn the presence of Johnny Adair. Brid Rodgers voiced the questions of many in the *Irish News* on 8 July: 'Who speaks for the Orange Order? Is it the Grand Master, who has condemned the violence? Or is it Harold Gracey . . . ?'

There were the usual condemnations of violence by way of press statements from Orange headquarters, but William Thompson, MP for West Tyrone, called for an urgent rethink of the strategy: 'Many people including myself support the Orange Order in their stand . . . but when we get to a situation where they are supported by paramilitaries who attack police and hijack cars, it loses sympathy among the Unionist population.'

Harold Gracey's refusal to condemn violence was no surprise to anyone with a close knowledge of events. Prior to the church parade in 1999 he had been asked by the Orange leadership in County Armagh to sign a wide-ranging statement condemning violence and calling for exclusively peaceful protests. He refused to do so until the section condemning violence was removed!

As the second Drumcree Sunday approached, Gracey called for a general stoppage on Monday 10 July from 4 to 8 p.m., intended to bring Northern Ireland to a standstill. The Rev. Dr Warren Porter wrote in the *Sunday Times* on 9 July: 'Christian principles, Orange principles, ordinary prudence, not to speak of common sense, all demand that the Drumcree stand-off be stood down.' But stood down it was not, for pride and prejudice demanded, 'We stand firm in our principles.' Thankfully common sense prevailed to the extent that there was no great response to the call for a stoppage. Most businesses closed early to allow staff to go home. At tea-time on the evening of 10 July Belfast resembled a ghost town.

On the evening of 13 July, in an interview with Mark Simpson on the Northern Ireland BBC News, Robert Saulters conceded, when pressed, that the protests should be called off. They had indeed served no useful purpose. The members of Portadown District Lodge were still encamped on the hill at Drumcree.

In the autumn of 2000, the Orange Institution was again to present an incongruous image to a bewildered world over its position on the Civic Forum which had been established as part of the Belfast Agreement. No approach had been made by the Institution to the government during the initial establishment of the mechanisms for the selection of personnel to serve on this body. Nominating bodies had been established over the summer. This fact was in the public domain. There was no mention of the Civic Forum at the Grand Lodge Meeting on 14 June, yet on 11 August, by which time the selection process was well advanced, the Institution sent a letter to the First Minister, David Trimble. On 25 September, no doubt in preparation for the Grand Lodge meeting on 30 September at which the Civic Forum was discussed for the first time, Orange headquarters issued the following press release, in which the contents of the letter to Trimble are implied:

> The Grand Orange Lodge of Ireland has expressed regret and amazement at the fact that its commitment to community life in Northern Ireland has not been recognised through appointment to the Civic Forum.
>
> Whilst individuals who are members of the Orange Institution have been nominated (and we wish them well in their appointments) the simple fact is that the Orange Order as a body has been overlooked.
>
> It appears to us to be totally incredulous [*sic*] that the Prime Minister, Rt Hon. Tony Blair MP, can recognise the important role of the Orange Order and the contribution it makes to the life of society in Northern Ireland whilst those responsible for the appointments to the Civic Forum cannot.

This was clearly an attempt to embarrass and discredit Trimble, who was now the chief hate figure for the leadership. This duplicity had not gone unnoticed by many within the Institution. The leadership had given no encouragement whatever to the implementation of the Belfast Agreement. Now they gave the appearance of wanting to make use of one of its benefits by participating in the Civic Forum, yet they had made no approach to be considered for involvement while that forum was being set up.

At the Grand Lodge meeting on 30 September the Grand Master reported that he had set up a committee of four to look at the parades issue. He would not disclose their names, but it was later revealed that the committee's convenor was the Assistant Grand Treasurer, William McKeown, and the other members were Thomas Haire, Rodney Stewart and the Rev. Alan McCann.

On 13 October a letter was sent to all district lodges by the Executive Officer, George Patton, seeking opinions on Grand Lodge policy regarding the Parades Commission and 'Sinn Féin/IRA Residents groups'. The purpose of this letter was difficult to decipher. Were the leadership trying to get themselves off the hook of the 14 June decision of the Grand Lodge, a decision made because of their unwillingness to give leadership? Were they trying to lead from the rear, as usual? Perhaps the significance of the poor response to the most recent rally had begun to sink in. In a BBC (NI) interview, George Patton said: 'It's simply being done to look at what we have been doing right and what, if anything, we have been doing wrong.'

On 9 September 2000 a rally took place to mark eight hundred days of the protest. Denis Watson and George Patton addressed the rally and continued to pledge their support for the protest. The *Irish News* on 11 September reported that one hundred people had attended. The *Belfast News Letter* of the same day devoted two short paragraphs to the rally but did not state the numbers who attended.

News of the existence of the 'review committee' first came into the public domain in an article in the *Sunday Times* by Vincent Kearney on 20 October, headlined 'Orange Order to vote on ending parade talks ban'. This may have been technically inaccurate, as the committee had no power so to do, but of course this would not have prevented the leadership using the 'review committee' for their own ends. As was seen in other areas over these years, rules were made up as you went along. However, this was a high-risk strategy, for it would expose the leadership to the wrath of the hardliners who were now the dominant force within the Grand Lodge.

Vincent Kearney made the connection between this effort and the previous week's failed attempt by Dunloy Orange Lodge Master Davy Tweed to get leave to seek a judicial review using newly introduced European Union human rights legislation. The leadership of the Institution had been building up hopes on this legislation being the mechanism under which they would have the right 'to walk every road in Ulster'. Kearney also revealed in his article that Portadown District's legal advisor, Richard Monteith, had advised them that they would have to meet the Parades Commission before going to the courts. One did not have to be a trained legal mind to acknowledge this. No legal redress can be sought if the legal process has not been exhausted. In the case of the Parades Commission it had not even been embarked upon. The officer team of Grand Lodge steadfastly refused to acknowledge the existence of the Parades Commission, referring to them as an 'unelected quango'. At a meeting of Grand Lodge on 1 August 1998, the Rev. Martin Smyth had called the commission 'a political appointment designed to destroy the Institution.'

In April 1998 Grand Lodge had accepted a report from the Parades

Strategy Committee advising 'Non-acceptance of the Parades Commission'. That was one hook from which it was going to be difficult to be freed. For the district lodges to favour talking to the Parades Commission would mean bypassing Grand Lodge's decision to follow that 'non-acceptance' strategy. On 3 February 2001, the 'Committee to review current parades strategy' (established by the Grand Lodge on 30 September 2000) reported to a special meeting of the Grand Lodge with a 'Parades Policy Document' which was circulated to those present and discussed for over two hours. Such was the paranoia that each copy of the document was numbered and had to be returned at the end of the discussion, or given to the Inside Tyler, whose job it is to guard the door during meetings, if members had to leave for a comfort break. Such was the lack of interest in this important subject that only 115 members bothered to turn up. This should have sent a clear message to the leadership, but not only were they not going to talk to the Parades Commission, they had not realised the lack of support from their own membership for their hardline stance.

The substance of the 'Parades Policy Document' was that the leadership would engage in publicly challenging the role of the Parades Commission. The 'change' of policy indicated by the media in the following days was not as much a change as a sidestep; they would protest at the Parades Commission's determinations, but they would not talk to the Commission itself. No total figures were given for the responses to the survey of district lodges. In reply to a question, it was said by one senior officer to have been 'inconclusive'. Later another senior member of Grand Lodge maintained that the result was 'overwhelmingly' in favour of speaking to the Parades Commission, while another claimed it was against. Only one of these three answers could be the truth. We may never know which.

This uncertainty about the reaction of the rank-and-file membership was disclosed at the 'Forward within the Community' conference of 18 January 2003. At the end of this conference the Grand Master asked for a show of hands as to whether to meet with the Parades Commission and with cross-border groups or bodies that included Sinn Féin/IRA. The official report reads:

> In each case there was an overwhelming vote not to become involved in these. The Grand Master then stated that it would appear from this that Grand Lodge has got it right and is representative of the Institution. He went on to say that with this confirmation he would like

> to make it known that 'the tail will not wag the dog' and the policies of Grand Lodge must be adhered to.

This was not the only attempt in this period to change tack on the Drumcree issue. In December 1999 the South African human-rights lawyer Brian Currin had been approached to see if he could achieve anything to resolve the now six-year-long dispute. One hundred and eighty copies of his 2,700-word report were delivered to the Grand Secretary on 1 February 2001, in preparation for the 3 February special meeting of Grand Lodge. Although the document was lengthy its contents were clear:

> Your final decisions will have a huge impact on whether or not Drumcree is settled this year and for the future.
>
> History will judge your decisions this weekend as being of the most important decisions ever taken by the Orange Order.
>
> I make this plea because I know that all of you are committed to the preservation of your traditions and culture. I would, therefore, hope that the decisions you take enable you to participate comprehensively and fairly in processes and debates which will undoubtedly impact on the future of Orange traditions and culture in Ulster.

Currin had studied the legal background to the Parades Commission's powers as well as analysing its guidelines and actions in the context of human rights law. He said:

> The Parades Commission has, since 1998, consistently taken into consideration: attempts by the organisers to reach accommodation with the local residents; the threat of public disorder; the demographic balance along the route and the potential restrictions on the rights and freedoms of local residents; past behaviour of participants; and the broader political conflict in Northern Ireland.
>
> Following its own Guidelines and principles of International Human Rights law the Commission does not regard the Right to Peaceful Assembly as an absolute right and has not hesitated in restricting that right whenever it believes it is justified in doing so.
>
> The Guidelines developed by the Parades Commission, although intended to address the unique problems associated with the right to peaceful assembly and processions in Northern Ireland, are fairly and firmly based on international human rights norms and standards.

> Because of the unique problems associated with parades in Northern Ireland, there are, however, significant differences in application between Northern Ireland on the one hand and Great Britain and Europe on the other. Contrary to what you may have expected, the approach adopted in Northern Ireland to public processions is significantly more generous than the norm in Europe.
>
> My own conclusion is that in Europe the right to peaceful assembly is a fairly soft right. The interests of public safety, the prevention of disorder and the protection of the rights of others take relatively easy preference.
>
> In my respectful view, the Public Processions NI Act of 1998 and the body it created, the Parades Commission, provide a key to the preservation of cultural diversity in Northern Ireland. If that key is thrown away, the consequences for Orangeism, its culture and traditions will be dire.
>
> Ironically from your perspective, given the approach to freedom of assembly in Europe, the Parades Commission could be the saviour rather than the destroyer of the parading tradition in NI. However, for that to happen the approach to parades in NI will have to be a collaborative one, involving both traditions, the Parades Commission and Government.

While the press on Monday 5 February quoted liberally from this document, which had fallen into their hands over the weekend, nowhere did they reveal that it had been neither presented nor discussed at the special meeting of the Grand Lodge. The usual lack of leadership was revealed once more at this meeting when, after the lengthy discussion on the 'Parades Policy Document', it was intimated that Currin's report had been received. The members were showing signs of exhaustion and there was no enthusiasm for considering another document. No attempt was made by the leadership to communicate its significance.

By any standards this was not an honourable and open treatment of Brian Currin's document, which had cost the Institution nothing, whereas an opinion of counsel would have cost thousands of pounds that the Institution could ill afford given the spiralling costs, kept under cover, of their new premises. Currin had done the leadership a great service by presenting to them the combined product of his legal expertise and his intellectual assessment, and still they were unwilling to face the truth.

On 6 February the full text of his report appeared in the *Irish News*. Some of the radio and television news reports indicated that the document had not been dealt with at the Grand Lodge meeting. As usual there was no one available from the Grand Lodge Headquarters to comment.

A legal opinion entitled 'Freedom Of Peaceful Assembly: Parades In Northern Ireland', by Austen Morgan, a London-based barrister close to David Trimble, became public in March 2001. His advice was strikingly similar to Brian Currin's. Morgan said that the Institution should learn from its own best practice, and make use of the Human Rights Act of 1998 as well as the European Convention on Human Rights. He went on to state:

> The loyal orders should recognise the Parades Commission. It has been created by parliament. It has the power to make 'legal' determinations. Active engagement can only improve the position for particular lodges etc.
>
> Genuine interaction is at least tactically necessary, and it would be difficult to persuade a Northern Ireland court there was any merit in the no contact with convicted (republican) terrorists position (especially given the role of loyalist paramilitaries in 2000 and earlier).

Morgan gave the Orange Order 'a choice between two scenarios':

> EITHER: a stand for principle, involving a boycott of the Parades Commission, a refusal to talk to former republican terrorists, a failure to obey the law and increasing disregard of all legitimate authority, a public relations disaster at home and abroad affecting 'the Ulster people' generally, increasing pro-nationalist stances by the United Kingdom government under pressure from Dublin, more Drumcrees, and a continuing loss of members, leading to a rump organisation at once impotent and despised;
>
> OR: an intelligent response to very difficult circumstances, involving engagement with (but not necessarily support for) the Parades Commission, engagement with local residents and genuine community leaders, a complete rejection of all republican and loyalist violence, articulated support for the rule of law in a tolerant, pluralist democracy premised on diversity, undoing some of the damage to Northern Ireland, increasing responsiveness from the United Kingdom government and exposure of surviving intolerance in the Republic of Ireland, tackling the Drumcree issue, and preventing the decline in numbers, and consequent loss of status in the majority community.

Much of this had been recommended before, either in various written reports or in statements in Central Committee or Grand Lodge. The reader will note a striking resemblance to the analysis which I had sent on 5 May 1997 to all the County Masters.* No one took any action then, nor did they now.

Although Morgan does not state in his opinion who had asked for the advice, Chris Ryder and Vincent Kearney state in *Drumcree: The Orange Order's Last Stand* that it was William Thompson MP. Thompson received the document in August 2000 and, according to Ryder and Kearney, 'copied it to Robert Saulters, the Grand Master. Saulters did not like what he read either, and the report was never circulated to Grand Lodge members.'[4] At a meeting on 28 March 2001 Saulters denied any knowledge of Morgan's opinion. It might well have been the case that this document, like so many other letters and documents, was conveniently mislaid. Ryder and Kearney suggest that the leaders were 'actively promot[ing] ignorance to pacify unthinking hardliners and traditionalists and prevent unrest'.[5] Evidently someone was also keeping the Grand Master in ignorance.

The weekly protest following the service of morning prayer had been suspended in March 2001 because of the outbreak of foot-and-mouth disease. This however did not stop people from gathering on Drumcree Hill as Portadown District marked one thousand days of the dispute on Sunday 1 April 2001. The editorial of the *Irish News* on 2 April captured the widely held opinion:

> Orange figures were less than forthcoming when it came to assessing precisely what they had achieved during this period of time. However, any objective observer could only conclude that the Drumcree initiative had been nothing less than disastrous for the Portadown Orangemen. Their basic objective of securing a march along the Garvaghy Road is as far away as ever, and the overall reputation of their organisation is in tatters. Should the Orange Order decide to engage in full talks with the Garvaghy Road residents, and cooperate effectively with Mr Currin and the Parades Commission, then nationalists must react positively.

At a protest rally to mark the thousand days of the Drumcree stand-off, on 5 May 2001, Harold Gracey displayed his own example of foot-and-

* See Chapter Four, pp. 93–4.

mouth disease when he made what were considered by some to be threatening remarks towards the police: 'We know where you come from. You come from the Protestant community, the vast majority of you come from the Protestant community, and it is high time that you supported your own Protestant people.' These remarks were widely condemned by the community but not by senior officers of the Institution.

An opinion poll in the *Belfast Telegraph* on 23 May revealed that sixty-four per cent of the Protestant community had answered 'Yes' to the question 'Should Orangemen at Drumcree enter into dialogue with Garvaghy Road Residents' Coalition?' When asked about their 'preferred outcome' of the dispute at Drumcree, sixty-one per cent indicated that 'The Orangemen should have some form of parade at Drumcree but only with the agreement of the Garvaghy Residents' Coalition.' This poll had no impact whatsoever on the Orange leadership. It is doubtful if they even discussed its contents or its implications for the wider interests of Orangeism.

The illogicality of Grand Lodge's policy of not talking to the Parades Commission turned to farce in the run-up to the 2001 Drumcree church parade. In previous years prominent Orangemen such as Arnold Hatch and Mark Neale, members of Craigavon Borough Council, had talked to the Parades Commission about the parade. Chris McGimpsey and Jim Rodgers from Belfast City Council, both Orangemen, had also talked to the Parades Commission about the problems on the Ormeau Road. That year, in the run-up to the Whiterock Parade on 30 June, the Rev. Martin Smyth, the former Grand Master, and Nigel Dodds, newly elected MP for North Belfast and also an Orangeman, visited the Parades Commission on the 29th. They were followed on 3 July by a delegation from Craigavon Borough Council which included the newly elected councillor David Jones, press officer for Portadown District Lodge. All this made Grand Lodge's policy look foolish, the more so given the violence and carnage which had been witnessed in previous years.

The Grand Orange Lodge of Ireland finally made a submission on behalf of Portadown District to the Parades Commission on 5 July 2001. This bore all the hallmarks of the incompetence of the past, especially in dispensing with the Currin and Morgan documents. The chairman of the Parades Commission, Tony Holland, had let it be known on 4 July that he anticipated a 'major development' in relation to the Drumcree parade. What exactly this major development was is a matter of dispute. Some suggest that Portadown District officers were going to present themselves to the Parades Commission to argue their case for being allowed to go down the Garvaghy Road. It is also suggested that Grand Lodge officers, who would have regarded this as mutiny, forcibly stopped it. Instead the twenty-four-page submission was drawn up and its contents were disclosed to the two Unionist ministers, Sir Reg Empey and Michael McGimpsey, who were to meet the Commission at 11.30 a.m. on 5 July. The ministers arrived on time but the document did not. The Commission telephoned the Grand Lodge Office and were told that it was on its way by courier. Perhaps Grand Lodge officers assumed that by using a courier they were not having any contact with a body which they refused to recognise.

It is not clear whether the document eventually arrived by courier or by fax, but in any case it was fruitless. In substance it stated that Portadown District would enter into a Civic Forum with the Garvaghy Road residents on Saturday 7 July only if the parade was allowed to proceed on the 8th. The Orange leadership had evidently still failed to learn the lesson that this conflict would not be resolved by making conditional offers at the eleventh hour. They gave the impression that they were negotiating from a position of strength, which was certainly not the case. The situation was further confused when a Grand Lodge spokesperson was quoted in the *Belfast Telegraph* on 9 July as saying: ‘At the moment the policy of Grand Lodge remains no formal contacts with the Parades Commission.’

This ineptitude in communicating was all the more surprising considering that in 2001 the public relations company ‘Reputation Matters’, run by Stephen Chambers, had been brought in to train four members from each County Grand Lodge in media presentation, at a cost of £250 per head. The company was to be employed again for a one-year period from 1 March 2002, at a cost of £27,000.

The Drumcree church parade on Sunday 8 July passed off with the traditional confrontation and speeches at the security barricade at the bridge, following the morning service. That Harold Gracey was under instruction from senior officers of the Institution was evident, as he was more subdued than the previous year. However he still lambasted the *Belfast Telegraph* and went on to criticise the journalist who had exposed his ‘vigil’ at Drumcree as a sham.

Robert Saulters read a prepared speech which bore the hallmarks of the PR consultant. Stephen Chambers had cleverly used the words of the Parades Commission’s chairman of the previous week when he made reference to ‘banking progress for the future’, but had *too* cleverly incorporated quotations from Edmund Burke and Aristotle, which were not characteristic of Saulters. Some perceived the statement as a 'shift in thinking', but Denis Watson was quoted in the *Irish News* on 11 July as saying that the signs were being 'misread'. This was borne out by his attack on the Parades Commission from the platform at the Twelfth demonstration in Keady, County Armagh.

At 'Drumcree Eight' on Sunday 7 July 2002, following the handing over of a letter of protest by Portadown District to Assistant Chief Constable Stephen White, violence erupted in which twenty-four police personnel were injured, four of whom were hospitalised. All the PR in the world could not put a good spin on scenes of Orangemen assaulting and taunting members of the police.

This was followed by the customary vocal condemnation of violence by the Institution and further promises of discipline. Not to let the Institution off the hook, Brid Rodgers, the MLA for the area, called on the Orange Order to help the police by giving them the names of those involved. Perhaps she had in mind the Particular Qualifications which state that an Orangeman 'will, as far as in him lies, assist the magistrates and civil authorities of these kingdoms in the lawful execution of their duties, when called upon to do so'.

On BBC Radio Ulster the following morning the Executive Officer, George Patton, said in relation to the incident the previous night: 'We will be investigating . . . we will deal with this.' The promises of discipline by the leadership soon turned to pledges of support and no one was to be disciplined. After a number of Orangemen were arrested and some were held on remand, Denis Watson, the Grand Secretary and County Master of Armagh, speaking at the Twelfth in Newtownhamilton, called for 'Christian love and tolerance towards our brethren who have asked for repentance [*sic*] for their actions'.

As a result of the Weston Park agreement between the British and Irish governments in July 2001, the review of the Parades Commission led by Sir George Quigley reported in November 2002. The report recommended the separation of the 'mediation' role from the 'determinative' role of the Parades Commission by the establishment of two separate bodies, a Parades Facilitation Agency and a separate Rights Panel to rule on human rights issues. A press release from Grand Lodge said:

> Sir George Quigley's report vindicates our long-held view that instead of reducing tensions, the Parades Commission has actually made things worse. In its rulings the Commission has consistently taken the path of

> least resistance by banning or restricting traditional Orange parades and caving in to the threat of violence from a number of unrepresentative and politically-motivated nationalist residents' groups.
>
> We welcome any move that recognises the need to balance the concerns of those who oppose marches with the fundamental human rights of others seeking to celebrate their culture and traditions in peace and without giving offence to anybody.

The press release also described senior officers as 'looking forward to participating fully' in the consultation process. The oft-repeated objection to the 'quango' nature of the Commission, now being replaced by two 'quangos', seemed to have been forgotten.

The days preceding 'Drumcree Nine' in 2003 saw a total U-turn on the part of Portadown District. At an emergency meeting of the District Lodge on 3 July the membership endorsed the decision of the leadership to enter into direct talks with the residents. It was later to be revealed that a senior Orangeman, believed to be Denis Watson, tried to scupper the peace deal by leaking it to the press. This eleventh-hour decision did not of course resolve the dilemma, but on Sunday 6 July 'Drumcree Nine' passed off uneventfully with the now 'traditional' protest at the police barrier, after which the members of Portadown District and their supporters went home for their traditional Sunday lunch.

This U-turn by Portadown District had followed the City of Londonderry Grand Lodge's decision to enter into a local agreement, a decision which led to the resignation from office of its Master, Alan Lindsay, Deputy County Grand Master Dougie Caldwell and County Grand Chaplain the Rev. Stephen Dickinson. It was also revealed in the *Belfast News Letter* on 12 July that the Ligoniel lodges had had talks with the Commission about their Twelfth parade past the Ardoyne shops in North Belfast.

With a serious reduction in the membership of Portadown District Lodge, 'Drumcree Ten' in 2004 posed little by way of a security threat. *Belfast Telegraph* reporter Michael McHugh estimated the numbers on parade at 'around 500 Orangemen from across the province', a massive drop from previous years. Internal conflict within the Grand Lodge because of the Portadown District officers' attendance at a Parades Commission-sponsored visit to South Africa in February, and their more recent involvement in a Parades Commission clinic in Portadown, meant that, in contrast to previous years, Grand Lodge officers were conspicuous by their absence.

The question of talking to residents' groups, while highlighted by the annual confrontation at Drumcree, was not restricted to County Armagh. In June 2004, in order to resolve difficulties over the annual Whiterock parade in West Belfast, traditionally held on the last Saturday in June, the North and West Belfast Parades Forum was established, consisting of representatives of loyalist paramilitaries, local clergy and the Orange Order including the 'Belfast County Grand Master', as described in the letter sent by the Forum to the Parades Commission on 25 June undertaking to 'meet with representatives of the Springfield Road Residents' Association and the Parades Commission'. This was a clear commitment to meet not only with the commission but also with representatives of Republican paramilitaries.

Senior officers of the Institution, including Robert Saulters, supported the efforts of the Forum and had been kept fully informed. The fact that Sean 'Spike' Murray, chairman of the Springfield Road Residents' Association, was named in the *Sunday Times* on 1 June 2005 as a possible replacement for Gerry Adams on the Army Council of the IRA did not seem to deter senior officers, when mentioned at the Grand Lodge meeting on 15 June 2005. However, when on 30 June BBC Northern Ireland reporter Brian Rowan revealed that 'meetings had taken place between a senior Republican in West Belfast, Sean Murray, and William Mawhinney, the Master of No. 9 District Lodge', things took the inevitable twist. Although they had been informed in an open meeting of the Grand Lodge about both the West Belfast and the Londonderry negotiations, the Grand Master, Robert Saulters, and Deputy Grand Master the Rev. Stephen Dickinson issued a press release on 1 July claiming they were 'disturbed by the events in Londonderry and West Belfast and regret that members got involved in such meetings'. What dismayed many faithful Orangemen was that the Grand Orange Lodge of Ireland, which claims to be 'a Christian organisation . . . Christ-centred, Bible-based, Church-grounded', could refuse to talk to anyone made in the image of God.

Liam Clarke, in the *Sunday Times* of 4 July 2004, had summed up the situation:

> The Orange Order has been beaten and its defeat is largely of its own making . . . In any other organisation but the Orange Order, such a reversal of fortunes, such a failure of strategy, would provoke a rethink and a cleanout of senior management. The Order has lost the battle to march and is fast losing the battle for relevance. Yet to listen to the

> pronouncements of the Grand Lodge you could be forgiven for thinking that its bosses ran the province . . . What must be maddening to many Orangemen is that their analysis of the opposition to their marches was largely correct but their leadership succeeded in losing the battle.

Not only had the Drumcree debacle affected Portadown District, the birthplace of the Order, but the whole credibility and even the future of the Institution were now at stake.

Chapter Nine

Bricks without Straw: the Work of the Education Committee

> *'When you educate a man in mind and not in morals, you educate a menace to society.'*
>
> Franklin D. Roosevelt

At the time of the formation of the state of Northern Ireland in 1922, an attempt was made to create an all-embracing state system of education. The minister of education's 1923 bill proposing a purely secular system was widely condemned by the churches and the Orange Institution, who felt a deep sense of betrayal. At the time of crisis Unionist politicians had sought the support of both the churches and the Institution, but now that they had achieved political power they were disregarding the churches' spiritual emphases. The churches, understandably unwilling to see 'religious' schools transferred to secular educationalism, united under the United Education Committee of the Protestant Churches (UECPC) to oppose the bill. After much pressure from this body and the Orange Institution, accompanied by a very strong groundswell of Protestant opinion, the Amending Education Act of 12 March 1925 removed the secularising sections from the 1923 Act. In practice this permitted teachers to give religious instruction and enabled schools' management committees to enquire into the religion of applicants for teaching posts. The matter was still not completely resolved, as the government declared its unwillingness to enshrine these changes in schools' 'deeds of transfer'. A resumption of pressure led to the resignation of the then Minister of Education, Lord Londonderry.

The problem was one of management and control. The Protestant churches and the Loyal Orange Institution were finding it difficult to understand why a parliament which could fund Roman Catholic schools and a training college which were entirely denominational, both in character and in control, could yet refuse to fund schools or a teacher-training college with a non-denominational character.

The controversy was not satisfactorily resolved until the introduction of the 1930 Education Act, in which the churches were justly given the right of representation on management committees. The issue of teacher-training colleges kept the pot on the boil until 1932, when it was agreed by the Northern Ireland government that there should be representatives of the churches on the Stranmillis Teacher Training College Committee of Management.

The Grand Orange Lodge of Ireland had formed a committee in 1925 to 'keep in touch with the situation', and in 1928 the Education Committee came into being, prompted by a resolution from County Tyrone Grand Lodge responding to the controversy over 'deeds of transfer'. Its membership was appointed by Grand Lodge but was not restricted to members of that body. Rooted in this history, and wary of political promises, the Education Committee continued to monitor the educational system through many and varied changes until its demise on 14 June 2000. A large and important part of its work was a watching brief, continually responding to various changes and challenges within the educational sector, which may have given the impression that it was a reactive committee. To begin with, it would appear that the committee was concerned only with the state's educational provision sector, on the Protestant ethos of the transferred schools, and not with education in general. The wider and increasingly urgent need of educating the membership and the general public was yet to be addressed.

I joined the Education Committee in 1984, from which time my name appears in the official reports of Grand Lodge though it did not appear on the list of members of the committee until I was appointed chairman on 13 December 1989. I was appointed convenor on 9 December 1992 and Arnold Hatch became chairman. The committee kept a look-out for young, intelligent members to strengthen its work, and three who joined in these years deserve mention. Graham Montgomery, a teacher of history and politics at a Lisburn school, and David Richardson, then a primary-school teacher in West Belfast, later a research student and presently a minister of the Church of Ireland, brought a special insight, wisdom and knowledge to the work of the committee, as did Henry Reid, a farmer from County Tyrone, with his enthusiasm and vision. Others already serving on the committee who rose to the challenge and enthusiastically promoted its work were Richard Whitten, a history teacher, Cecil Kilpatrick, the retired Chief Forest Officer, and W. B. Loane, a farmer from County Fermanagh.

From the mid 1980s it became evident that the committee needed to be more than an internal talking shop. Under the convenorship of the Rev. Fred Baillie, the committee proposed to Grand Lodge that a 'one-off' education levy be raised from all the brethren within the Institution. Grand Lodge agreed this in December 1986, and the resultant funds gave the Education Committee the financial freedom to pursue areas of educational interest with vigour.

A job description or 'mission statement' for the committee was adopted by the Grand Orange Lodge of Ireland in June 1989:

> The function of the Education Committee will extend to all those areas which have any bearing in the field of education.
>
> The Committee will monitor the present and continuing system of Education in Schools, Colleges, Universities, etc., and bring to bear such influences as may be possible, to ensure that the education system reflects a broadly based Protestant ethos.
>
> The Committee will engage in the process of continuing to educate the Brethren of our Institution and the general public in the truths and principles of the Reformed Religion, and our historical and cultural heritage.

Within its specific parameters this broad statement gave both guidance and direction to the work of the Education Committee. Pursuing these aims, the committee over the years made representations to the Department of Education for Northern Ireland on a number of issues, such as the teaching of a common history course in all Northern Ireland schools. The committee also produced two papers for internal consumption: 'Integrated Education' in 1988 and 'Education for Mutual Understanding' in 1990.

In response to the Department of Education for Northern Ireland's consultative document 'Educational Administration in Northern Ireland', submissions were made to the minister responsible and copies were circulated to every lodge. We kept up a correspondence with the department, especially with reference to the Council for Catholic Maintained Schools, and made written and personal submissions on education to the Northern Ireland Forum on behalf of the Institution. Our booklet *The Order on Parade* was submitted to the North Commission as an appendix to the Grand Lodge submission.

Following our mission statement, the committee took the message of Orangeism out into the wider community as well as paying particular attention to the education of our own membership. As our work expanded, we made an appeal to the Institution at large in 1994 for new members who had 'a willingness to be a working participant and not a passenger'. Sadly, we did not receive any positive response.

From 1989 to 2000 the committee produced various booklets in accordance with the aims set out in the mission statement of 'continuing to educate the brethren of our Institution, and the general public, in the truths and principles of the Reformed Religion and our historical and cultural heritage'. This series began with *Ulster Special Constabulary*, *The Enniskillen Men* and *The Siege of Londonderry*. To mark the bicentenary of the Institution the committee produced *The Formation of the Orange Order*, a 166-page hardback making available the papers of Colonel William Blacker (1777–1825) and Colonel Robert H. Wallace CB, CBE, DL (1860–1929) to a wider audience.

To mark the bicentenary of the 1798 Rebellion, the committee published two booklets: *Murder Without Sin*, being edited extracts from the publication *Orangeism: Its Origin and History* by Ogle Robert Gowan, first published in Toronto in 1859; and another reprint from the major official history of the Order, *The Sunshine Patriots: The 1798 Rebellion in Antrim & Down*. This was an excerpt from R. M. Sibbett's 1938 work *Orangeism in Ireland and throughout the Empire*. County Antrim and County Down Grand Lodges supported the Education Committee in this project and took responsibility for the sale of three thousand and five thousand copies respectively. The large print run of this publication facilitated the financing of a commemorative dinner on 12 June 1998, attended by guests from the Republic of Ireland and from England. The booklet was placed on the list of official publications recommended by the Department of Education for Northern Ireland; this we believe was a first for the Order.

In 1997 the committee published a booklet on the Protestant perspective of Saint Patrick. This was sent to every Second Level educational institution throughout Ireland. The publication was launched on St Patrick's Night 1997 with a cross-cultural discussion in St Patrick's Trian, Armagh, involving Dr Richard Warner, Fr Paul Symonds, Nelson McCausland and myself. The evening was sponsored by the Community Relations Council and the discussion was chaired by James Hawthorne, former controller of the BBC (Northern Ireland). By the end of 1998, with the publication of *William of Orange – A Dedicated Life*, the committee had seventeen listed publications in print, as well as various other materials.

Not all the publications were strictly 'historical' in character. The booklet *The Order on Parade* was launched at the bicentenary parade at Loughgall on 23 September 1995 and provoked a wide media response due to its topical nature. The purpose of the publication was to help to make the case for parading better understood after the events at Drumcree in July 1995.

The Education Committee discovered that a lot of archival material had been transferred from Dublin when the Grand Lodge Office was moved to Belfast during the Civil War and was now in the safe keeping of the Rev. John Brown, a Grand Chaplain of the Order and in his younger days a notable figure. He was unwilling to part with it until someone was authorised to care for it. Accordingly the committee set out a policy for the cataloguing of this substantial material. The Grand Lodge accepted this on 2 June 1992 and appointed an archivist and assistant archivist. The work of the archivists continues under the careful and accurate eyes of Cecil Kilpatrick, a former member of the Education Committee and the author of a number of its publications. He is assisted by David Cargo, the Grand Director of Ceremonies of the Grand Lodge, as they compile an inventory of the archives held by Grand Lodge and those available elsewhere.

Over these years the Education Committee initiated a more outgoing approach in other areas too. Contact with other theological traditions was encouraged through the attendance of members of the committee at various cross-community conferences and projects, peace groups and the Glenstall Ecumenical Conference in June 1997, which I received the approval of the Grand Secretary, John McCrea, to attend. At all of these events we had unfettered opportunity to explain the principles and work of the Order.

The cultural and political divide was crossed again when the Education Committee took up membership in the Irish Association in 1996, after addressing the Association's meeting in Dublin on the evening of 15 March 1996. This significant event was attended by such notable people as the British Ambassador, Mrs (later Dame) Veronica Sutherland, the veteran Irish politician Conor Cruise O'Brien and the commentator and journalist Eoghan Harris. It led to many doors being opened for our educational work in the Irish Republic as ambassadors of the Orange Order.

On 5 March 1997 a meeting was held at the invitation of the minister of state at the Department of the Taoiseach, Avril Doyle TD, in Leinster House, Dublin. It had become known that the Order was proposing to commemorate the 1798 Rebellion and reflect upon its significance for Irish Protestants. Naturally this was of great interest to the Southern constituency. The meeting was attended by, among others, Professor Tom Bartlett, the Irish government's advisor on 1798, and Senator Dr Mary Henry. David Richardson and I represented the Education Committee. The Central Committee of the Grand Lodge was kept fully informed of all this activity.

This visit caused some media interest and heightened the profile of the Institution. Although it was made clear to reporters outside Leinster House that our interest was purely academic and historical, it was reported by the BBC in the context of the blocking of roads the previous summer.

The committee's interest in the commemoration of the 1798 Rebellion led to invitations to write articles for publications including the *Irish Times* and the *Irish Catholic.* We took part in a Gaelic Television programme on the Rebellion and were commended by Eoghan Harris in the *Sunday Times* on 6 September 1998. All this helped to improve the public perception of the Institution and present a more reasonable, if not academic, image. This progressive and proactive approach was recognised by the media as something of a novelty. As Orangemen became more approachable to the media so the media became more approachable to Orangemen.

As we advanced towards the summer of 1997 with 'Drumcree One' and 'Drumcree Two' behind us, it was evident that we had still to create a better understanding of the principles and values of the Institution among the population at large. The committee discussed the possibility of an information leaflet for wide circulation and agreed the text and layout of the publication on 28 February, opting for the inclusion of the Basis of the Institution rather than the Qualifications. It was at this stage that the Grand Secretary, John McCrea, began to display negative reactions to the work of the committee.

Having left the final draft before printing with the Executive Officer, we received a telephone message instructing us to hold the printing, as it would 'need the approval of the Central Committee'. None of our other publications had gone before Central Committee, and no one was any the wiser as a result of the next Central Committee meeting, on 9 May. The objection from John McCrea and the Grand Treasurer, Mervyn Bishop, appeared to be the omission of the Qualifications. It was carefully explained that we had opted for the Basis since it was shorter. Professional communicators would probably tell us that the leaflet contained too many words as it was.

This appeared to satisfy, but the next objection from the Grand Secretary was that 'King William was facing the wrong way – he was facing one way on the front and another way on the back'. Some members were astounded that this should be offered as a serious criticism. Dr Warren Porter commented that 'it suited us as we don't appear to know whether we are coming or going'.

While the production of the leaflet went ahead, and one hundred thousand copies were printed and taken up by the County Grand Lodges for distribution over the Twelfth period, this episode revealed that there was dissatisfaction in some quarters with the Education Committee. This negative attitude continued in relation to the Parades Commission. On 25 July 1997 I received an invitation for the Education Committee to meet with the Parades Commission, which noted our 'many publications and other recent initiatives aimed at enhancing understanding of the Orange Order'. I consulted the chairman, Arnold Hatch, and we agreed that since the Grand Lodge had not yet issued any direction on contact with the commission, and since the request was specifically to explore our 'views on what steps' the commission might take 'in pursuit of the educational dimension' of its remit, we ought to meet them on the suggested date of 12 September. The correspondence from the Parades Commission was read to the Executive Officer, who expressed no objection, and we then wrote to inform the committee members.

On 7 September *Sunday Life* carried a story about the proposed meeting, claiming that the Education Committee was 'split down the middle' and that 'letters had been exchanged between committee members and Rev. Kennaway'. In fact only one member of the committee had written concerning the meeting, not to me but to the Executive Officer. He had evidently misread the letter convening the meeting. We assumed that members of the Education Committee would know that the meeting was intended to discuss education. A member of the committee had evidently passed on incomplete information to *Sunday Life*. This matter was not helped by an incorrect ITV Teletext report on 12 September which suggested that the committee was going to discuss or negotiate over parades.

In the light of this I discussed the matter with the Grand Master, who affirmed that the Grand Lodge had not given any advice on the matter and that he personally had no problem with us going, adding, 'When you elect a committee you let it get on with the job.' The Education Committee met on 12 September, the day of the meeting arranged with the Parades Commission, discussed the matter and decided to proceed. The Grand Secretary, who had made no previous approach or suggestion to us, was present for the first time. He advised against going and said that it would 'undermine the Grand Master'. This appeared strange in the light of the Grand Master's own comments.

It was this meeting that was blockaded by a group of protesters from the Spirit of Drumcree. Their negative and aggressive approach typified a hardline Protestantism which regards talking as compromise, and compromise as surrender. During the disturbance Graham Montgomery intimated to another committee member that he might resign from the committee as a result of this abuse. He was alarmed to read this conversation repeated in *Sunday Life* a few days later!

The meeting with the Parades Commission went ahead that day, though slightly later than planned, with very positive discussions on the possibility of producing a CD-ROM for use in schools. The commission indicated that they would like to help us to get our message across to the wider community, particularly to those of a different background and tradition. As we made clear in our subsequent press release: 'The issues of parades in 1997 or 1998, or any possible legislation were neither raised nor discussed as these topics are outside the remit of the Committee.'

At its subsequent regular meeting on 19 September, the Education Committee unanimously affirmed its complete confidence in the actions of its convenor and chairman, especially concerning the conduct of the meeting with the Parades Commission. We reported to the Central Committee, which wholeheartedly supported and encouraged our work in this respect, and a report was subsequently made to the Grand Orange Lodge of Ireland on 10 December.

At the Education Committee's November meeting, in the light of these events, we discussed three particular areas of concern. I delivered a written report on collective responsibility, confidentiality and decision-making, as it was becoming evident that some members of the committee had views on these things which did not follow the tradition of the Institution.

Prior to the 10 December meeting of Grand Lodge a report appeared in the *Belfast Telegraph* quoting David McNarry as saying, 'The education committee were entitled to meet the Parades Commission as individuals. What we need to find out is on whose authority they went and who did they indicate they were representing?'[1] The same article reported that he had said, 'I am pleading to all attending as delegates or visitors to embrace dignity and decorum. I am imploring them to make their points inside the meeting before saying anything outside on the street.' This was something of a self-contradictory position.

Grand Lodge accepted the Education Committee's report, but at the same meeting it was decided, without much thought or discussion, to have no contact with the Parades Commission until the newly-formed Parades Strategy Committee had reported. The Education Committee therefore had no further contact with the commission, even though our remit included the education of anyone who needed to know the principles of Orangeism. We might justifiably have gone to see the Pope if a door of opportunity had opened.

The Grand Lodge meeting revealed some other underhand activities. The name of Nelson McCausland was proposed as convenor of the Education Committee by Robert Heyburn, a member of Ballymacarret District Lodge in Belfast and a professed disciple of Ian Paisley, on the grounds that 'some of us do not like the direction the Education Committee is taking'. He did not specify what he meant. The Education Committee had already agreed its membership and officers to submit to Grand Lodge and at no time did Robert Heyburn or his lodge write or speak to the committee concerning this 'direction'. Heyburn's proposal failed, receiving only seven votes.

At this same meeting Thomas Ross, District Master of Glenavy District, also went against the customary practice of the committee of which he was a member by proposing David Hall for membership. The committee had previously decided that Hall should be invited to meet with us to see if he felt that he could make a contribution.

In February 1998 a letter was apparently handed in to Grand Lodge headquarters at 65 Dublin Road by Stephen Nicholl, the Secretary of Antrim District Lodge. The letter was never forwarded to me as convenor, yet Nelson McCausland presented a copy of it to the committee meeting on 20 February. The Executive Officer, who was in attendance at the committee at this point, said that he knew nothing about the letter. My subsequent requests to Stephen Nicholl for all Education Committee correspondence to be sent to me went unanswered.

Suspicions increased when I received a telephone call on 17 June 1998 from a Mr Hugh Scullion asking why there had been no response to his correspondence. Hugh Scullion was of the nationalist tradition and had been involved with the Northern Ireland Civil Rights Association in the past. The purpose of his attempt to contact the Education Committee was to involve us in an education process with the community in Bellaghy, to try to relieve the parades situation. He subsequently sent me a copy of the letter which had gone astray, as well as another letter handed in to the House of Orange on 18 March 1998 which had also never reached me.

One can only wonder how many other items of correspondence had gone 'missing', and what false impressions were given to individuals or lodges who thought that the Education Committee had ignored their correspondence.

I discussed this matter with the Executive Officer, George Patton, who denied any knowledge of these two letters. As all correspondence, whether addressed to me personally, 'The Convenor' or 'The Education Committee', was as a matter of course opened in 65 Dublin Road, this made one wonder if the letters had not met with the approval of some individual and had therefore disappeared into the 'big black hole'. This was the term used by many within the Institution to describe the final resting place of various items, including correspondence and decisions of Grand Lodge, which the leadership wanted to forget.

This inadequate handling of correspondence was becoming increasingly obvious. On 6 October 1995 the Central Committee had set up a committee to meet with some members of the Ulster Unionist Council. The letter requesting a meeting was not written until 26 October. Yet this was the time when the Spirit of Drumcree group was beginning its campaign, one issue of which was the relationship of the Institution to the Ulster Unionist Party. Similarly, the letter of 6/7 April 1997 from the Parades Commission was not acknowledged for three weeks and was never replied to in substance.

Over the summer of 1998, even the Grand Master fell foul of the 'big black hole'. Two days before the 1 August special meeting of the Grand Lodge a former member of the Institution, the Rev. John Dickinson, delivered a letter by hand to 65 Dublin Road, giving it to Mervyn Gibson, a student for the Presbyterian ministry who had been helping out in the Grand Lodge Office over the summer. The letter was addressed to the Grand Master and was handed over with the instruction that 'I want Bobby [i.e. the Grand Master] to get this letter before the meeting.' In the four-page letter the Rev. Dickinson set out clearly the reasons why he had resigned from the Orange Order, reacting to a remark allegedly made a few days before by David McNarry to the effect that if members were leaving they were not giving reasons. Several weeks later, when no acknowledgement or reply had been forthcoming, it was discovered that the Grand Master had never received the letter. A copy was then sent to his home address, to which he replied stating that several significant items of correspondence had not been passed on to him.

The major event in 1998, as far as the Education Committee was concerned, was the 1798 Commemorative Dinner held on 12 June in Parliament Buildings, Stormont. Even this was to reveal the 'big black hole' syndrome. Two years previously the Grand Lodge had given permission to the Education Committee to organise this dinner. Yet the Grand Secretary, John McCrea, claimed to be unaware of it as late as March 1998. The Grand Secretary, as anticipated, did not come to the dinner. Since 1984 he had not come to anything the Education Committee had organised.

After the meeting of Grand Lodge on 10 June, just two days before the dinner, a press release was approved by the Executive Officer to be released the following day. It gave details of the event, 'designed to be broad and inclusive of Civic and Academic interests throughout Ireland', and noted that 'Guests will include the Lord Mayors of Belfast and Dublin, senior academics and journalists from both sides of the border'.

The following day, it was established after several attempts at clarification that this press release had not been issued. The Executive Officer's secretary told me that it was 'not approved by the Grand Secretary and the Grand Master'. I asked if that meant that they had not yet seen it in order to approve it, or that they had seen it and not approved it. She did not know.

Later in the day I managed to speak to the Executive Officer. I was told that both the Grand Secretary and the Grand Master had seen the press release and had not approved its release; they felt that it should have been presented to the Grand Lodge! This was something completely new in the practice of the Institution.

The half-yearly report of the Education Committee, which included details of the dinner, had been received at Grand Lodge. Only one person objected: Joel Patton, the leader of the Spirit of Drumcree faction, who in his usual aggressive fashion objected to the Mayor of Dublin attending the dinner. The Mayor in fact wears the chain of office presented to the Corporation of the City of Dublin by William III of 'glorious, pious and immortal memory'.

The Grand Master Robert Saulters did not attend the dinner either. He had written it in his diary and had agreed to come, but I received a letter from him claiming that attending would 'again bring the wrath of many members down on me and Grand Lodge Officers'. This letter was amazing, and more so as time went by. The Grand Lodge on 10 June had accepted the report and only one person had objected to the Mayor of Dublin being invited. Whatever else it might have done, the Grand Master's declining would certainly not have preserved harmony.

The Commemorative Dinner went ahead with ninety-one people attending. There were thirty invited guests, thirteen of them from the Irish Republic. Academia, taking in all the major Irish universities, and journalism were well represented. Professor Brian Walker gave an excellent after-dinner lecture on 'The Lessons of '98'. Sponsorship for the project had been received from Co-Operation North, the Community Relations Council: Cultural Diversity Programme, the Northern Ireland Tourist Board and Edenderry Print. If the success of the evening is to be measured by the number of positive and encouraging letters which followed, then it was a resounding success.

While the work of the Education Committee was not always appreciated by everyone inside the Institution, some of whom appeared to feel threatened by its increasing impact on the public perception of the Order, it was appreciated by many. On 23 June 1996 I was preaching at the annual service of Ballynadrentagh LOL 1059, of which Lord Molyneaux is a member. He told me: 'That committee of yours could be the salvation of our outfit.' Later the Commission on the Loyal Orange Institution in Ireland commended our work, saying that the 'Education Committee has been influential in effecting a considerable improvement in our public image but the Commission is mindful that such good work can be undermined by irresponsible criticism'.

There was however no let-up on the attack on the work of the committee. These attacks often took place 'behind backs', and not in accordance with basic democratic, let alone Christian, principles of the Institution.

The meeting of Central Committee on Friday 4 December 1998 was adjourned to meet the next day, when I was unable to be present because of a meeting of the Education Committee, as senior officers, also being *ex officio* members of the committee, were aware. This was one of the few Central Committee meetings for which an agenda was published. There was no reference on the agenda to any business concerning the Education Committee, yet this did not prevent matters being raised in my absence and that of other members who had been unable to return for the postponed meeting, and a resolution was put forward for the next meeting of Grand Lodge that the Grand Master should appoint a 'Committee to consider the constitution and remit of the Education Committee'. At the subsequent meeting of the Grand Lodge on 9 December, after 5 p.m. when I and many others had left, this recommendation was accepted.

According to the Grand Lodge report of the meeting, correspondence was read from Belfast County and Carrickfergus District 'querying aspects of the composition and workings of the Education Committee'. There was no communication with either myself or the chairman of the committee with regard to this until we received a letter dated 18 February from the newly appointed Grand Secretary, Denis Watson, informing us of the setting up of the 'Committee to consider the constitution and remit of the Education Committee'.

This letter was read at the meeting of the Education Committee on 19 February, when members were unable to throw any further light on the subject. As a result I wrote to the Grand Secretary asking to know the names of those on the new committee and the background to the decision. In reply we were informed that the brethren serving on the committee were Rt Wor. Bros R. Stewart, J. McCrea JP and R. Kells MBE, and W. Bros D. Davison and C. Shilliday. (Colin Shilliday later resigned.) We were also informed that the decision to appoint the committee had been taken following a recommendation from Central Committee in response to communications received. There was no information forthcoming as to the nature of the communications.

This was beginning to look like a replay of the Grand Committee of the previous year. The inclusion of John McCrea also revealed a lot. He had been present at the Grand Committee hearing when some members of the Education Committee had brought charges against members of the Spirit of Drumcree. Now he was a member of this 'Committee to consider the constitution and remit'. Since he was also, as Grand Secretary, an *ex officio* member of the Education Committee, this raised suspicions of a conflict of interest, as did the inclusion of Drew Davison, the former Secretary of County Antrim Grand Orange Lodge. He had been involved in the hearing of the charges against David Tweed and William Smith concerning the Spirit of Drumcree blockade on 12 September 1997 and, it was believed, had initiated the secret talks in Magheragall Orange Hall with the Spirit of Drumcree in January 1998. Obviously, given the make-up of this committee, the writing was on the wall for the Education Committee.

Around this time Drew Davison invited Graham Montgomery to dinner and informed him that there was a place in the Orange Institution in the future for him and for me, but that we should not 'rock the boat'! Davison was of course not the originator of this message; he was only acting as the messenger of a higher power, who was unwilling to get his hands dirtied.

The 'Committee to consider the constitution and remit of the Education Committee' was apparently in no hurry. There was a preliminary meeting on 23 February 1999 and a full discussion on 19 March 1999. A further meeting was called and later cancelled.

Some members of the Education Committee felt that a campaign to undermine the effectiveness of our work was being given spurious legitimacy by the creation of this committee. Ordinary, perhaps less well-informed members of the Order could be asking, 'What has the Education Committee been doing?' But this was not the only attempt to undermine the work of the Education Committee. The Grand Treasurer, Mervyn Bishop, wrote to me on 28 February 1999 saying that at the meeting of Grand Lodge on 9 December 1998 he had been asked for a breakdown of costs of the 1798 Commemorative Dinner and had been unable to provide the details. I answered his letter, reminding him that as Grand Treasurer he should have been fully aware of the income and expenditure for this event as all these matters were handled by the Grand Lodge Office. I also reminded him that I had kept him fully informed throughout the planning stages from the spring of 1996, prior to Grand Lodge giving its approval, and that he had responded positively when I outlined the financial package drawn up around the production of the booklet *The Sunshine Patriots*. I attached a breakdown of income and expenditure with a balance of £1994.65 in credit, although he should have been able to find this information in his own records. When the report of the 9 December 1998 meeting of Grand Lodge was published, it revealed that the originator of the question concerning the financing of the dinner was John McCrea, the past Grand Secretary.

My letter explaining the financing of the dinner was read to the next meeting of Grand Lodge on 27 March, but, unable to let this matter rest, John McCrea proposed that it 'be given to the Investigation Committee'. According to the minutes of the meeting of 9 December 1998 and the letter from the new Grand Secretary, Denis Watson, the new body was 'a Committee to consider the constitution and remit of the Education Committee', not an 'Investigation Committee'. Was this incompetence in the use of language or a Freudian slip? Future events were to reveal the true answer to that question, but at the Central Committee meeting on 17 September 1999 members were assured in categorical terms that there was only one committee and that its remit was, as stated, 'to consider the constitution and remit of the Education Committee'. John McCrea apologised and admitted that 'Investigation Committee' were the words he had used. His admission and apology were of course accepted.

Nothing further was heard until the Grand Secretary wrote on 1 October 1999 requesting 'Minutes of the Education Committee'. After consultation with the chairman, Arnold Hatch, we replied that the business of the Education Committee was conducted through the House of Orange and that the minutes were therefore available from the Executive Officer, George Patton. However, when we were interviewed by the 'Committee to consider the constitution and remit' on 22 October, the first question asked of me and of Arnold Hatch was, 'What was the difficulty over the minutes?' We pointed out that the Executive Officer had the minutes, but we were informed that he did not have the 'certified minutes'. We replied that we had not been asked for the 'certified minutes', and on 12 November wrote to Rodney Stewart, the convenor of the 'Committee to consider . . .', to clarify the sequence and substance of the correspondence. We then received a specific request for the 'certified minutes of the Education Committee for the last three years' from the Grand Secretary, who apologised for being insufficiently specific in his previous letter. We supplied them promptly as requested.

As by this stage the boundaries of trust had well nigh been crossed, the chairman and I personally delivered the above letter and the minutes to 65 Dublin Road. We asked for, and received, a signed receipt from the Executive Officer.

The interviews with the 'Committee to consider . . .' took place individually with such members of the Education Committee who responded. Not all those interviewed were asked the same questions. For example, the officers of the committee, the chairman and I were not asked anything about the meeting with the Parades Commission on 12 September 1997, nor were some other members. Yet this was one of the matters dealt with in the final report. Again, I was the only one interviewed concerning the 1798 Commemorative Dinner. During this interview the Grand Treasurer, Mervyn Bishop, again stated that he had no problems with the financing of the dinner. Only John McCrea was arguing that the dinner, taken on its own, made a loss. I went over the facts outlined in my letter of 9 March to the Grand Treasurer, showing how the dinner had been financed by the production of *The Sunshine Patriots* and that the enterprise as a whole had made a profit.

Nothing further was heard from this committee until, at the closing of the Central Committee meeting on 3 March 2000, Rodney Stewart announced that its report would be made to Grand Lodge on 18 March. This was unprecedented. Reports are normally first considered by Central Committee, but then the Central Committee would have been more sympathetic to the work of the Education Committee.

Because many members of the Education Committee suspected what the result of the Grand Lodge meeting would be, three members attended as visitors: Arnold Hatch, Cecil Kilpatrick and Graham Montgomery. Richard Whitten, also a member of the Education Committee, was present in his capacity as a representative from his district lodge. The report was delivered verbally by Rodney Stewart and accepted by the Grand Lodge on the proposal of David McNarry. On 21 March the Education Committee received a written copy of the report's recommendations. The work of the Education Committeee was to be 'sub-divided into three areas for operational purposes', namely education, publication and public relations. Details were given of the reporting procedures which were to apply for each of the three new committees. It was recommended that 'the composition of the new Committees should be reviewed by the Grand Lodge Officers with the present Chairman and Convenor and reflect the expertise required to deal with the various issues. The members of this Grand Lodge Committee will be prepared to assist the Grand Master for a further period, should this be necessary.' Further strictures were proposed relative to the appointment of members and the offices of chairman and convenor. It was recommended that I should 'head up the Publications Committee, in view of [my] interest and experience in this field'. The recommendations concluded that 'all funds or levies relative to Education should remain in one account and continue to be administered by the Executive Officer', and that expenses budgets should be agreed and approved by the Grand Treasurer.

We were not sent the whole of the report, despite our requests. My suggestions for dates for meetings were also ignored. Not only were those in authority avoiding my request for a copy of the report, but they were hiding behind the decision of Grand Lodge. After various attempts to obtain a copy of the report had failed, it was with some surprise that we received a letter, not from the Grand Secretary but from the Executive Officer, George Patton, which enclosed 'further details' of what the report had contained. This letter was received on 18 May, the day before the next scheduled meeting of the Education Committee.

REPORT FROM COMMITTEE CONSIDERING THE CONSTITUTION AND REMIT OF THE EDUCATION COMMITTEE

During the course of our meetings with the Officers and Members of the Education Committee it was disturbing to find that the Members of the Education Committee were not all aware of the detail of some of the identical subjects placed before them. Your Committee were unable to find evidence of adequate feedback or reports from the Convenor and/or Representatives following attendance at Conferences, Seminars, or Meetings.

The Committee were unable to find evidence to support the case that Delegates and Representatives are appointed by the Education Committee. It was noted that in most cases the Education Committee were represented at outside Conferences etc. by the Convenor or Brethren selected by the Convenor and Chairman. It is accepted that it may be difficult for the Education Committee to make appointments when events occur between Meetings.

However, there is no evidence to suggest that a report is always presented at the next meeting, to advise of the attendance and the reasons for attendance and selection.

The Committee were disturbed to find that the Education Committee, following representations to the Author of the Book entitled 'The Committee', had received correspondence from the Author's legal representatives in the United States of America and failed to advise the Grand Master and/or the Grand Secretary of possible legal action. The Education Committee Convenor sought legal advice from an individual solicitor on a personal basis and as a result the Grand Lodge Solicitors were not consulted for legal advice.

The question of the Education Committee meeting with the Parades Commission has already been discussed in detail by Grand Lodge and Central Committee. However, in examining the remit of the Education Committee it was necessary to re-visit this matter.

Taking into consideration the following:

A. The remit of the Education Committee.
B. The advice given on the day by Senior Officers of Grand Lodge.
C. The concern of some Members of the Education Committee.
D. The fact that Central Committee had considered a letter from the Parades Commission without reaching a decision.

It is considered it was inappropriate for the Education Committee to meet the Parades Commission.

Following an examination of correspondence by the Convenor, the Committee concluded that at the quarterly meetings of the Education Committee the Members are not being presented with complete details. In addition when circular or group letters are being sent to internal Lodges and/or Officers, the Grand Secretary should in the first instance be issued with a copy of the correspondence and the reasons for issue.

> On examination of the Minutes of the Education Committee at their Meeting on the 20 November 1992 the Committee decided 'with regard to the future of the Educational Committee that the Offices of Convenor and Chairman should rotate'.
>
> At the Grand Lodge Meeting on the 9 December 1992 the Convenor in his report stated 'The recommendations of the Committee as to Officers and Membership, has been submitted and dealt with in the Election of Officers'. The report was adopted by Grand Lodge. Since the change of Officers in 1992, the Education Committee have not implemented their own decision to 'rotate the Offices of Chairman and Convenor', which was approved by Grand Lodge.
>
> All available correspondence and the Accounts for the 1798 Anniversary Dinner held in Parliament Buildings, Stormont, were reviewed and discussed with the Convenor of the Education Committee and the Grand Treasurer.
>
> At this stage, the only comment the Committee would make is 'that they regret that the Officers of the Education Committee did not adopt a more open policy in relation to the management of this event, with their Committee and Grand Lodge'.

The 'further details' concluded:

> Following examination of Minutes, Records, and Correspondence, Interviews and lengthy deliberation the Grand Lodge Committee concluded that during the past three years the Education Committee have not totally worked within their remit.
>
> We would request Grand Lodge to commend the work of the Education Committee plus the enthusiasm and commitment of the members. However, the lack of communication on occasions has set the committee on courses which have caused them to operate outside their remit.
>
> Your Committee considers with the assistance of Grand Lodge in accepting our findings and recommendations that the Education Committee will proceed to work in the future for the benefit of the Institution as a whole.

At the meeting of the Education Committee on 19 May we were joined by Grand Lodge officers, as suggested in the report: the Grand Master, Robert Saulters, the Grand Secretary, Denis Watson, the Grand Treasurer, Mervyn Bishop, Assistant Grand Secretary Drew Davison,

Assistant Grand Treasurer William McKeown and the Executive Officer, George Patton. This was the first time since I had joined the Committee that so many *ex officio* members had attended. When discussion arose concerning the report from the 'Committee to consider the constitution and remit of the Education Committee', the chairman pointed out that we could not implement a report which we did not have. When asked why the report had not been furnished to members, the Grand Master said that there was only one copy, which was locked in the safe in the House of Orange. He would not allow it to be distributed in case it was leaked to the press. After further questions he conceded that members of the Education Committee could read it in the House of Orange by arrangement with the Executive Officer.

I pointed out that the committee was still unaware of the origins of the 'Committee to consider . . .', in spite of having asked. We had been kept in the dark contrary to the spirit of brotherhood and the Scriptures (Matthew 18:15). I also pointed out that the commission which had looked at all the structures of the Institution including the Education Committee had recommended no change. There was no reply to this.

We pointed out that the 'further details' supplied by the Executive Officer the previous day made reference to two sub-committees; the recommendations appeared to make reference to three sub-committees, while the Grand Master had made reference to four sub-committees. The Grand Treasurer said that the members of the three sub-committees would also be members of a General Committee. Mervyn Gibson pointed out that this was not what the recommendations said. There was confusion as to which committee the convenor would belong to or if there would be three convenors.

Graham Montgomery queried the statement in the 'further details' criticising the Education Committee for not adopting a more open policy in the management of the 1798 Commemorative Dinner. He said that he had been fully involved and found nothing to support the allegation. He also asked for evidence to substantiate the claim, made twice in the 'further details', that the Education Committee had exceeded its remit. Cecil Kilpatrick handed a copy of the remit to Robert Saulters and asked him if he could show the committee where its terms had been broken. Graham Montgomery pointed out that it was important for us to know this so that we would not exceed our remit again. There was no reply. Because of the long embarrassing silence, Graham Montgomery suggested that the Grand Master might need time to consider that question further and get back to us. The Grand Master agreed, but no response ever came.

At the following Grand Lodge meeting on 14 June it was pointed out to Robert Saulters that he had failed to answer that question. He made the excuse that he thought that he was to reply in writing. The Grand Secretary told him that was not what was understood. No answer was ever given to this question, and therefore at no time did anyone in authority, or in the 'Committee to consider . . .', ever point out precisely where the Education Committee had allegedly exceeded its remit.

The Grand Master's insistence that he would not release the report, but that we could read it in the Grand Lodge Office, came as a shock to all present. After Robert Saulters had left the meeting the Grand Secretary, Denis Watson, was asked why, in our fruitless correspondence, he had not stated this. He told us that he was unaware of this, and that obviously the Grand Master had just decided it that evening.

The mystery turned to farce when, on reading the report in the Grand Lodge Office, we discovered that it was little different from what had already been communicated in the two documents already furnished to all members of the Education Committee. The farce reached its zenith seven days later, when the two documents appeared in the published report of the Grand Lodge meeting of 18 March. This report is sent to every member of the Grand Orange Lodge of Ireland, and also to every private, district and county lodge secretary. The print run must be in the region of two thousand copies. Reports are professionally printed and therefore this one must have been ready for publication, in order to meet the print deadline, all the time we were attempting to acquire a copy.

This raised again the question in the minds of those actively involved in the work of the Education Committee, as well as various senior county officers: 'Was the Education Committee to be offered on the altar of sacrifice for the purpose of peace with the Spirit of Drumcree?'

To bring the attention of the Grand Lodge and the Institution at large to the errors in the report, we prepared a response to be delivered at the next scheduled meeting of the Grand Lodge on 14 June 2000. We expressed our concerns that we had not been given access to a report which we were expected to implement; that the spirit of Scripture contained in Matthew 18 had been ignored; that the 'Committee to consider . . .' had ignored the constitution of the Education Committee, which was part of its remit; that we were accused of going beyond our remit, yet the Grand Master could not give us any examples of this; and that the meeting with the Parades Commission should not have been considered, as the Education Committee had been supported by the Central Committee in its actions. Our concern was that the 'Committee to consider . . .' had been selective in its use of material and that its recommendations were based on a report which was factually flawed. This report was debated but not accepted.

I then sought and received the permission of the Grand Master to read a letter of resignation from myself as convenor, Arnold Hatch as chairman, Cecil Kilpatrick, W. B. Loane DL, Graham Montgomery, Dr David Richardson, Henry Reid and Richard Whitten. The reasons we gave in the letter were the manner in which the 'investigation' had been carried out, the flaws in the report and the fact that the Grand Lodge, in accepting the report, had transgressed the rules of Christian discipleship.

Halfway through reading the letter a point of order was raised by Dawson Bailie, the Belfast County Master. The Grand Master put it to me that resignations should be made to private lodges, but the Grand Secretary quickly interrupted him, pointing out that this was with reference to a committee of the Grand Lodge.

The Grand Master would not let me continue to read our letter of resignation, in spite of previously agreeing that I could. Thus we were deprived of the basic courtesy afforded to members of parliament at Westminster, where resignation statements are traditionally heard without interruption. The letter was tabled and I left the Grand Lodge meeting.

Those of us who had resigned issued a statement to the press the same day:

> In the light of the speculation, which is surrounding the events in Grand Lodge concerning the Education Committee, we need to put the record straight.
>
> It is a matter of great sorrow that we, the majority of the Education Committee, felt that we had to resign, but in the light of the recent behaviour of the senior officers of Grand Lodge, we concluded that we had no other option.
>
> The Grand Lodge Officers have behaved in a way which has stood the principle of brotherhood on its head by instigating an 'investigation' behind the backs of the Committee. To make matters worse they withheld the full Report, which was the result of that investigation.
>
> Such behaviour is, in our opinion, both unbrotherly and unchristian, and therefore, as we had no other option open to us, we have, with regret, resigned.

Media reaction was quite sympathetic. BBC Ceefax carried the news on 14 and 15 June:

> Members of Orange Committee resign – 8 members of an Orange Order Committee have resigned their position. One of the members of the Education Committee, Graham Montgomery, said it had 'become impossible to present a coherent and intelligent argument in favour of the Order'. Mr Montgomery added that this was because of restraints placed upon the Education Committee.

The *Belfast Telegraph* gave it front-page coverage the following evening. I appeared on the BBC Northern Ireland radio programme 'Good Morning Ulster' on 15 June as well as on the UTV evening news and the BBC Northern Ireland investigative programme 'Hearts and Minds'. Positive and encouraging letters appeared in the press from the Rev. Dr Warren Porter and the Rev. Ken Newell. Arnold Hatch said in the *Portadown Times* that 'the Grand Lodge of Ireland should be examining itself'. As expected the leadership refused to appear in public, but they issued a statement condemning the fact that we had spoken to the press.

Liam Clarke in the *Sunday Times* on 18 June and Malachi O'Doherty in the *Belfast Telegraph* on 20 June commented both favourably and accurately on both the background to the resignations and the message which the resignations conveyed. Ruth Dudley Edwards said in a perceptive article on the general direction of the Institution in the *Belfast Telegraph* on 30 June 2000, 'What starkly illustrated the state of affairs was what happened with the Education Committee. Under the leadership of the Rev. Brian Kennaway, its members did more in a few years to make to outsiders a credible case for Orangeism than had the Grand Lodge of Ireland in two centuries.'

Writing of the 18 March 2000 meeting of the Grand Lodge in the 'Afterword' of the paperback edition of *The Faithful Tribe*, published in June 2000, Ruth Dudley Edwards said:

> At the same meeting the Order also opted to implement the conclusions of a report designed to trammel the Education Committee, whose convenor, Brian Kennaway, and several talented colleagues, had done so much to improve the image of Orangeism at home and abroad. They were not shown the report, but were informed of its conclusions. It criticised them for going beyond their powers in speaking at conferences and seminars, and for the manner in which they had organised a highly successful dinner at Stormont.

Some months following the mass resignation yet another member of the

Education Committee felt unable to continue in the prevailing circumstances. The inequitable conduct of business was revealed as some individuals were asked to reconsider their resignations. Cecil Kilpatrick was asked by the Grand Master, the Rev. William Bingham approached Richard Whitten and the ninth member to resign received a letter from the new committee. All declined, and the chairman of the newly constructed Educational Affairs Committee, Thomas Ross, reported to the Grand Lodge on 12 June 2002 that their search for new members had failed.

It is worth noting that in the event the Grand Orange Lodge of Ireland failed to implement its own report, as the three or four sub-committees envisaged in the report were never established. The object of what John McCrea called the 'Investigation Committee' had been achieved with the resignation of the majority of the Education Committee.

It was to be the end of an era in more ways than one. It was not only the end of a progressive incarnation of the Education Committee, but also the end of the committee itself, which had begun its life in 1928. The new committee dealing with education was to be known, according to the Grand Lodge Report of 30 September, as the 'Committee for Educational Affairs'. Thus the Grand Orange Lodge of Ireland managed to do to the Education Committee what they had accused the government of doing to the Royal Ulster Constabulary – destroying its operational capability, disbanding it and setting up a replacement under a new name.

Chapter Ten

In Office but not in Power

> *'We give the impression of being in office but not in power.'*
>
> Norman Lamont MP, Chancellor of the Exchequer 1990–3

The method of the choice of the Grand Master of the Grand Orange Lodge of Ireland is, for many, shrouded in mystery. There are no guidelines laid down in the Laws and Ordinances except when it comes to the actual election, which takes place in 'Open Lodge'.

In past generations, when there was some prestige to be gained by holding the highest office in the Orange Institution, it was occupied by the aristocracy. These gentry were quite often appointed to the Grand Master's chair without having held senior office previously within the Institution. The rank and file of the Institution were happy that this should be so. The break from that tradition was to come with the election of John Bryans in December 1969. Bryans was County Grand Master of Belfast from 1958 until 1969. The method of selection for the Grand Master's post, being relinquished by Sir George Clark, was that a group of senior officers made up of the Grand Master, Grand Secretary, Grand Treasurer, some of the Grand Chaplains and others, would meet and approach a suitable successor. Evidence indicates that it was the Rev. Martin Smyth and the Rev. John Brown who pushed for John Bryans to be approached, although he was then eighty-four years of age. A native of County Monaghan, where he was born in 1885, John Bryans was a committed Christian and a lay preacher in the Methodist Church. He was re-elected annually until the election of the Rev. William Martin Smyth in December 1972.

When Bryans indicated he was relinquishing the chair, a similar procedure was adopted. As the senior officers met to consider this position there were two possible names, those of the Rev. Martin Smyth and Canon S. E. Long. Canon Long made it clear that there were three reasons why he could not accept the position. He did not have the time, he could not afford it and his family would not accept it. The Church of Ireland bishop R. C. Elliott, who was one of the Grand Chaplains involved, indicated that the first two objections could be taken care of, but the third was a personal matter. The Rev. Martin Smyth indicated that he would be prepared to accept the post. Accordingly his name was tabled at the subsequent meeting of the Grand Orange Lodge of Ireland in December 1972, where he was elected Grand Master. Smyth, an ordained minister of the Presbyterian Church in Ireland, held the office of County Grand Master of Belfast until December 1973. He was elected MP for Belfast South in February 1982.

Up to this time a general pattern had developed in the selection of a Grand Master, which effectively became the 'custom and practice' when a successor was being sought. This same custom and practice was followed on four occasions during Smyth's term of office when he indicated that he wished to relinquish the office. After he had served ten years, Smyth intimated his intention to stand down. Sir George Clark, who had served as Grand Master from 1959 to 1969, chaired a committee in an attempt to select a successor to present to the Grand Lodge. Although Dr Michael Dewar, a member of the senior officer team, insisted that they 'should not have another clergyman', a number of individuals were approached including Lord Brookeborough, the Rev. Robert Coulter and the Rev. Warren Porter, who at that time was minister of the congregations of Bellaghy and Knockloughrim, having completed his chaplaincy with the Royal Air Force. However, no successor could be decided upon at this time, nor in 1988 when Smyth again attempted to lay down the reins of office.

In 1990 a committee of senior officers and County Masters attempted to find a successor. The names of a number of possible suitable persons were tabled at a meeting on 19 November and they were accordingly written to by the Grand Secretary, Walter Williams. They included the Rev. Dr John Lockington, later to become Moderator of the General Assembly of the Presbyterian Church in Ireland. None was willing to take on this responsibility at that time and so the Rev. Martin Smyth was persuaded, not only by circumstances but by the persuasive voice of James Molyneaux, to remain in office and stand again for election.

In 1995 a similar attempt failed for different reasons. Tom Reid, the County Master of Tyrone and senior County Master, chaired a committee to search for a successor to the Grand Master. An approach was made to Clifford Forsythe, MP for South Antrim. He agreed to take the position, but the whole thing collapsed when it was realised that he had been divorced and remarried. So it was that Smyth held office until the election of Robert Saulters in 1996.

When Smyth had succeeded the ageing John Bryans as Grand Master in December 1972, there had been an air of expectancy throughout the Institution. Smyth was one of a growing number of evangelicals within the Presbyterian Church who had consistently advocated that the church should stand more firmly on her Reformed Confessional standards. There was the expectation of a similar impetus for the Institution to return to its traditional religious values.

The Rev. Martin Smyth's tenure of office unfortunately coincided with social and demographic changes which produced a steady decline in the numerical strength of the Institution, from some sixty thousand members to around forty-three thousand. Other disappointing trends became evident in these years, such as the failure of the Grand Lodge to deal with the numerous 'Clubs' within Orange Halls and so distance the Institution from the sale and consumption of alcohol. Orange Halls tend to be in the hands of management committees under the authority of trustees. While originally the local lodge or lodges may have been the controlling influence in the management of the hall, with the passage of time these connections sometimes became very loose. An increasing number of Orange Halls created facilities for the sale of alcohol by designating a room for that purpose, thereby circumventing Law 5 of the Constitution, Laws and Ordinances, 'No Lodge shall meet in premises licensed for the sale of intoxicating liquor.' Evidently this Law was being broken both in spirit and in practice. It was not the intention of earlier generations to enforce total abstinence, but to distance the Institution from alcohol and its associated social problems.

The first attempt to strengthen Law 5 took place by way of a Notice of Motion tabled on 14 June 1978 by the Rev. John Brown, Grand Master of County Antrim, to amend the law to read: 'No Lodge shall meet in premises, any portion of which is licensed for the sale of Intoxicating Liquor, or is occupied by a Licensed Club.' When this matter came up for discussion at the meeting of the Grand Orange Lodge of Ireland on 14 December 1978, the words 'or supply' were added after 'sale', on the advice of the Grand Lodge solicitors.

Notices of Motion to change Laws required either a unanimous decision of Grand Lodge, in which case it became law immediately, or three consecutive meetings of the Grand Lodge with a majority vote in favour. This motion passed its first two readings comfortably but failed on the third, with forty-five in favour and forty-seven against.

A second attempt to make the same change to Law 5 in 1987–8 failed in its second reading by sixty votes to thirty-three. This decrease in support for attempts to distance the Institution deserves explanation. If the amendment had passed, many Orange Halls would have to dismantle the social clubs attached to their premises if they wanted Orange Lodges to continue to meet there. At the first reading of this amendment the Grand Master had clearly expressed his embarrassment at the social club operating in North Belfast Orange Hall, within the bounds of the congregation of Alexandra where he had served as minister from 1963 until 1982.

Some district and county lodges instructed those who were members of the Grand Lodge to vote against this amendment at its second reading. While some might argue that this 'instruction' was a negation of civil and religious liberty and the rights of conscience, it was disappointing to note that many of those who voted against the amendment were professing evangelical Christians. The Grand Master was surprised and bewildered by the result of the vote. There were many members of the Grand Orange Lodge of Ireland who held privately to the conviction that there should not be any sale of alcohol in Orange Halls, but they evidently lacked the will to display those convictions in Grand Lodge meetings.

This was an example, to be repeated in the years to follow, of the unwillingness of the Institution to make difficult decisions. While there was an admirable aim of trying to keep everyone 'on board', there was not the realisation that keeping on board those at one end of the spectrum meant losing those at the other end. These two incidents no doubt contributed to the reduction in both quality and quantity of the membership of the Orange Institution.

It should also be noted that the second reading in 1988 coincided with the meeting of the General Assembly of the Presbyterian Church in Ireland, so that few members who were Presbyterian ministers could attend to vote. I had pointed out this coincidence of dates at the previous meeting of Grand Lodge but to no avail, although Grand Lodge had previously decided not to meet during the annual meetings of the main churches. Of course whether the attendance of Presbyterian chaplains would have made any difference to the voting is a matter of speculation.

In the spring of 1996 the Rev. Martin Smyth made it abundantly clear that he was not going to seek re-election the following December. He acquainted the Central Committee of this in good time so that they could seek out a successor. For reasons unknown the established pattern was not followed. Indeed nothing was done until the late autumn of 1996 when, after some County Grand Masters had been called together, approaches were made to Lord Brookeborough, Roy Kells and the Rev. Dr Warren Porter. The name of Denis Watson, the County Grand Master of Armagh, was circulated later as another possible candidate. I was also contacted by the Grand Secretary, John McCrea, and the Grand Treasurer, Mervyn Bishop, who asked me on 5 December to consider letting my name go forward. I can well recall my reaction, knowing that the Central Committee was to meet next morning and the Grand Lodge was due to meet the following week: 'You would need to give me a couple of weeks to think about that!' Next morning, prior to the meeting of the Central Committee, I declined.

Such was the chaotic state of the organisation that these things were left to the last possible moment. It appeared to be a matter of the County Masters sitting around and attempting to coax each other to 'take it'. Eventually Robert Saulters agreed to take it 'if nobody else will'. Accordingly his name was presented to the Central Committee and agreed. I overheard one individual, who had been a member of Central Committee since 1987, asking, 'Who is that?' Robert Saulters had been a member of Central Committee since the beginning of 1985. He was duly elected to the office of Grand Master of the Grand Orange Lodge of Ireland on 11 December 1996.

Immediately following his election, Saulters was asked at a press conference about remarks he had made the previous Twelfth, as County Grand Master of Belfast, when he accused Tony Blair, then leader of the Labour Party in opposition, of betraying his faith by marrying a Roman Catholic. He confirmed his statement that Blair was disloyal. Saulters was also asked if he would go to Harryville in Ballymena, County Antrim, to show support for the Roman Catholics who were being picketed going to Saturday evening Mass.* He said he would go if he were invited. A few days later he was invited by one of the peace groups, but declined, saying that he would go when it suited him.

It is worth remembering that the Grand Orange Lodge of Ireland at its half-yearly meeting on 11 December 1996 had responded to the intimidation of Harryville Catholics by passing the following lengthy resolution, released to the media:

> The Grand Orange Lodge of Ireland, in common with all other citizens who desire to uphold the rule of law and the principles of civil and religious liberty, deeply deplores the recent upsurge in sectarian

* See Chapter Three, pp. 53–5.

> violence and strife in the Province, manifested in the burning of Churches, Orange Halls, Schools and other property; in the eviction of families from their homes, the boycotting of businesses and the obstruction of people, Protestant and Roman Catholic, attending their places of worship. In the name of the Truth and the Faith for which we stand we utterly condemn all such actions. We are sure that all right-thinking people will join us in such condemnation. Nothing can justify activities which are in breach of the Law of God and therefore contrary to the solemn obligations to which we are all pledged.

When some individual members of the Education Committee met with the Grand Master on 3 January 1997 the projected visit to Harryville was mentioned, and he stated that he intended to go on the evening of 11 January. He invited some of us to go with him, and asked for arrangements to be made to liaise with the parish priest and the RUC. He also thought that it would be a good idea to have a banner which would state clearly and concisely that Orangemen stood for freedom to worship. He also undertook to speak to the Grand Secretary, John McCrea, and the Executive Officer, George Patton, to invite them to come as well.

When I spoke to the Grand Master and Dr Porter the evening before to confirm the arrangements, Saulters said that the parish priest did not want us and that the RUC was not happy. I contacted the parish priest, and it was confirmed that we were 'one hundred per cent welcome' and that there were no difficulties. The RUC in Ballymena also stated that they had no difficulties whatever and their opinion was that it 'would be helpful'. Someone was at work behind the scenes with what has become fashionably known as 'black propaganda', or more colloquially 'the hand of the godfather'. As part of the whispering campaign, it was being said that Dr Porter and I had 'put pressure on the Grand Master to go to Harryville'. Apparently passing resolutions is one thing but doing anything practical about them is another. It was a case of words speaking louder than actions.

On the evening of Saturday 11 January, the Grand Master went to the Church of Our Lady in Harryville, accompanied by myself and other senior Orangemen: the Rev. Dr Warren Porter, Assistant Grand Master, Colin Shilliday, Assistant Grand Treasurer and *ex officio* member of the Education Committee, the Rev. Ian McClean, Grand Chaplain of County Antrim, the Rev. Derek McMeekin, Deputy Grand Chaplain and minister of 1st Ahoghill Presbyterian Church, and Graham Montgomery, District Lecturer of Magheragall District Lodge and also a member of the

Education Committee. The Grand Secretary and the Executive Officer were unable to attend. As parishioners went in and later came out from Mass, we stood outside the Church behind the banner which read 'Orangemen support civil & religious liberty for all'. We were cordially greeted by many of the parishioners who were pleased to read the wording on the banner.

This support for the Roman Catholics of Harryville was one of those very rare occasions when the principles of the Loyal Orange Institution of Ireland were actually put into practice, but the events surrounding it still leave one in bewilderment.

Speaking to the journalist Gary Kent for an article which appeared in the *Irish Post* on 15 March, the Grand Master was asked if he thought that it would be useful if others went to Harryville. He said he thought that if Ian Paisley went, the picket would be stopped in weeks. Was he aware that Paisley had called for the protest to stop?

Photographs in the press showed some protesters wearing Orange collarettes. Very few had the courage to show their faces to the cameras, but some were identified. One individual turned out to be from a lodge in Broughshane, but the County Lodge failed to get his lodge to discipline him. The Grand Orange Lodge of Ireland subsequently passed a resolution on 11 June 1997 that 'Failure to enforce this discipline will also be recognised as defiance of superior lodge authority and will be dealt with, in accordance with the Laws and Ordinances of the Institution.' Like so many other resolutions before and since, it was not implemented.

The County Grand Orange Lodge of Antrim may not have had the will to pursue this disciplinary matter, but the civil courts certainly did. In the months to follow a number of the Harryville demonstrators appeared in Ballymena Magistrates' Court. One who was regarded as a persistent offender, Ivan Arthur Kilpatrick, was given a fifteen-month prison sentence. Others received suspended sentences and fines.

In the same *Irish Post* interview with the Grand Master, Gary Kent wrote:

> Disciplinary action is also promised against any Orange Order members who participated in Harryville pickets whilst wearing their Orange collarettes. Saulters has himself studied the photographs but has said he couldn't identify any participants. There would be definitive action by June, if not before.

This interview suggested that the new Grand Master was his own man and was willing positively to implement the resolutions of the Grand Lodge. The single act of his going to Harryville had an enormous impact on the public image of the Orange Institution worldwide. The *Sunday Times* the following day reported the event under the headline 'Orangemen march to support Catholics', quoting the Grand Master as saying: 'Our motto is civil and religious liberties and quite frankly I don't think it is right if people are intimidated like this going to their church.' The *Belfast Telegraph* on 13 January presented the event under a picture and the headline 'Freedom Protest'. The *Irish News* on the other hand, in its editorial, dismissed allegations from the Ormeau Concerned Community Group that it was a 'cynical stunt' but commented that 'Orangemen have some way to go'. A news article in the same edition was headlined 'Orangemen's support welcomed'.

Robert Saulters, formerly known as the Grand Master who had insulted the future prime minister Tony Blair, was now known as the Grand Master who went to Harryville. Unfortunately, he was later to express regret for having done so.

Things were not all sweetness and light. Some hardline members suggested that the Grand Master had broken the rules of the Institution by 'encouraging' Roman Catholics to attend Mass. Even in his own County Grand Lodge of Belfast he had to endure criticism from some small-minded members of Belfast's No. 6 District, Ballymacarrett. These 'super Prods' should have reflected on the words of Sir Edward Carson in 1921: 'I would be ashamed to lead a party who persecuted any man for his religion, just as I would not tolerate any man persecuting me because of mine.'[1]

The *Orange Standard* made reference to the Harryville incident in October 1999. The unnamed writer stated, under the headline 'Unfair media bias on Patton':

> At the time of the Harryville protest in Ballymena by loyalist elements, the Orange Order took a brave and principled stand for freedom – for civil and religious liberty – and Orangemen including the Grand Master Wor. Bro. Robert Saulters, along with County Grand officers of Antrim, and the Ulster Unionist Mayor of Ballymena, James Currie, went to Harryville to make their stand and helped to persuade their angry co-religionists to drop their protest.

Other prominent brethren who had participated with the Grand Master in his stand for civil and religious liberty at Harryville were 'airbrushed' out of history. They were out of favour. No one can tell why, but the suspicion was that they were too keen on recalling the Orange Institution to its basic principles of fraternity and tolerance, and not sufficiently committed to the confrontational policies being currently promoted.

After the courageous initiative of Harryville the Grand Master took another courageous step. On 8 February he travelled to London, accompanied by his County Secretary Tom Haire, Graham Montgomery and me, and met with Dr Ruth Dudley Edwards and the recently released IRA prisoner Sean O'Callaghan, who briefed us on IRA/Sinn Féin tactics to trap the Orange Order into confronting the security forces over the issue of parades. As Ruth Dudley Edwards made clear in *The Faithful Tribe*, it was she who arranged the meeting, 'where Sean spelled out republican strategy, laid bare the trap into which the Orange Order were falling in contentious areas and particularly in Portadown, and gave strategic and tactical advice'.[2]

On 12 April 1997 Eoghan Harris, the Irish journalist and media consultant, conducted a 'Hands-on Media Training Seminar' at the invitation of the Education Committee. As Robert Saulters undertook interviews with Eoghan it became evident that he was not going to be great at handling the media. However, throughout 1997 he continued to present a positive and moderate image of the Institution.

On 2 May the Grand Master, Denis Watson, Roy Kells and I attended a dinner in Dublin with the British Ambassador, Veronica Sutherland. Among the invited guests were Senator Pascal Mooney, Minister Joan Burton from the Department of Foreign Affairs, Liam Kavanagh, the Labour TD from Wicklow, and Sean O'Huiginn, Second Secretary at the Department of Foreign Affairs, who was later to become the Irish Ambassador to the United States.

The only hiccup that year came on the weekend of 17–18 May when it was publicly intimated that John Hume and the Grand Master intended to visit the residents on the Garvaghy Road. This had resulted from a one-to-one meeting which Saulters had had with Hume in spite of being advised not to undertake such meetings unaccompanied. In the absence of the Grand Secretary, on 19 May the Rev. Dr Warren Porter and I spent the best part of the day dealing with this situation. A press release was issued by the Grand Master in which he stated: 'There would appear to be some misunderstanding following a recent Press Release from John Hume, MP. In keeping with the Policy of Grand Lodge, I will not be meeting with anyone who has any connection with IRA/Sinn Féin.' This was the first overt indication of the Grand Master's inability to handle sensitive issues.

On 28 and 29 November 1997 Saulters attended a conference at Hatfield House, the home of the Marquess of Salisbury. The purpose of the conference was to gel together some form of Unionist unity as the negotiations at Stormont, under the chairmanship of Senator Mitchell, were drawing to a conclusion. It was the opinion of the Friends of the Union, who had organised the conference, that the Orange Order should be strongly represented, as the Institution was seen as a vehicle in which that unity might be cemented. The strong representation, which the Grand Master approved, consisted of Saulters, Dr Porter, Denis Watson, the Rev. William Bingham, Graham Montgomery, Henry Reid and me. The conference was held under 'Chatham House rules', which forbid the attribution of comments, but the Grand Master's speech on the Public Processions Bill was well received.

Prior to the Grand Lodge meeting of 11 December 1997 Robert Saulters gave an interview to Brendan O'Neill, which appeared in issue 367 (January 1998) of *Fortnight*. He said with reference to the right of the Parades Commission to decide on parades: 'This is unacceptable . . . The police should be the ones who should decide on a contested parade, not some unelected body.' This ignored completely the stated position of the chief constable that the RUC did not want to have to take decisions and then to police the decisions they had taken. Saulters is also quoted as saying: 'The Parades Commission should understand that we either have the right to do something or we do not. There can be no middle ground on the issue of rights.' Yet Canon Long had argued in Chaplains' Conference on 3 May 1997:

> The refusal to accept any restriction on Orange Order marches is not sustainable, if in the wake of that resolution there is certain to be violent confrontation, injuries, destruction of property and maybe dcaths . . . Rights arc worth maintaining but no right is without responsibility . . . The Institution is more than its public processions.

The Grand Master received a response from Alistair Graham, the chairman of the Parades Commission, in the following edition of *Fortnight*, concluding: 'I am disappointed that at this stage we should find it necessary to explain to Mr Saulters what the Commission is all about.'

At the end of 1997 Robert Saulters was persuaded to remain as Grand

Master for another year. Whatever and whoever the persuasive powers were, there was a dramatic change in his attitude as we approached the Grand Lodge meeting, and the events of 1998 were to bear little resemblance to those of 1997, as he has acknowledged to me in correspondence.

One of the Grand Master's first engagements of this New Year was a dinner I had arranged in Dublin on 26 January. Along with Denis Watson, County Armagh Grand Master, and Colin Shilliday, the Deputy Grand Treasurer, he met among others Tom Mitchell, Provost of Trinity College, John N. Kenna, the chief executive of IBEC-CBI, T. K. Whitaker, the well-known public servant and economist, and Douglas Gageby, former editor of the *Irish Times*.

Prior to the event it had been revealed in the press that 'secret' meetings had taken place involving the Grand Master and Grand Secretary and the Spirit of Drumcree faction. When some of the guests questioned the Grand Master, he expressed the opinion that relations between the Spirit of Drumcree and Grand Lodge could be resolved. This was a dramatic U-turn from his public statements following the occupation of the Grand Lodge headquarters by the Spirit of Drumcree the previous month. Similar U-turns were to follow over the next months, and years, to such an extent that no one could tell what was coming next. 'Unpredictable' and 'unreliable' are the kindest words to describe an inherently decent man's bizarre policy swings.

Saulters' credibility as a public leader took a further tumble in April 1998 when he was asked for his reaction to the Belfast Agreement. His immediate response was, 'I don't like this about the Irish language.' The Agreement contained the following:

> . . . the British Government will in particular in relation to the Irish language, where appropriate and where people so desire it:
>
> - take resolute action to promote the language;
> - facilitate and encourage the use of the language in speech and writing in public and private life where there is appropriate demand;
> - seek to remove, where possible, restrictions which would discourage or work against the maintenance or development of the language.

To many the response of the Grand Master appeared ridiculous. After all the provision for the teaching of Irish was to apply only 'where appropriate and where people so desire it'. Was this not in keeping with the respect for 'civil liberties' often proclaimed by the Institution? Like many in the Protestant community the Grand Master had allowed himself to be duped into thinking that the nationalist community was the sole custodian of the Irish language. To accept such a position was a denial of the past, when many Protestants, particularly Presbyterians, were involved in various revivals of the language. It was also an insult to his distinguished predecessor as County Grand Master of Belfast from 1885 to 1898, the Rev. Dr Richard Routledge Kane, who according to R. M. Sibbett had a 'distinguished career in the interests of Protestantism and civil and religious liberty throughout the Empire'.[3] Dr Kane was not only a great advocate of the Irish language but a patron of the Belfast Gaelic League, founded in 1895. It is said that he signed the minutes of lodge meetings in Irish. According to James Winder Good in *Ulster & Ireland*, he said, 'My Orangeism does not make me less proud to be an O'Cahan.'[4]

In *The Twelfth 1986*, published by the County Grand Orange Lodge of Belfast, Canon S. E. Long gives an excellent biography of Kane entitled 'Belfast's Orange Champion', but fails to mention his advocacy of the Irish language and his connection with the Gaelic League. Canon Long probably knew that those reading the article would have little sympathy with this important element in Kane's life. The politicising of the Irish language by ultra-nationalists has borne bitter fruit within the Unionist constituency, where prejudice has fed on the propaganda which seeks to airbrush the Irish dimension from the historical portrait of Orangeism. Dr Kane, Colonel Saunderson and their ilk would scarcely recognise the 'anti-Irish Orangeman' of the present day.

Robert Saulters may not have been an ardent student of history, but as Secretary of Belfast's No. 9 District from 1977 to 1982, he ought to have remembered that the members of 'Ireland's Heritage' LOL No. 1303, which existed in No. 9 District within Belfast County from 1970 to 1982, carried a banner with the Gaelic inscription '*Oidhreacht Éireann*'.

The Ultach Trust, whose objective is to 'widen the appreciation of the Irish language's contribution to Northern Ireland's cultural heritage and increase knowledge of the language', is totally opposed to the exclusive association of the language with any single political or religious tradition.

The Grand Master's credibility in the eyes of those inside and outside the Institution steadily decreased throughout 1998. At a press conference and photo call on 21 May, the day before the Referendum on the Belfast

Agreement, he refused to answer any questions put to him. Later in the year he was unable to give the necessary leadership after the murder of the three Quinn children in Ballymoney. At the end of July 1998 a U-turn over talking to residents' groups signalled what was to become his standard practice of statement and denial in the months and years ahead. At a Central Committee meeting on 2 October, as reported in *Sunday Life*, Saulters announced his decision to resign. This was not followed through, and was not even mentioned at the subsequent meeting of the Central Committee, on 4 December.

The Grand Orange Lodge of Ireland met on 9 December 1998 and re-elected Robert Saulters as Grand Master for the third successive year. The direction in which he was taking the Institution became more obvious with the appointment of two Assistant Grand Masters: John McCrea, who had just relinquished office as Grand Secretary, and Rodney Stewart of Ahoghill, well known for his anti-Agreement stance. The new Grand Secretary was Denis Watson, County Master of Armagh. Watson had revealed himself as a dedicated opponent of his fellow Orangeman David Trimble, and enthusiastically joined the anti-Agreement camp. He was elected to the new Northern Ireland Assembly for the term 1998–2003.

As Harold Wilson once said, 'A week is a long time in politics.' On that basis, a year in the Orange Institution is a millennium. At the end of his first year of office Saulters was being applauded by the press for the projection of a moderate image, particularly after the occupation of the House of Orange by the Spirit of Drumcree. Twelve months and many indecisions later the estimate of his leadership was very different. How and why the change took place is a matter of speculation. Until his return from the Hatfield House conference at the end of November 1997 Saulters was what many regarded as his 'natural self', moderate and unassuming, the typical decent Ulsterman. After Hatfield House, the questions being asked by those close to him were: has someone got at him? Has he been threatened with resignation by some of his senior officers? It was certainly known that he had been at loggerheads with John McCrea, who had not only attempted to keep him out of negotiations with the Spirit of Drumcree faction but was perceived by many to be trying to straitjacket him.

His change in attitude did not go unnoticed by the press. In the *Belfast Morning Telegraph* of 19 December 1998, Larry White may have had in mind the words of the nineteenth-century French politician Alexandre Auguste Ledru-Rollin, 'Ah well! I am their leader, I really had to follow them,' when he listed his 'awards' for 1998. His second award was 'A compass' for Saulters, 'so that he can see which way the institution is going before he makes any decision'.

As the final year of the millennium began the Grand Master attended various Installation functions. One such was the Installation of the officers of County Fermanagh Grand Lodge in January 1999, where Roy Kells was the new County Master. Was it simply blindness which led the Grand Master to declare on that occasion, 'The Institution has never been more united than it is today'?

The public performance of Robert Saulters throughout 1999 did not add to the integrity of the Institution. On leaving the Apprentice Boys Memorial Hall in Londonderry following the Grand Lodge meeting on 2 June, he was asked by a reporter if he believed that there was an 'absolute right' to march. He replied that there was. Such a comment displayed a lack of knowledge. Was the Grand Master not aware that he was contradicting the Institution's own publication, *The Case Against the Parades Commission*, which acknowledged that 'absolute freedom of assembly could lead to chaos and anarchy and there must be checks on it'?

In all fairness we must assume that he was aware of the Strategy Committee's document. That being so, however, other questions arise. Did he not accept its affirmations, or did he not understand its implications? Other documents would have given the same message. In June 1998 the General Assembly of the Presbyterian Church in Ireland had passed a resolution, 'The issue about parades and protests has to do with conflict between two groups of people holding to two sets of rights, neither one of which is absolute.' This was a reflection of Biblical teaching. A fundamental tenet of Protestant Reformed theology is that man has no absolute rights. Life itself is a gift of the grace of God. The only 'absolute right' is damnation! This is affirmed in Article 9 of the Thirty-Nine Articles of the Church of Ireland and in Question 84 of the Shorter Catechism.

The report of February 2001 by Brian Currin and the opinion by Austen Morgan in March 2001 would both also affirm that the right to parade/march was not absolute. The Northern Ireland Human Rights Commission would also examine the European Convention on Human Rights and report in March 2001 that the Orange Order had no 'absolute' right under European law.

This being so, Saulters' support for the Long March at the June 1999 Grand Lodge meeting was another act of gross ill judgement. He may well have been right in claiming that it was 'the only show in town', but that does not necessarily mean that it was worthy of support. The continued public perception of the Long March as an 'anti-Agreement March' further committed the Institution to the projection of a continuing negative image.

Saulters' interviews with the media in June and July 1999 caused confusion and consternation. On the evening of 5 July 1999, in an interview on Downtown Radio, he suggested, as he had done previously in July 1998, that he would favour talking to residents' groups. He repeated this in an interview on the Ulster Television programme 'Insight' the following evening, saying that he would 'call the bluff' of the residents' groups and talk to them. An Orange Order spokesman said the next day, 'Mr Saulters has stated that he has been misquoted in the context of a much longer interview': another example of 'statement and denial'.

The reputation of the Institution suffered yet again, but during subsequent meetings of Central Committee and Grand Lodge these embarrassing public retractions of the Grand Master were never mentioned. Neither of course was the spoof interview by the comedian Sacha Baron Cohen, aka 'Ali G', with the Executive Officer, George Patton, first broadcast on Channel 4 and often repeated since, to the detriment of the image of the Institution. Such was now the self-denial evident within the Orange Institution that many of its leading figures seemed to be living in a world of make-believe.

There were no further major public pronouncements from the Grand Master in 1999. Those in charge managed to keep him on the approved path, and the meeting of Grand Lodge on 8 December saw him returned for his fourth term of office. The media largely ignored the event. The Institution progressed into the new millennium apparently having learned none of the lessons of the past and ill-prepared for the future. A policy of inertia had taken control. One prominent Orangeman commented to me at the end of 1999: 'It is not historians who will be researching the Orange Order in the future, it will be forensic scientists.'

Saulters' 'misunderstandings' continued throughout 2000, most noticeably when he said on 13 July in an interview with Mark Simpson for BBC Northern Ireland that the Drumcree protests should be called off as they served no useful purpose. When the press sought further comment the following day, 'no one was available'.

The sterility and uncertainty of the leadership was further revealed by the events of the Grand Lodge meeting on 3 February 2001. Saulters had originally asked Brian Currin to present his report personally to the Grand Lodge, but later asked him to submit a written presentation instead. Saulters undertook to circulate this for discussion, but when the document was delivered no such circulation or discussion took place. The *Belfast Telegraph* of 22 February reported:

> Orange chief executive George Patton said today that Grand Master Robert Saulters told Grand Lodge members about the report and 'they weren't terribly interested'. But that contrasts with an explanation given by Grand Lodge Secretary Denis Watson, who said the document 'was not considered by the Grand Master and his team because of the late stage it was presented to us'.

The leadership were obviously embarrassed and took steps to cover their tracks. In an interview with Mervyn Jess for the BBC on 30 March marking a thousand days of the Drumcree protest, Saulters said that he had only received Currin's document 'half an hour before the meeting'. Mervyn Jess did not ask if he was unaware of the content of the document, nor why the Grand Lodge Office or the Grand Secretary had not passed it on to him if, as *Sunday World* had reported on 11 February, copies had been delivered to the Grand Secretary the day before the meeting. *Sunday World* had further reported:

> Top Orangeman Robert Saulters told us yesterday: 'There was no point in presenting it. The first six pages were all about discussions with the Garvaghy Road committee. There was no point in presenting that to the Grand Lodge. It would have been irrelevant.' . . . He said a decision was taken not to present what was meant as a discussion document.

One of the most significant events during the reign of Robert Saulters was an addition of a new paragraph to Law 13. At the meeting of the Grand Lodge on 30 September 2000, the Grand Master proposed a Notice of Motion to amend Law 13 to read:

> The Grand Master of the Grand Orange Lodge of Ireland shall be empowered to suspend or expel from the Institution any member of the Grand Lodge who has offended against the Institution as a whole, in his judgement. In that eventuality the member so suspended or expelled shall have the right to appeal to the Grand Committee and notice of his

> intention to appeal must be communicated in writing to the Grand Secretary within 7 days of the decision having been communicated to him.

This Notice of Motion was formally proposed by the Grand Master at the next meeting of the Grand Lodge on 13 December 2000, seconded by Robert McIlroy, the County Antrim Grand Master. Because seven voted against it, a second reading was given at the next meeting of the Grand Lodge on 5 May 2001, when nine voted against. The third and final reading was on 13 June 2001, when it passed by ninety-eight votes to eight with three abstentions.

The passing of this Law indicated the depths to which the leadership of the Orange Institution had stooped. Not only was it contrary to the principle of natural justice to suspend or expel members without a hearing, but it displayed a distinctive lack of knowledge of what the Institution really stood for. It was not unlike the powers once taken upon himself by a certain King James II to imprison without trial, to suspend laws, to dismiss judges without a hearing. The freedom-loving peoples of these islands were fortunate three hundred years ago that a young prince called William came along to stop him before he went too far!

By this single act the combined leadership of the Orange Institution had betrayed the memory of William III, Prince of Orange. They had in effect become Jacobites, betraying the whole concept of Orangeism. This was the establishment of the principle of the 'Divine Right', not of kings, but of the Grand Master.

There had been a previous attempt to give similar power to the Grand Master in June 1983. In that case wiser counsels had prevailed, but such was now the constituency of the Grand Orange Lodge of Ireland that there was no one to give such counsel or refer to the precedent of 1983, let alone speak forcibly against the change.

The Grand Master exercised this new power on 5 June 2003. He suspended David McNarry from membership of the Institution 'for a serious breach' of Law 10, which states: 'Any member who speaks on radio or television must first obtain permission from one or more of the Grand Master, Deputy Grand Master, Grand Secretary, or Executive Officer of the Grand Orange Lodge of Ireland.' David McNarry had said on BBC Radio Ulster on 4 June that many Orange Halls had difficulty getting insurance cover. This suspension was not to last long. Following the exchange of correspondence between his solicitor and the Grand Lodge, David McNarry received a letter from the Grand Lodge's legal adviser, David Brewster, towards the end of August, advising him that the suspension was lifted with immediate effect.

Ironically the Grand Lodge of Ireland which had given this power to the Grand Master included in its membership the self-same David McNarry. In that sense he was a victim of his own decision.

Drumcree Sunday 2002 was worse in public relations terms than anything that had gone before. The violence which erupted after the service of worship led to the arrest of fifteen individuals, most of whom were members of the Institution. This was followed by the now customary promises of discipline.

I responded to various invitations from the media and contributed articles to the *Irish Times* and the *Irish News* in which I endeavoured to uphold the authentic values of Orangeism.[5] I pointed out that contradictory messages were being sent out to a disbelieving world and that previous promises of discipline had come to nothing. To expect discipline now was 'hope triumphing over experience', and 'I for one [would] not be holding my breath'. I also called for discipline to be public, in order to restore credibility in the Protestant and Unionist community.

After I addressed the triannual conference of the Ancient Order of Hibernians in September, I received a letter dated 2 October from the Grand Master, which accused me of 'sniping at the Institution and Grand Lodge Officers in particular'. Most of this letter made little sense and I therefore responded asking the Grand Master for 'an honest face-to-face discussion on a one-to-one basis'. Saulters wrote in reply that he had asked seven questions in his first letter, to which he would welcome a response, but because I considered the original letter to be grammatically unintelligible and intellectually incomprehensible I responded with certain caveats.

Evidently my reply did not satisfy the Grand Master. I received a letter on 1 March 2003 instructing me to attend a meeting of Central Committee on 14 March. The letter said that 'The Members of Central Committee are seeking clarification from you in respect of comments made in correspondence to Grand Lodge Officers and newspaper articles attributed to you.' I responded asking for details of these 'comments', 'in order to facilitate a productive meeting'. Although no response was made to my request, I attended the meeting on 14 March.

The Grand Master and other members made limited attempts to deal with the substance of what I had written. They also raised the interpretation of Law 10, contrary to the letter of instruction to attend, of which they had to be reminded several times. None of the questions put during the forty-minute meeting indicated any lack of understanding of what I had written either in correspondence or in newspaper articles. I can only conclude that clarification was not the issue, and that it was an attempt to intimidate me.

I received another letter from the Grand Secretary, Denis Watson, on 27 March in which he drew my attention to Law 10 and accused me of making 'inaccurate statements'. He said that he had enclosed 'a copy of procedures', but there was no enclosure with the letter. I replied dealing with these issues and again offered to meet privately, in a spirit of brotherhood, with any member of the Central Committee. No response ever came, although I repeated this correspondence a month later, on 12 May 2003.

Robert Saulters' re-election for the ninth successive year on 8 December 2004 was accompanied by changes in the leadership team. In an unprecedented event, Denis Watson was challenged and defeated, by seventy-eight votes to forty-one, for the office of Grand Secretary by Drew Nelson, a Banbridge solicitor. A year later, with no one else apparently willing to take the post, Saulters was unopposed and confirmed in office again. By then Drew Nelson's elevation could be seen as clearly progressing the Institution's move in the direction from 'faith' towards 'culture' that had steadily accelerated during the years Saulters was 'in office but not in power'.

Chapter Eleven

'Egg on our Face': the Referendum

'If a house is divided against itself, that house cannot stand.'

Jesus (Mark 3:25)

The crucial weaknesses within the Institution became even more apparent during the Referendum debate on the Belfast Agreement in 1998, creating bitterness which still prevails.

More than one member of Central Committee counselled that caution should be exercised lest this issue become divisive within the Order. It was pointed out that if the Order appeared to give direction to its members on how to vote, and it then transpired that the directions were not followed, we could end up with 'egg on our face'. There was some historical precedent for this advice.

One of the first major issues to confront the Grand Orange Lodge of Ireland after it was formed in 1798 was the abolition of the Irish parliament by the Act of Union of 1801, which united the parliaments of Great Britain and Ireland. This was a direct result of the failed United Irishmen's rebellion of 1798. The Irish parliament was far removed from a democratic parliament in twenty-first century terms. The franchise was restricted to those who held a forty-shilling freehold, regardless of religion.

The Institution at large was divided on the issue of the Act of Union. Many of the aristocratic brethren held seats in the Irish parliament, yet this did not prevent a special meeting of Grand Lodge on 13 December 1798 declaring:

> . . . that as many persons who are enemies of the Orange Institution have endeavoured to injure and divide it by involving us in debates on political questions, particularly by the present question of the Union, that the Masters of the different lodges in Dublin are entreated to discourage as much as possible any discussion or decision in their respective lodges upon that or any other political subject as such

> conduct must tend to create division and produce injury and ruin to the Institution.[1]

R. M. Sibbett claims in *Orangeism*, though he does not identify his source, that at the end of 1798 when legislative union was first mooted Grand Lodge advised those under its jurisdiction

> . . . strictly to abstain from expressing any opinion pro or con upon the question of a Legislative Union between this country and Great Britain, because that such expression of opinion, and such discussion in Lodges could only lead to disunion; that disunion might lead to disruption; and the disruption of the Society in the existing crisis would but promote the designs of the disaffected, and, in all human probability, lead to the dismemberment of the Empire.

Sibbett also points out, 'At the same time, the brethren were informed that, as citizens of a free state, they were at liberty to act at they pleased in regard to the question.'[2] Obviously the founding fathers of the Orange Institution took the principles of civil and religious liberty seriously, unlike some in leadership today.

The quality of the leadership was such in 1798 that although the majority of the members of Grand Lodge probably would have opposed the Act of Union, they had the wisdom and courage to act for the good of the Institution as a whole. Two of the major influential figures within the Institution in these early years stood in opposite camps on the issue. Thomas Verner, the Grand Master of Ireland, representing the northern gentry, favoured the Act of Union while John Claudius Beresford, the Grand Secretary, was opposed to it. Probably most Irish Protestants in 1800 tended to see their parliament as a protection of their position. Had such wisdom and courage been displayed concerning the Referendum debate on the Belfast Agreement much hurt, anger and division could have been avoided.

When the Agreement was reached in Belfast on Good Friday, 10 April 1998, the politics of Ulster divided in usual form – for and against! The Central Committee of the Grand Lodge met the following day to make preparations for the Grand Lodge meeting on 15 April. It did not require great powers of historical analysis to see where we were. Twenty-five years previously Unionists had been asked to share power with the SDLP, a non-violent nationalist party, but refused. The power-sharing executive had been brought down by street violence. A quarter of a century on,

Unionists were being asked to share power with Republicans. If as a community they refused this time round, where would they be in another twenty-five years' time? They would not be asked to share power with anyone! As I thought of sharing these sentiments with Central Committee I was encouraged to hear another member of Central Committee make exactly the same comment without any prompting.

I drew the historical parallel of the 1880s, when the Protestants of Ulster briefly flirted with Parnell's Land League out of self-interest. The Protestants of Ulster were just as interested as their southern neighbours in the 'three Fs': fair rent, fixity of tenure and freedom to sell. They supported Parnell in spite of being urged not to do so by their leadership. In fact, in the County Tyrone by-election of 1881 the radical Liberal T. A. Dixon, who evidently had the support of Orangemen, defeated the County Grand Master Colonel W. S. Knox.

It was pointed out that self-interest would take precedence over everything else in this referendum. If its proposals received widespread support we would look very foolish if we were seen to oppose it. When I spoke to the Grand Master after the meeting he admitted quite frankly that if we opposed the Belfast Agreement we could indeed have 'egg on our face'.

The two most difficult aspects of the Belfast Agreement, not only for those within the Orange Institution but for all who had a respect for law and order, were the possibility of the inclusion of Sinn Féin in government and the early release of prisoners. Of these two, it was the second which people found most difficult to stomach. Selective memory, if not an ignorance of history, had overlooked previous early releases as a result of the end of hostilities, but those who understood that reasoning still found it repulsive in the extreme to contemplate the release of vicious criminals, most of whom showed no sign of remorse.

Dr Eamon Phoenix, in an article in the *Belfast Telegraph* on 21 April headlined 'Prisoners still hold the key 80 years on', reminded all concerned of various releases in the past, from the early release of the three thousand interned and ninety-seven sentenced to life imprisonment as a result of the Easter Rising of 1916, to those released as part of the negotiations for a truce in 1921 and a result of the historic pact of 30 March 1922 between Michael Collins and Sir James Craig. In this pact they agreed to 'arrange for the release of political prisoners for offences committed before the date thereof'. The Tripartite Agreement of 3 December 1925 between London, Dublin and the Northern Ireland government paved the way for the release of IRA prisoners within six months. As a result of the murder of an RUC constable in 1942, six IRA men were convicted and sentenced to death. One was executed and five had their sentences commuted to life imprisonment, but were released by 1950. They included Joe Cahill, who was to stand as a Sinn Féin candidate in North Antrim in the Assembly Elections in June 1998. Brian Faulkner, as minister of home affairs in the Northern Ireland government, released those interned as a result of the IRA campaign of 1956–62 almost a year *before* the IRA officially ended its campaign. Dr Phoenix concluded: 'Understandably, the release of prisoners responsible for many heinous crimes poses a difficult moral dilemma for many citizens. Yet the modern history of Northern Ireland suggests such releases have been a central part of government policy since the 1920s.'

The release of prisoners may have been a bitter pill to swallow, but there was a historic precedent – or as they say in some circles, it was traditional. All this fell on deaf ears. The television media did not take the subject up with any degree of intensity, perhaps because of the abundance of news coverage of other relevant events. The population of Northern Ireland, who had suffered so much, were on an emotional wave and understandably reason could all too easily give way to prejudice. As Samuel Johnson put it: 'Prejudice, not being founded on reason, cannot be removed by argument.' I would want to rephrase that quotation to read: 'Prejudice, not being founded on reason, cannot be removed by argument – only by grace.'

In the run-up to the Grand Lodge meeting on 15 April 1998 there was much speculation in the press. In *Sunday Life* on 15 March the Executive Officer, George Patton, was quoted as saying that the Orange Order 'will recommend a "yes" or "no" vote, depending on the outline of any proposal put to the electorate'. Later on he made it clear that he was going to vote 'No' and would be giving his complete support to the 'No' campaign.

In a front-page article in the *Belfast Telegraph* on 13 April, Paul Connolly and Noel McAdam wrote: 'Further pressure on Mr Trimble may come on Wednesday when around 120 members of the Grand Orange Lodge of Ireland vote on the Agreement. Both Unionist and Orange sources predict the Lodge – the Orange Order's ruling body – will vote against the deal effectively making it official Orange policy.' The following evening, in what appeared to be an attempt to present a different picture, an article by Noel McAdam and Martina Purdy wrote:

> Belfast Grand Master [*sic*] John McCrea said: 'The whole basis of the Institution is civil and religious liberty, so it is very difficult for the

> Lodge to tell its members exactly how to vote. It has to be for everyone's conscience. I am still studying the document but I have several reservations and would like more convincing particularly in areas like the north–south bodies and prisoner releases.'

This on the face of it was a very encouraging statement, in line with the attitude of our forefathers in 1800. But there is a certain inconsistency, if not contradiction, between McCrea's statement and George Patton's. The uncertainty was to get worse. While there often appears to be 'fog' surrounding any attitude expressed by the Orange Institution, this was to be an extraordinary confusion.

At the meeting of Grand Lodge on 15 April there was a very tense atmosphere. A press release was read to the media which included the statement: 'The Grand Orange Lodge of Ireland takes note of the acceptance by the participants to the talks process of the document of 10th April 1998 but failing clarification of certain vital issues cannot recommend it to the people of Ulster.' More details of the meeting were communicated in the *Belfast Telegraph* on 16 April:

> Lord Molyneaux proposed that the Order seek clarification on aspects of the agreement such as decommissioning . . . someone called for a 'No' and this was overwhelmingly rejected despite having the support of Joel Patton. Twenty voted for the 'No' but 73 voted against it . . . The Orangemen were not prepared to throw the agreement out.

The *Belfast Telegraph*'s interpretation was quite correct. The Grand Orange Lodge of Ireland did not come out against the Agreement. Some interpreted the resolution delivered in the press release on 15 April as a NO vote. This interpretation was patently wrong, in the light of the fact that the resolution put as an amendment to the meeting that 'This Grand Lodge says NO to the Agreement' was, according to the Grand Lodge Report, lost by seventy votes to twenty two. That was and remained the official position of the Grand Orange Lodge of Ireland, the ruling body of the Institution, which was never recalled to review its decision.

There were those within the Order who would not accept the democratic decision of the meeting. Ironically, these 'super-loyalists' were actually following in the Gaelic Republican tradition of Eamon de Valéra. In the 1920s he likewise had continued to oppose a democratically reached decision, even though he had undertaken to accept the Treaty agreed by the Irish delegation to London, providing the cabinet accepted it also. When the cabinet did so, he reneged, claiming that he would accept it if it was endorsed by Dáil Éireann. When the Dáil endorsed it he still refused to accept it, and said that he would accept it if the country approved it in an election. When the country overwhelmingly accepted the Treaty, de Valéra still refused to accept the majority vote of the Irish people, and led the Free State into civil war. Not for the first time the historically minded observer could see where extremes can meet.

After the vote which forestalled the specific rejection of the Belfast Agreement had been taken, Joel Patton and some others, including visitors, left the meeting and addressed reporters outside on the Shankill Road. Patton affirmed with typical vehemence that if the Grand Lodge officers were not going to give leadership, he would. Signs of such leadership appeared later that evening when a number of people, including at least one in Orange regalia, picketed the home of Ken Maginnis, MP for Fermanagh and South Tyrone. According to the *Belfast Telegraph* on 16 April, 'Mr Patton confirmed it was his supporters who picketed Ken Maginnis' Dungannon home last night and defended the move because it was a "peaceful protest".'

It is a great pity that those who call for democracy do not always submit to the democratically expressed will! It is clear that for them, democracy is 'my way or no way'.

The Ulster Unionist Party executive had meanwhile endorsed the Belfast Agreement by a majority of some seventy-one per cent. Two days after the meeting of Grand Lodge on 15 April, the Ulster Unionist Council, made up of some eight hundred delegates, endorsed the Agreement by a majority of 540 to 210, a seventy-two per cent vote in favour. Given that the Council had up to 113 delegates coming directly from the Loyal Orange Institution and that many of the other delegates from the branches were also members of the Order, it would be fair to estimate that at least half of the Orange delegates had voted in favour of the Agreement. There is little reason to doubt that a similar proportion voted in favour at the actual Referendum.

The public perception of the position of the Orange Order at this stage, in the run-up to the Referendum, was that it was opposed to the Agreement. Even the normally perceptive Paul Connolly of the *Belfast Telegraph* failed to spot the camouflage used by elements in the Grand Lodge hierarchy to mask the real state of affairs. On 2 May he wrote: 'The Order's rejection of the Good Friday Agreement after a Grand Lodge meeting yesterday was seen as a blow to the Yes campaign.' But there was no meeting of the 'Grand Lodge' on 1 May. There was a meeting of District Masters on that date, when soundings were taken as to the attitude of the membership, but neither District Masters nor County Masters can make policy for the Institution. Only the Grand Orange Lodge of Ireland has the right and authority to do that. Grand Lodge Officers may have made a decision, County Masters may have made a decision, but 'Grand Lodge' never met to make any further decision on the Belfast Agreement after 15 April 1998.

On 27 April the Grand Secretary, John McCrea, wrote to David Trimble, leader of the Ulster Unionist Party. His letter expressed the opinions of 'Grand Lodge', as if the Grand Lodge had met and discussed the various issues raised. This of course was not the case. As Trimble's reply was not sent until 5 May it could not have been considered at the meeting of District Masters on 1 May. For the record, this reply in which Trimble answers McCrea's concerns under his original headings is reproduced here:

> Dear John,
>
> You wrote to me on 27 April expressing the concerns of Grand Lodge about the Stormont Agreement. I have set out below detailed responses to each of those concerns. Could I preface them with some general remarks?
>
> Any negotiated arrangement will involve pluses and minuses. The real question concerns the balance that is struck at the end of the day. There are important gains for us in the Stormont Agreement.
>
> The Irish territorial claim will disappear. Dublin will be recognising, not just the existence of Northern Ireland, but its legitimacy, accepting that it is for the people of Northern Ireland alone to determine its status. For these reasons alone it is right to say that the Union has been strengthened.
>
> Moreover direct rule, which has done so much to undermine the Union, will end. In its place will come an Assembly, in which our elected representatives will take decisions which hitherto were taken by persons who were not accountable to us. Of course it is not a return to simple majority rule. There will be vetoes, but every nationalist veto will be matched by a unionist veto. Until now there has been an indirect nationalist veto exercised through Maryfield and unionists were helpless. The British Isles body is also a gain being an explicitly unionist concept.
>
> There are uncertainties for the future, as if the future was ever anything but uncertain. The question is can we cope with the

challenges of these uncertainties better with the institutions of the Stormont Agreement than without them. I sometimes think that unionists have become so accustomed over the last 25 years to defeat that they cannot cope with the possibility that they might have achieved something. It is also a problem that we lack so much confidence in ourselves. We do not have to assume that all future developments will be negative. We must be prepared to get off our knees and take on the problems, believing that we can cope with them.

The Stormont Agreement does not solve all our problems. It is not a unionist wish list. But it creates a platform which we can occupy and use in order to make further advances. Having been salami sliced by others, can we not turn the slicer round?

We should also not overlook the significance of showing moderate nationalists that we think there is a place for them too in Northern Ireland. Repeatedly at UUC conferences and AGMs I have talked of the superiority of the Union as a place where different identities can live together within a genuinely multi-national and multi-cultural state. It is true. We should draw confidence from the multi-faceted strength of our Union and its ability to attract others.

The following were your main concerns together with my comments thereon:

1. (a) Decommissioning

We want decommissioning. We have always wanted it. But it will not be achieved unless the government insists on it. Last June the new government changed its position. We recognised at the time that that was a set-back for us. We engaged on a detailed consultation to decide what our response should be, and as you know the Party collectively decided that we would not let this set-back drive us out of the talks.

In the Stormont Agreement matters have improved to the extent that there is now a time frame for the completion of decommissioning and the government has said that it should begin immediately. The need for decommissioning is also explicitly cross-referenced to involvement in the administration.

(b) [Author's note: here reference is made to a paragraph which would appear in the final Agreement. David Trimble's reply clarifies the numbering of paragraphs which McCrea had queried.]

2. RUC

At the Party Executive on 9 April, I advised that the Commission would be along the lines of a Royal Commission with an international element. The appointment of an establishment figure in the shape of Chris Patten confirms that expectation. The really important issue is preserving the integrity of the RUC. You will have noted the public commitments by the Secretary of State and the Prime Minister that paramilitaries are not about to be recruited into a two tier police force. We will have, however, to continue to be vigilant on this issue as it was and will be an issue irrespective of talks or agreements.

As Ken Maginnis MP has been warning for years there are elements in the NIO who see the sacrifice of the RUC as a way of appeasing paramilitaries. It is for this reason that we are opposing the Police Bill that is currently going through Parliament. This Bill is perhaps just as big a problem for the RUC as the Commission.

3. Assembly

Strand One does indeed contain safeguards that go beyond those in the Welsh and Scottish Bills, and, realistically, it was not and will not be possible to restore a local assembly without some safeguards. The special voting provisions on key issues provide that on such issues a decision must be supported by at least 40% of nationalists and 40% of unionists. This carries with it the danger of deadlock. But there is a unionist veto as well as a nationalist veto. At present the Northern Ireland Office takes all decisions, subject to an indirect nationalist veto operating through Maryfield. There is, at present, no unionist veto at all, but under this there will be a unionist veto on all issues.

The general words of the pledge of office have to be read in the light of the particular provision in paragraph 2 of Strand Two. The latter reads, 'If a holder of a relevant post will not participate normally in the Council . . . The First and Deputy First Minister . . . to be able to make alternative arrangements.' This sentence was inserted at our insistence precisely to avoid giving certain members the opportunity to make a martyr of themselves.

4. Prisoners

We share Grand Lodge's distaste for prisoner release. But we recognised that this was outside our power to affect. As you know it is hedged with various safeguards and that approximately one third of the prisoners affiliated to qualifying groups would be released anyway over the next two years. In the event of a genuine peace this is not without precedent, including similar action by Unionist governments, though they did it without publicity! In any event a 'no' vote will not prevent a similar scheme being introduced if government think it expedient in the future.

5. Sinn Féin in administration

We too are opposed to the suggestion that unrepentant terrorists be included in any administration. It would be contrary to the clear text of the agreement. See the commitment to non-violence and exclusively peaceful and democratic means in the Pledge of Office (page 10), and the requirement that those who do not use only democratic non-violent means be excluded or removed from office (para 25, page 8, to which the need for decommissioning on page 20 is expressly crossed [*sic*] referenced (para 1)).

We recognise the concern that these requirements could be fudged. Indeed governments have fudged such matters in the past. But this is different. We will be there. It will require our involvement. We can if necessary simply say no and walk away. We would like, however, to solve the problem without having to walk away. That is why we obtained an undertaking, from the Prime Minister, to which we will hold him. As was said to the Ulster Unionist Council, we do not intend to serve alongside unrepentant terrorists and we intend to be the judge of what constitutes one.

6. Cultural issues

Paragraph 5 on page 20 is, to put it mildly, pretty meaningless. 'Sensitivity' and 'mutual respect' have no necessary meaning. 'Arrangements will be made' – what arrangements? – made by whom? This is a battle to be fought in the future. The battle cannot be avoided, for these issues will arise whatever we do. The question is, will we be better placed to succeed with an Assembly or without one?

7. Dublin role

The North/South Ministerial Council (NSMC) does not in itself have any power. No functions are devolved to it. It is simply a place where Ministers meet. Ministers may have power. But they do so by virtue of their own elected body, i.e. the Assembly. In the NSMC Ministers cannot do whatever they like. The Agreement is quite clear on this. 'All operating in accordance with the rules for democratic authority and accountability in force in the Northern Ireland Assembly . . .' (Para 2, page 11, see also para 6, page 12 which emphasises need for 'defined authority' and need for approval if any departure from defined authority).

These are the procedures for agreeing any scheme for co-operation. Co-operation in itself has never been controversial within unionism, if there is a mutual benefit. Of course a scheme for co-operation has to be implemented. This is a job for officials acting through existing channels for specifically created quangos (implementation bodies). Such quangos are not and would not become political bodies, and all would be accountable to the NI Assembly. They are the same concept as the Carlingford Lough Commission, Foyle Fisheries or the joint committee that ran the Belfast Dublin railway in the fifties.

8. British Irish Council

This is a totally different concept to the Anglo-Irish Agreement. The idea of a British Isles wide body was first mooted by Sir John Biggs Davison and promoted by him and Martin Smyth under the name of Islands of the North Atlantic (IONA). Replacing the Diktat by such a body has been party policy since 1987. The Council is a purely consultative body to facilitate discussion and co-operation. I believe that it will be welcomed by the new devolved institutions in Cardiff and Edinburgh, and it will enable us to put matters suggested for north/south co-operation in their proper context where appropriate. Perhaps the most significant aspect is the fact that the Irish Republic is coming into a British Isles based body where it will be developing a relationship with all the constituent elements of the United Kingdom.

The creation of a secretariat to service the British Irish Council is not significant. Maryfield is significant because in addition to servicing meetings of the Intergovernmental Conference it was the channel by which Dublin exerted influence on NIO policies and public appointments. It could do this because the Anglo-lrish Agreement gave Dublin the right to act on these matters. Those parts of the Anglo-Irish Agreement are not in the Stormont Agreement. Dublin has lost its right to influence appointments and the policies of the NI departments. The only hangover is in relation primarily to security co-operation (paras 5 to 7 on page 15) and how the Assembly will be represented. Most of Dublin's role has been eliminated and what little remains now continues in our presence. Ten years ago we would have been delighted to have achieved so much.

9. Signature

The appearance of the words 'of Ireland' after Northern Ireland on page 29 is a misprint. The words do not appear in the final text of the

> Agreement as approved at Stormont on 11 April nor do they appear in the Command Paper presented to Parliament last week (Cm. 3883).
>
> I am also attaching some relevant papers. The prisoner release scheme, a memorandum on constitutional matters and the two letters from the Prime Minister. I appreciate you may have seen these before but it may be handy to have them again.
>
> Finally may I wish the Grand Master and the Grand Lodge delegation all the best for the meeting with the Prime Minister on Thursday.

The contents of this letter, and even the fact that it had been received, were not disclosed to Grand Lodge. Like other correspondence, it entered the 'big black hole'. A copy was sent privately to me and later authenticated by David Trimble.

The front page of the *Orange Standard*, 'the official newspaper of the Grand Orange Lodge of Ireland', of May 1998 carried a five-inch headline: the single word 'NO'. The article under the headline presented the case for voting 'No' in the Referendum: 'As it presently stands, the agreement reached at Stormont on April 10 is something which very few unionists, if they are patently honest, could live with.'

Denis Watson, the County Grand Master of Armagh, also appeared to embrace 'de Valéran' democracy. A member of the Ulster Unionist Party's executive, which had initially endorsed the Agreement by seventy-one per cent, he decided to stand in David Trimble's constituency as a 'No' candidate in the Assembly Elections which were to be held in the month after the Referendum. Watson's contribution to the Institution had been enormous, but this reduced his credibility considerably. The fact that such a high-profile Orangeman should stand for election in clear opposition to the leader of the Ulster Unionist Party, himself a brother in the Order, further added to the confusion as to the attitude of the Institution to the Belfast Agreement.

Watson was subsequently elected for the Upper Bann constituency to the Assembly whose existence he opposed. Under the proportional representation system he had required some four hundred of David Trimble's transfer votes in order to succeed.

He was not alone in making his position clear on this issue. The Rev. Dr Warren Porter, Grand Chaplain, came out in support of the Belfast Agreement. Interviewed for the *Sunday Observer* on 17 May, he said: 'I support [the deal] because the constitutional position of Northern Ireland is safeguarded and it opens the door to peace.' In the *Irish Times* on 19 May, he stated:

> The paranoia about the Belfast Agreement which is gripping a section of Orangeism at the present time is being fed by scare-mongering on the part of some who should know better . . . there are areas in the document which arouse genuine feelings of revulsion in many hearts, and no doubt those feelings are not confined to members of the pro-Union community. Nobody seems to be entirely happy about every aspect of the agreement. Yet . . . many Orangemen are going to be in the yes camp.

Once again in rather strange circumstances, the *Belfast Telegraph* informed the world on 2 May that the Executive Officer, George Patton, had revealed that the 'Order had been seeking to speak to Mr Blair since last July'. The prime minister apparently was 'very keen' to meet the Orange Order, but 'sources today blamed a "breakdown in communication" over the affair'. Such a 'breakdown in communication' was an all too common excuse at that period.

The front-page article also revealed the Executive Officer's personal opinion that such a meeting 'is not necessary . . . I have had enough clarification after listening very carefully to what has been said in parliament and other places.' Yet, the article stated, 'Leading Orangeman David McNarry issued a statement urging the Order to meet Mr Blair.' In the event a meeting with the prime minister in London was hurriedly arranged for 7 May. In the light of the conflict of opinion between George Patton and David McNarry, some wondered just which was the Executive Officer. It ought to be borne in mind that the Executive Officer was the paid official of the Institution and that, as we had been frequently told, he had no opinion in his official capacity.

George Patton's remarks in a radio interview on the morning of 2 May caused at least one member to resign in protest. The Rev. John Dickinson, a member of a lodge in County Down and a Deputy Grand Chaplain of the Grand Orange Lodge of Ireland, wrote in his resignation letter:

> Over the last three or four years I have struggled as a Christian with the things which have been exercising our movement. I have managed to cope with the sense of shame I have felt at the events of successive Drumcrees and with the frustration caused by the shortsighted policy

> adopted over contact with the Parades Commission. The final straw came this morning when I awoke to hear George Patton on the radio news telling me that the Orange Order has decided that it is opposed to the Agreement. I particularly resent his comment that no true loyalist can vote 'yes'. If he is speaking for the Order, what happened to the idea that we are a brotherhood and a broad church?
>
> Over the last fourteen years or so of my membership, wherever I have gone in Orange circles North and South of the border, I have found only friendship and wholesome company. But the Order for which Messrs Patton and McCrea claim to speak is not the one I joined and has apparently no room for private judgement and freedom of conscience.

At a meeting of some informed friends of Ulster in Whitehall on 4 May, the fear was expressed that the Orange delegation would not impress the prime minister and his officials at the upcoming meeting. Indeed, Downing Street's reaction might be that if that was the best the Institution could put forward, there was nothing to be feared from the Orange Order.

The meeting between the prime minister and the Orange delegation of Robert Saulters, John McCrea and George Patton on 7 May brought no satisfactory results as far as the officers attending were concerned. This was the message they communicated to a meeting of County Masters the following day. The leadership would appear at this stage to have aligned itself firmly with the 'No' campaign. The official position of the Institution remained as stated on 15 April, only that it could not 'recommend' the Agreement to the people of Ulster.

The *Belfast Telegraph* reported on the day of the Downing Street visit: 'A final verdict is unlikely to emerge before further talks with senior officers at County and Local level over the next week.' The Rev. William Bingham is quoted as saying, 'There are many Orangemen who are open to be persuaded to vote Yes. The Order should not seek to persuade members to vote Yes or No, but should seek clarification on matters of concern and then let the people make up their own minds.' The Rev. Dr Warren Porter also sought, unsuccessfully, to lead his brethren into adopting a position where each man would be left to his own conscience in the matter, without any direction from the Order, a religious organisation, in a matter that was purely political.

The eight 'northern' County Grand Lodges discussed the Referendum within their respective county lodges. While the majority came out in opposition to the Agreement, counties Down, Tyrone and Fermanagh resolutely refused to give a directive, much to the disgust of the hardline element.

Various attempts were made to try to get the Orange leadership to see sense, not to convince them to come out for the 'Yes' campaign but that they should have the same discretion as their predecessors, thus avoiding a split in the Institution. One of these attempts included a breakfast with Lord Robert Cranborne, the Conservative leader of the House of Lords, on 11 May, during his visit in support of the Unionist 'Yes' campaign. Robert Saulters, George Patton, Denis Watson, the Rev. William Bingham and I were all present. I can well recall Lord Cranborne's stunning remark after the discussion had reached the proverbial 'brick wall'. Quoting Samuel Johnson's observation that nothing concentrates the mind like a hanging in the morning, he added: 'You have just disproved that.'

Grand Lodge officers issued this press release on 12 May:

FINAL POSITION
Grand Lodge Rejects The Agreement

> Since the publication of 'The Agreement' we have given it careful and detailed consideration. We had hoped that it would offer such a real prospect of peace that we could positively endorse it. Sadly that has not been the case.
>
> Grand Lodge at its Meeting on 15 April decided that failing clarification of certain vital issues we could not recommend the Agreement.
>
> Clarification was sought from a variety of sources including a request for a Meeting with the Prime Minister.
>
> Before meeting Mr Blair we were aware that Her Majesty's Government as one of the parties to a multi party agreement could not unilaterally vary or amend it. We thought it right however to meet the Prime Minister, to express our concerns and listen carefully to his responses.
>
> Having heard the Prime Minister's response we are confirmed in our opinion that those matters in 'The Agreement' that we find objectionable are unalterable and we have communicated this to our County Grand Masters for transmission to their Members.
>
> The Orange Institution is an organisation committed to Civil and Religious Liberty and as such cannot instruct anyone how to vote, and would urge everyone to read and study the Agreement. However in light of the clarification received and for reasons previously

documented the Grand Orange Lodge of Ireland is unable to recommend the Agreement to the people of Ulster.

On 13 May the *Belfast Telegraph* ran extracts from the statement under the headline 'DUP hails the Orange no to the agreement'.

These different signals made the Institution look very foolish in the modern world. The Grand Orange Lodge of Ireland had not met to consider the situation. This was a unilateral decision by the officers of Grand Lodge, who would appear to have convinced themselves that they *were* the Grand Lodge.

The day before the Referendum one of the most surprising episodes of the whole campaign occurred in the House of Orange. The past Grand Master the Rev. Martin Smyth set up a press conference and arranged for the present Grand Master, Robert Saulters, to read a statement in support of the 'No' campaign. Those current Unionist MPs who were opposed to the Agreement, with one notable exception, were joined by others prominently involved in the 'No' campaign for a press statement and photo-call. The one exception was Jeffrey Donaldson, MP for Lagan Valley, who along with other senior Orangemen had attempted to persuade the Grand Master not to take part. According to Donaldson and Canon S. E. Long, who both spoke to the Grand Master immediately before he left to attend the photo-call, he said he was not going to take part. Apparently his mind was changed for him when he arrived at 65 Dublin Road. Obediently he read the statement prepared for him, and he refused to answer any questions.

This episode more than any other caused an enormous amount of disquiet among Orangemen who supported the Agreement, particularly those who were members of the Ulster Unionist Party and who subsequently stood in the elections to the Assembly. Clearly it was a display of political partiality.

The Referendum went ahead on Friday 22 May, and, as they say, 'the rest is history' – Ulster's history. Seventy-one per cent of an eighty-one per cent turnout of the Northern Ireland electorate voted Yes. In any normal society, such a resounding vote would be the end of the matter. Not so in Ulster. The bitterness of the campaign had not gone away. This was abundantly evident throughout the Institution, in spite of the contents of 'Information Sheet No. 2' issued by the Grand Lodge Office in the early part of August.* This unspectacular attempt to rewrite the history

* See Chapter Five, pp. 118–20.

books was a palpable failure. Many people throughout the Institution were 'cold-shouldered' and sidelined, either because they had publicly stated that they were in favour of the Agreement or because they were perceived to have been in favour. In fact relationships within the Institution became much too strained for many good God-fearing members. Some believed that their only alternative in the circumstances was to drift out, thus increasing the general haemorrhage of disenchanted members over the years. One can only hope that the bitterness over the division of opinion on the Belfast Agreement will not be as deep and long-lasting as the division over the 1921 Treaty in the Irish Republic.

The continued negative attitude to the Belfast Agreement is indefensible coming from an organisation professing loyalty to the Crown, since the Queen endorsed the Belfast Agreement in her Christmas 1999 message to the nation by referring to 'the very welcome progress in Northern Ireland.'

As a professedly religious organisation the Orange Institution should have known that the Lord Jesus Christ said, 'By their fruit you will recognise them' (Matthew 7:16). Making statements and press releases is simply not enough. The *Belfast Telegraph* recognised this weakness in its editorial of 14 August 1998, commenting on the content of the 'Information Sheets' just released:

> The Orange Order's 'full support' for the Northern Ireland assembly is also somewhat mystifying when set against the institution's original opposition . . . To make matters worse, the Drumcree protest was hijacked by the No campaign, and once again the Orange leadership has failed to assert itself . . . A resolution of that dispute would do more to help the Order's image than any amount of fancy information sheets.

The unwritten truth of the matter, as far as the hardline element were concerned, is that they did not accept the validity of the 'Roman Catholic vote'. In their view it was as if the Reform Act of 1832 had never been passed. Only 'Protestant' votes counted for them, and by some strange process they had persuaded themselves that the majority of these had been cast against the Agreement.

The opposition of the leadership to the Belfast Agreement was cemented on 12 December 2001 when the Grand Master, Robert Saulters, appointed two vocal opponents of the Agreement as his Assistants. The appointment of the Rev. Stephen Dickinson and William Ross, former MP for East Londonderry, made the Grand Orange Lodge of Ireland a 'cold house' for traditional Orangeism.

Chapter Twelve

A Heritage Lost? Principles and Practice

> *'The Orange Institution will survive as long as it is true to its Biblical basis.'*
>
> The Rev. Martin Smyth, Grand Master, Grand Orange Lodge of Ireland 1972–96

By this stage the reader might well be asking: 'How could an organisation with such Christian foundations find itself in such a mess? How did all this come to pass? Where and how did all this go so badly wrong?' To a large extent it has been the 'March of the Termites', a gradual shift away from fundamental core values.

The Grand Lodge meeting on 9 December 1998 approved the statement: 'The Orange Institution is a Christian organisation! It has clear and precise attitudes to the Christian faith and the practice of it.' Immediately prior to this it had received a report of a meeting with the prime minister in which the delegation of senior officers had called for 'an end to the demonisation of our Institution and its recognition as a *cultural organisation*' (italics mine). The Grand Lodge thus had mastered the ability to make two confusing, if not entirely conflicting, statements within the space of an hour. An organisation whose leadership has no clear vision of what it is supposed to be will inevitably contradict its principles by its practice. Of course, the Orange Institution is no different from any other organisation in that leadership often falls into the hands of those least able, when those with the gifts and ability are unwilling to put themselves forward.

While there always was and always will be something of a divergence between principle and practice, as there is in the churches, the present position of the leadership in giving direction, if not encouragement, to this divergence is something completely new. As long as fallen humanity remains there will always be some element of hypocrisy in any human society, but it is sad in the extreme to find it in this blatant unblushing form exercised within an Institution which claims the Christian name.

While it is evident that society today is less religiously oriented than a hundred years ago, the openly sceptical attitudes and the overt opposition to the teaching of the Reformed Church, particularly in questions of morality, exhibited by many within the Orange Institution are an embarrassment to many of its chaplains as well as to the devoted minority of members who still adhere to the religious principles of the Order. Many within the Institution today do not have any credible Church connection. In fact many do not have even a nominal membership of any Church, despite the written rules of the Order. When, as sometimes happens, the minister of a church hears about a dishonest application and approaches the lodge involved, quite frequently absolutely nothing is done about it. By bringing into membership over the years individuals who have had little or no interest in the Protestant Reformed religion, the Institution has not only done itself a disservice but has enabled that particular calibre of individual to rise in the ranks of Orangeism. Is it any wonder then that many of those in leadership at the present are motivated by an agenda other than the Protestant Reformed religion? As a highly respected senior officer in County Fermanagh has often expressed it, 'the problem is what we let in at the bottom'. However, while this is a serious problem its impact is not universal. It would appear to be much less of a problem west of the River Bann, where commitment to the cause of the local church is taken much more seriously and where the bulk of the Protestant communities are much more religiously motivated.

A core value of evangelical Protestantism is honesty. This also is enshrined in the history of Orangeism. It appears in the original Qualifications of 1798 which direct that an Orangeman should let 'honesty and integrity direct his conduct'. The present Qualifications read: 'His conduct should be guided by wisdom and prudence, and marked by honesty, temperance, and sobriety; the glory of God and the welfare of man, the honour of his Sovereign, and the good of his country, should be the motives of his actions.' Yet honesty is not seen as a hallmark of the of the Institution's recent behaviour. Dr Warren Porter presented a paper to the Central Committee on 21 March 1998 entitled 'Are We Hypocrites?' in which he drew attention to the contradiction between principle and practice. He gave three examples of maintaining the refusal to talk to the Parades Commission and other groups on principle and demonstrated that in practice various talks and contacts were taking place. The paper produced no result.

Another core value of Orangeism which has come under the most thorough scrutiny in recent years is loyalty. What many found difficult to come to terms with in the practice of Orangeism were the demonstrations of loyalty so visible in the public view, combined with verbal and sometimes physical attacks on men obeying the Queen's commission. Nothing is more contradictory than to make expressions of loyalty to the state in the Twelfth resolutions and then to damage the structures of that state. The behaviour of Orange supporters at Portadown in 1998 was not only a sickening display of barbarity but gave many hostages to fortune when the report of the Independent Commission on Policing for Northern Ireland (the Patten report) came to be written the following year.

The bowing to the demands of the Spirit of Drumcree faction at the meeting of the Grand Orange Lodge of Ireland on 9 December 1998, coming after the 'hand-washing' that had been demonstrated at the Grand Lodge meeting of 1 August that year, led many to conclude that the situation was irredeemable. Having come to this conclusion, only one obvious course of action was left for these individuals.

While on many occasions the media analysed the situation correctly, both internally and externally, when they talked about a 'split' in the Orange Institution they were very far off the mark. They were using the extravagant language with which they were accustomed to put a sensational interpretation on events. The Orange Order does not split. It haemorrhages. Many of the most able members had become so disenchanted over the years that they drifted out quietly. By doing this of course they left the Institution even more impoverished, spiritually, intellectually and morally.

Many in the Orange Order like to play the 'numbers game' to project an image of the Institution which is numerically much stronger than it actually is. For example, the County Grand Orange Lodge of Belfast's publication *The Twelfth 1992* makes reference to '100,000 Orangemen' displaying 'continued commitment' at the Tercentenary Parade in Belfast on 29 September 1990. This figure of one hundred thousand, though often quoted, was far off the mark. When the Rev. Martin Smyth took over as Grand Master in 1972, the strength of the Order stood at some sixty thousand based on the capitation charge. But even in those days the myth of numbers was presented to an unquestioning world. In *The Ulster Unionist Party 1882–1973* John Harbinson writes of the Orange Order, 'With a present membership of between 125,000–130,000 this is obviously a formidable organisation in a community with a total population of 1,512,000.'[1] Harbinson gives his source for the figures just quoted as 'Interview with Rev. M. Smyth, 30 April 1969'. Perhaps Martin Smyth was thinking of both members and supporters, but that is not what is stated.

Based on the capitation charge, an annual sum per member of which a portion is allocated to the running of the Grand Lodge, there has been a dramatic reduction in membership over the last forty years. In 1964, when I joined, the membership stood on the verge of seventy thousand. In 2004 it numbered 36,998. This method of counting the membership is of course not totally accurate, as lodges have been known to make inexact returns. Yet Robert Saulters told the Select Committee on Northern Ireland Affairs on 15 November 2000 that the number of members falling under the jurisdiction of the Grand Orange Lodge of Ireland was 'in the region of around 60,000 to 70,000'.[2]

This playing of the 'numbers game' is not unique to the Grand Orange Lodge of Ireland. Referring to the situation in Canada in *The Sash Canada Wore*, Cecil J. Houston and William J. Smyth write: 'Accurate returns on the condition of the order in the nineteenth century were difficult to obtain and for decades the organisation operated with incomplete records. Orangemen, nevertheless, were not deterred from creating and propagating estimates of their numbers.'[3] There are some parallels to be drawn between the decline of the Orange Institution in Ireland and in Canada. Houston and Smyth reflect on the causes of the decline in Canada: 'With the growing sense of national assurance and weakening colonialism the order was anachronistic. It could not adjust because that would have required the rejection of its basic principles and it would be unable to survive as a garrison in a community that no longer had a place for its vigilance.' They list other factors which can be identified as being relevant to the situation in Ireland: 'growing secularisation and the decline in church going'; 'the increasing anachronism of the convivial possibilities which lodge membership provided'; the effects of 'new media'. They conclude: 'On practical and ideological grounds the Orange Order now appears redundant to Canadians, including sons of previously Orange families.'

In the September 2003 edition of the *Orange Standard* Brian Courtney wrote of the growth of the Institution in Canada and stated adamantly: 'There are still some 25,000 Orangemen in Canada.' Some wondered if his finger had inadvertently hit the '2' key, as '5,000' would have been a much more realistic figure!

The divergence between principle and practice did not go unnoticed by the wider community. In *Orangeism*, Kevin Haddick-Flynn, relating the situation following the Twelfth 1998, astutely observes:

> It was now quite clear that the Order was an ailing organisation, at war with itself and alienated from large sections of the public. Its basic problem lay, perhaps, in the glaring contradiction between what it purported to stand for and what it was actually seen to be. It claims to be based on Christian principles and on a premise of tolerance towards Catholics, although opposed to Catholic doctrine. Yet it has a well-attested reputation for bigotry, intolerance and inciting sectarian passions.[4]

In an age when the only acceptable intolerance is an intolerance of intolerance, there is no real place for an Orange Institution which cannot understand how its behaviour at Drumcree is perceived by the world at large as naked intolerance. Yet this should not have been the case. If the Institution had been true to its own declared principles as reflected in the Qualifications and Basis, and in the life of William III of the House of Orange, it would be better placed than many organisations to project the more acceptable tolerant image in the twenty-first century. Instead these foundation documents of the Orange Institution became a veneer to hide behind, and the heritage which the Institution claimed to maintain was increasingly neglected.

To many of those involved in its leadership, the Institution seems to be their total world. They have little interest outside the Orange Order, with its proliferation of meetings and ritual. When any merely human interest becomes so self-absorbing it damages the ability to 'see ourselves as others see us'. This is why the present leadership are unable to take a step back, learn from other disciplines and create a broad and inclusive vision for the Institution in the twenty-first century. Particularly since the signing of the Belfast Agreement in 1998 there has been, in many though not in all areas, a 'cold house' for those who are perceived to be 'moderate' or pro-Agreement. This, combined with the refusal of many to endorse the Drumcree stand-off with its associated violence, made the position of those who held firmly to authentic Orange principles even more precarious in many respects. The Institution's 1997 publication *What is the Orange Order?* proclaimed: 'The brotherly bond which unites the members is based on a spirit of *tolerance*, tolerance toward those within the brotherhood with whom there may be differences of emphasis and toward those outside the brotherhood who differ from us in religious persuasion.' Was this now 'dead in the water'?

A 'whispering campaign' in an organisation like the Orange Institution is a most successful way of manipulating events, because it is most successful among those who lack the ability to think for themselves. The whispering was carried on against those who were perceived to fall into a variety of categories: 'pro-Agreement', 'modern', 'liberal', 'progressive', 'radical' and 'smart'. Instead of the Orange Institution of the twenty-first century representing the broader inclusive political views of the Protestant constituency, as it did at the end of the eighteenth century, it came to represent a very narrow view of Protestantism.

The hardline image projected by the Institution toward those in the community who expressed opposition to particular parades was also directed towards those who sought to exercise their civil and religious liberty. Following my appearance on television during the summer of 2000, the secretary of my lodge, 'Christian Crusaders' LOL 1339, charged me with 'representing the Order in the media without permission'. The charge was eventually dismissed as neither I nor the BBC had claimed that I was there to 'represent' the Institution.

It should not be thought that I was out on a limb in expressing my concerns for the future of the Orange Institution. In November 2002, Mark Lawlor, a member of my lodge and the incoming Master of the Lodge of Research, resigned from the Order. Most of those who resign take the easy option and adduce 'personal reasons'. Mark Lawlor wrote a lengthy letter in which he covered many of the areas of concern to respectable Orangemen. Among other things he said:

> The Institution is intent on discarding the very principles and shared values of a belief in God, in the truth of the Reformed faith, in civil and religious liberty (toleration), in loyalty to the state and respect for the rule of law, in the importance of family life and in mutual brotherhood, which were its very *raison d'être*.
>
> The maintenance and promotion of the Reformed faith would appear to be the last of the leadership's concerns as Grand Lodge continues to issue statements on 'moral' issues, in circumstances in which it no longer has the moral authority to do so, with members intent on breaking God's law at every given opportunity. In doing so, the Institution has lost all credibility; it continues to alienate decent members and the wider public alike.

Had the Orange Institution managed to get itself into such a mess by a succession of mistakes that were clearly well-meaning though stupid, it might have attracted sympathy. Had the Institution's present standing been the result of lack of support, guidance and advice, the community might well understand it. But the sad truth is that over the recent years of betrayal the Institution has received the best of advice and offers of help from many quarters, which the leadership consistently and contemptuously dismissed. Perhaps this was because some of those who offered advice were not within the Orange fold. A number of the most helpful were certainly not of the Orange tradition, and their association with the leadership of the Institution was sometimes undertaken at considerable personal cost. Sean O'Callaghan, a former Republican activist, advised that 'the IRA would be delighted if Protestants turned against the state and started to oppose the security forces because that would prove their argument that the state was ungovernable'.[5] This advice was ignored by the leadership.

More detailed advice came from Dr Ruth Dudley Edwards, who was born and brought up in Dublin in the Roman Catholic tradition, where there was considerable sympathy for the Republican cause. She studied at University College, Dublin, where her father was professor of History, and later did post-graduate work at Cambridge University before embarking on an academic career of no mean achievement, as well as a spell in the British civil service. Her book *The Faithful Tribe: An Intimate Portrait of the Loyal Institutions* is the best independent work ever published on the nature of the Institution. It is an accurate reflection of the diverse nature of Orangeism and of how the Institution impinges on the lives of individuals and communities.

When *The Faithful Tribe* was published in June 1999, the leadership of the Institution were initially positive but not particularly enthusiastic. They failed to grasp the book's impact on the Institution's image in the world. The second edition reveals how the Scottish and English jurisdictions of the Institution assisted Dr Dudley Edwards at the launch, while the home of the Institution in Ireland displayed an inability to accommodate her. The book's launch at the Stormont Hotel in Belfast revealed the leadership's lack of social graces. While the Grand Master, Robert Saulters, made an acceptable speech, collectively the leadership displayed some of the characteristics of the old Russian politburo. No attempt was made to 'network' the wide variety of selected guests.

In the second edition Dr Dudley Edwards, in the interests of her own personal integrity and the truth, made some critical remarks about the Institution's leadership. As a result some of the leadership rewarded her with the title 'Fenian Bitch'.

The Executive Officer, George Patton, had written in *Steadfast for Faith and Freedom* in 1995: 'Obviously no one objects to criticism when it is justified and at times in its history the Order has had to accept such justifiable criticism, but generally this has been as a result of the actions of a few rather than the organisation as a whole.'[6] This language was sufficiently ambiguous to provide him with an escape route if he had fallen foul of the party line. The ordinary rank-and-file members were however, facing up to the implications of criticism. They were voting with their feet, and leaving.

Leaders of the business community also went out of their way to give advice and offer support, because of the damage inflicted on the whole community by the painful repetition of confrontation. Chris Gibson, the chairman of the Northern Ireland Branch of the Confederation of British Industry, and Sir George Quigley, chairman of the Ulster Bank and the Northern Ireland Economic Council, who was later appointed to chair a review of the Parades Commission, offered advice on many occasions. Both Gibson and Quigley played individual and collective roles in 'G7', the coalition of leading business figures and trade union representatives. The once-despised Irish Congress of Trade Unions also met with the leadership as late as 23 October 2002. The membership were never informed of that meeting.

Legal advice also came from many quarters, and, as we have seen, was often treated with contempt. The legal opinions of two of the top experts on human rights legislation, which cost the Institution nothing, were ignored. It is doubtful if the Grand Master ever received Austen Morgan's opinion, which was passed on to Grand Lodge Office for his attention by William Thompson, then MP for West Tyrone. The open, often-boasted democratic nature of Grand Lodge was abused by the failure to present or pass on the legal opinion of Brian Currin.

To treat with disdain the advice of experts from the business and legal field is one thing, but for a professed religious organisation to treat with contempt the advice of the leadership of the three main Protestant churches, who were constantly offering help in the late 1990s, is beyond excuse. During these years none was more willing and accommodating than Dr Robin Eames, the Church of Ireland Archbishop of Armagh. All the advice offered was lost in the 'big black hole'.

Arguably the most significant of these meetings took place towards the end of the Institution's '*annus horribilis*', on 2 December 1998 in the Methodist headquarters in Glengall Street, Belfast. There the Orange leadership team of Grand Secretary John McCrea, Assistant Grand Secretary Denis Watson, Grand Treasurer Mervyn Bishop and Executive Officer George Patton sat down with the three church leaders, the Rev. Dr

John Dixon, Presbyterian Moderator, the Rev. David Kerr, Methodist President, and Dr Eames. Pressed by the churchmen, the leadership team agreed that the Institution was religious rather than political and that it was founded on Christian principles. They further acknowledged that Scripture was of supreme authority, and that Christian behaviour is to be based on Scripture. Finally they agreed that 'any breaking of the Law cannot be acceptable' and that 'we cannot refuse to talk to anyone made in the image of God, and it is wrong to say that if we do not get our own way and walk down the [Garvaghy] Road the Reformed Faith or Protestantism is lost.' One of the Orange delegation even referred to those on Drumcree Hill as 'evil' and 'bloody-minded'.

The Orange leadership team agreed that they would put together a resolution encompassing these points. Had they done so they would have been supported by the three church leaders. But the greatest betrayal of Orange principle was now to take place. The leadership did what they thought they did best: nothing! The church leaders waited in vain. No resolution ever appeared.

On most occasions, in the presence of the church leaders, the Orange leadership were polite to their faces. Behind their backs it was a very different matter. They managed to treat them with such duplicity that they lost some of their few remaining friends.

The perceptive comment of Chris Ryder and Vincent Kearney in *Drumcree* summarises the events of this period: 'There is now a widespread feeling that Grand Lodge leaders actively promote ignorance to pacify unthinking hardliners and traditionalists and prevent unrest.' The leadership had placed the Institution on very shaky ground. Having failed to keep their word to the church leaders, they proceeded to indulge in farcical threats to both the public and the government. They knew that they would also fail to keep even their negative promises.

The Grand Lodge meeting of 27 March 1999 revealed the depths of despair into which the leadership had flung themselves. Even a child should know that one should not make threats, particularly threats which cannot be fulfilled. The Grand Lodge, however, threatened to take the whole membership of the Institution to Drumcree on 12 July 1999 if the situation was not resolved by that date. The Drumcree stand-off was not resolved by 12 July, but the Grand Lodge did not go as a body to Drumcree. The forty days it had given the prime minister to 'sort it out' was conveniently forgotten. It is doubtful if those delegated with the responsibility ever actually wrote to the prime minister in the terms of that resolution of Grand Lodge. The 'promote ignorance to pacify' doctrine was being pursued at great speed. Such was the lack of intellectual credibility within Grand Lodge that the failure of the leadership to implement its own resolutions was not raised at subsequent meetings of the Grand Orange Lodge of Ireland.

Visits to Downing Street ceased, as even the multi-faceted Tony Blair lost confidence in the Orange leadership. Their inability to deliver the goods was patently obvious. Going by previous experience, one can only speculate what undertakings the leadership had given to the prime minister, which they then failed to keep. What hope can there be for an Institution which is founded on an ideology which its leadership is ashamed to articulate, and to which it is unable to give vision and direction?

The end of the millennium year saw the resignation from the Institution of a member of fifty-five years' standing. George Williamson, District Secretary of Lisburn District, was quoted in the *Ulster Star* of 2 November 2000 and the *Belfast News Letter* of 5 November as stating: 'People are calling each other "brother" across the table but the same time stabbing each other in the back.' The fraternal nature of the Institution was at such a low ebb that this was a statement with which many could identify. In keeping with such a 'fraternal' atmosphere within the Institution, the 'black propaganda' machine created all sorts of other reasons for his resignation.

It was sad to see an organisation like the Orange Institution, which had in the past made such an important contribution to society, become trapped in a prison of its own making. By allowing the projection of an intolerant image of Orangeism, the leadership was denying the virtues and values of the life of William III, Prince of Orange. Their lack of courage to stand up to threats and thuggery showed how little they thought of the life of the one whose 'glorious memory' they supported.

It seemed that lessons had been learned when the Twelfth 2005 proved to be one of the most peaceful celebrations in recent memory. Commendations were forthcoming from many quarters for those who attempted to restore the tradition of a family day out, of which many had fond memories. I was invited to speak at the demonstration in Antrim, where I received a good reception and much encouragement.

As so often happens in the Orange Order, it was one step forward and two steps back. The positive commendations of the Twelfth were soon turned into denunciations by the events surrounding the Whiterock Parade of 10 September, organised by Belfast's No. 9 District Lodge and postponed from 25 June. Although the parade had been re-routed by the Parades Commission, the organisers had made no serious effort to render it more acceptable to the host community by the exclusion of paramilitary emblems. The bannerette of 'Old Boyne Island Heroes' LOL 633, bearing the likeness of Brian Robinson and the inscription 'LATE BRO. B. ROBINSON U.V.F. KILLED 2ND SEPTEMBER 1989', was clearly visible towards the beginning of the parade, and many of the accompanying bands were alleged to be paramilitary bands with direct connections to the UVF and the UDA. This was a clear breach of condition D laid down by the Parades Commission: 'There shall be no colour parties of any type, or flags, clothes, instruments, badges or emblems displayed which could be seen as associated with any paramilitary organisation.'

As the Whiterock Parade degenerated into disorder, loyalist gunmen fired on the army and police in the worst street violence seen in Belfast for ten years. In the hours and days to follow the violence spread to other areas of Northern Ireland. Chief Constable Sir Hugh Orde blamed the Orange Order. Precisely why and how the violence erupted is unclear. The result was clear – the good name of Orangeism was again presented to a bewildered world as a byword for confrontation and bitterness. As if the violence directed against the police and the army and witnessed by millions on television was not enough, the subsequent handling of events by the leadership turned this tragedy into a farce.

The farce began on Monday 12 September when Julian O'Neill of the BBC interviewed the County Grand Master of Belfast, Dawson Bailie. Bailie said that he was not making any statement, but refused to condemn the shocking violence directed against Crown forces. The next day in interviews with the media I had no hesitation in calling Bailie's refusal to condemn the violence 'diabolical'. On 14 September Lindy McDowell commented cynically in the *Belfast Telegraph*: 'And for anyone anywhere within the ranks who has been kidding themselves that their Order was finally getting to grips with the PR thing – two words – Dawson Bailie.'

Although both the Grand Secretary and 'Reputation Matters', the media consultants engaged by the Order, advised against it, a Grand Lodge press conference chaired by the Grand Master, Robert Saulters, was held in West Belfast Orange Hall on the morning of 14 September. Dawson Bailie, Belfast County Grand Secretary Tom Haire, the Deputy Grand Master the Rev. Stephen Dickinson, the Master of No. 9 District Billy Mawhinney and the No. 9 District Chaplain the Rev. W. J.

Malcolmson also attended. This press conference was preceded by a statement in which the central issue of the violence both during and following the parade of the previous Saturday was not addressed. While this statement bore all the hallmarks of the denial syndrome, its second paragraph stated that 'the most worrying thing about the weekend's events is the widespread feeling of frustration within the protestant community'. To many thinking people the most worrying thing *was* the violence!

During this conference the members of the press were dismayed as on three occasions Dawson Bailie said, 'I condone the violence.' Someone pointed out to him that perhaps he meant to say 'condemn'. He apologised and said that that was what he meant. The faux pas, if that is what it was, led to the circulation of a satirical picture on the internet, showing three primates bearing the head of Dawson Bailie and wearing Orange collarettes, captioned: 'Hear no evil – see no evil – talk no sense.'

The press conference continued in the farce mode. As Saulters and Bailie denied that any member of the Institution was involved in violence, the media replayed the scenes of violence over their words. Any good which had been achieved by the positive image of the Twelfth was undone. Again the good name of Orangeism was discredited not only by the violence against the police and army, which was bad enough, but by the contemptible response of those in leadership.

The violence was condemned by many political figures including the leader of the Ulster Unionist Party, Sir Reg Empey, and David Ford, the leader of the Alliance Party. The most significant condemnation, not only of the violence but of those associated with it, came from the Evangelical Alliance of Northern Ireland. In a press statement issued on 14 September they said:

> The Orange Order, which on its website claims to be Christ-centred, Bible-based and Church-grounded, has surely moved far from these roots when it calls people on to the streets knowing in all probability that would lead to civil unrest. It is unacceptable that the Order has been slow to speak out or unequivocally condemn the violence that ensued, particularly that perpetrated by its own members.

In the weeks which followed the police were determined to make arrests. They released photographs taken from CCTV footage of those they wished to question in relation to the violence. Many of these were Orangemen, some of whom were wearing Orange collarettes. The *Belfast*

Telegraph on 16 September summed up the feelings of most in its editorial: 'The attempt by Orange leaders to pin the blame on the PSNI is an insult to everyone's intelligence. The Order's credibility is at stake.'

All this violence again raised the question concerning the relationship between the Orange Order and paramilitaries. The answer came from Sammy Duddy, spokesman of the Ulster Political Research Group (UPRG), the political wing of the UDA. He was quoted in the *Sunday Times* on 18 September as saying:

> It's time to admit that the Orange Order has always used the paramilitaries as the big stick. They use them to police their parades through contentious areas. They use them as their army when it suits and then wash their hands if things turn out badly. It is time someone made the point of that. Certain sections of the UDA are now saying, 'No more are we going to be used by the Orange Order.'

The Orange leadership have yet to respond to this allegation!

The Grand Orange Lodge of Ireland has become a 'cold house' for those who hold to the traditional and authentic values of Orangeism. It is not so much 'Popery without' as 'dissension within' which has been the cause of the 'orderly management of decline', though as we have seen, even this has not been all that orderly.

Northern Ireland's first prime minister, Sir James Craig, later Lord Craigavon, once said: 'If Northern Ireland ever comes to an end, it will be because the Protestants started fighting the British.'[7] This wise and visionary statement could equally be applied to the Orange Order. It is the violence of recent years which has alienated members within and supporters without. Yet the negative impact of the violence itself could have been lessened if the leadership had taken a firm hand and exercised discipline. That they had not the courage to do so has been clearly demonstrated.

A heritage lost not as the result of losing a battle with the opposition, but through the lack of leadership and vision of its chief officers, must surely be a tragedy tinged by farce. That makes the loss all the harder to bear.

Appendix One

The Structure of Irish Orangeism before 1999

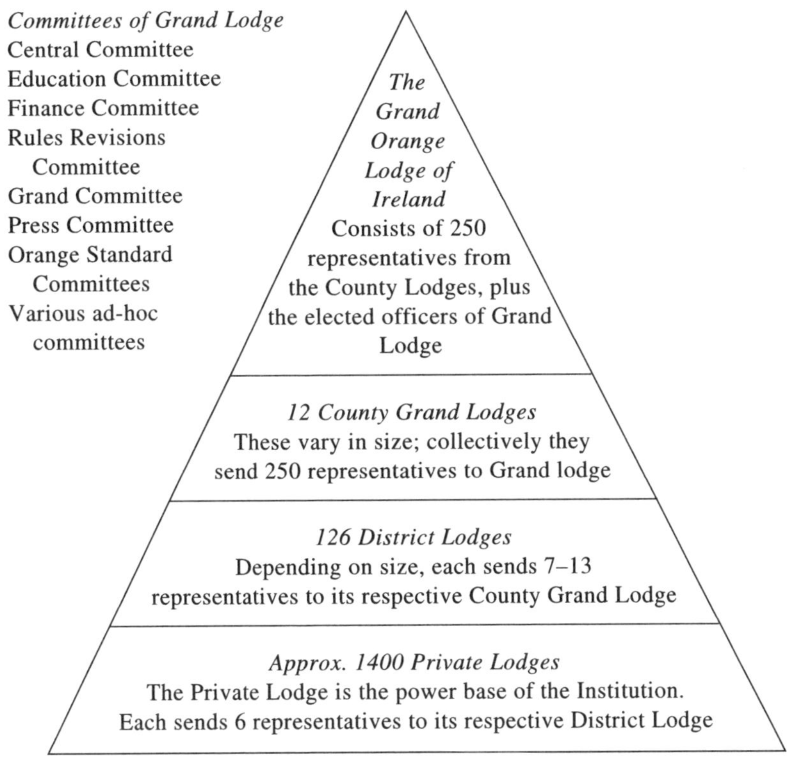

Note:

The diagram above shows the long-established structure of the Institution before 1999. Thereafter, under pressure from the Spirit of Drumcree, the Grand Lodge adopted a system whereby the 126 District Lodges are directly represented in Grand Lodge by one member from each. In addition, the number of Deputy Grand Chaplains has been reduced from 50 to 25, and the status of the 50 Deputy Grand Masters changed to that of non-voting honorary officers.

Appendix Two

The Standards of Irish Orangeism

The Qualifications of an Orangeman

An Orangeman should have a sincere love and veneration for his Heavenly Father; a humble and steadfast faith in Jesus Christ, the Saviour of mankind, believing in Him as the only Mediator between God and man. He should cultivate truth and justice, brotherly kindness and charity, devotion and piety, concord and unity, and obedience to the laws; his deportment should be gentle and compassionate, kind and courteous; he should seek the society of the virtuous, and avoid that of the evil; he should honour and diligently study the Holy Scriptures, and make them the rule of his faith and practice; he should love, uphold, and defend the Protestant religion, and sincerely desire and endeavour to propagate its doctrines and precepts; he should strenuously oppose the fatal errors and doctrines of the Church of Rome, and scrupulously avoid countenancing (by his presence or otherwise) any act or ceremony of Romish Worship; he should, by all lawful means, resist the ascendancy of that Church, its encroachments, and the extension of its power, ever abstaining from all uncharitable words, actions, or sentiments towards any Roman Catholic; he should remember to keep holy the Sabbath day, and attend the public worship of God, and diligently train up his off-spring, and all under his control, in the fear of God, and in the Protestant faith; he should never take the name of God in vain, but abstain from all cursing and profane language, and use every opportunity of discouraging those, and all other sinful practices, in others; his conduct should be guided by wisdom and prudence, and marked by honesty, temperance, and sobriety; the glory of God and the welfare of man, the honour of his Sovereign, and the good of his country, should be the motives of his actions.

(Last revised, December 1998)

Basis

The Institution is composed of Protestants, united and resolved to the utmost of their power to support and defend the rightful Sovereign, the Protestant Religion, the Laws of the Realm, and the Succession to the Throne in the House of Windsor, BEING PROTESTANT; and united further for the defence of their own Persons and Properties, and the maintenance of the Public Peace. It is exclusively an Association of those who are attached to the religion of the Reformation, and will not admit into its brotherhood persons whom an intolerant spirit leads to persecute, injure, or upbraid any man on account of his religious opinions. They associate also in honour of KING WILLIAM III, Prince of Orange, whose name they bear, as supporters of his glorious memory.

Values

The traditional values which are to be the objective of all Orangemen are ritually expressed as follows:

'We must all endeavour to disarm suspicion and antagonism. This can best be done by setting a good example in our daily lives, by living up to the high principles of the Order so that every section of the community will be compelled to admit that there is something in the Orange Society that elevates a man and raises him above the average of humanity. Something that makes him a better man morally, socially and intellectually.'

Notes

Chapter One: *The Place of Orangeism in Irish Society*

1. Alvin Jackson, *Colonel Edward Saunderson: Land and Loyalty in Victorian Ireland* (Oxford, 1995), p. 193
2. William Blacker, *The Formation of the Orange Order, 1795–1798: The Edited Papers of Colonel William Blacker and Colonel Robert Hugh Wallace* (Belfast, 1994), p. 116.
3. Ibid., p. 125.
4. Ibid., p. 126.
5. Ian McBride, *Scripture Politics: Ulster Presbyterians and Irish Radicalism in the late Eighteenth Century* (Oxford, 1998), p. 221.
6. R. M. Sibbett, *Orangeism in Ireland and throughout the Empire* (London, 1938), vol. 1, p. 443.
7. Official Reports, 5th Series, vol. 4 of Session 1914, p. 1752.
8. *Belfast News Letter*, 5 February 1921.
9. Edward Marjoribanks, *The Life of Lord Carson* (London, 1932), p. 68.
10. The Battle of the Boyne was actually fought on 1 July 1690, which became 12 July with the adoption of the Gregorian Calendar in 1752. When 12 July falls on a Sunday, as in 1998, the Twelfth celebrations are held on Monday 13 July.
11. Sibbett, vol. 1, p. 442.
12. Ibid., pp. 442, 443
13. Parliamentary Debates, 3rd Series, 30 March 1870, p. 960.

Chapter Two: *Religion or Politics?*

1. *Fair Sunshine: Character Studies of the Scottish Covenanters* (London, 1968), p. 77.
2. Sibbett, vol. 1, p. 451.
3. *Belfast News Letter*, 25 February 1800.
4. John F. Harbinson, *The Unionist Party, 1882–1973* (Belfast, 1973), p. 8.
5. W. D. Flackes and Sydney Elliott, *Northern Ireland: A Political Directory 1968–1999* (Belfast, 1998), p. 380.
6. Kevin Haddick-Flynn, *Orangeism: The Making of a Tradition* (Dublin, 1999), p. 315.
7. The description is given in both Haddick-Flynn, p. 315, and Jackson, *Colonel Edward Saunderson*.
8. Official Reports, 4th Series, vol. 99, p. 720.
9. Sibbett, vol. 2, p. 607
10. Haddick-Flynn, p. 317.
11. Ibid., p. 319.
12. *Sunday Life*, 9 May 1999, p. 18.
13. Ed Moloney, *A Secret History of the IRA* (London, 2002), pp. 468–79.
14. Constitution and Rules of the Ulster Unionist Party 18 (1) (a), adopted at its annual general meeting on 5 March 2005.

15. M. W. Dewar, J. Brown and S. E. Long, *Orangeism: A New Historical Appreciation* (Belfast, 1967), p. 188.
16. Ibid., p. 188.
17. Rev. Dr M. W. Dewar, *Why Orangeism?* (Belfast, 1958), p. 22.
18. Chris Ryder and Vincent Kearney, *Drumcree: The Orange Order's Last Stand* (London, 2001), p. 1.
19. Ibid., p. 333.
20. Billy Kennedy (ed.), *Steadfast for Faith and Freedom* (Belfast, 1995), p. 13.
21. Glenn Jordan, *Not of this World? Evangelical Protestants in Northern Ireland* (Belfast, 2001), pp. 117, 118.
22. Ibid., p. 131.

Chapter Three: *Decisive Discipline*

1. BBC (NI) 'Spotlight', 17 October 2000.
2. Cecil J. Houston and William J. Smyth, *The Sash Canada Wore: A Historical Geography of the Orange Order in Canada* (Toronto, 1980), p. 125.
3. Sibbett, vol. 1, p. 441.
4. Ibid., p. 452.
5. Peter Taylor, *Loyalists: Ulster's Protestant Paramilitaries* (London, 1999), p. 151.
6. Ibid., p. 151.
7. Ruth Dudley Edwards, *The Faithful Tribe: An Intimate Portrait of the Loyal Institutions* (London, 1999), p. 553n.
8. *Irish Press*, 14 June 1993.
9. *Irish News*, 29 March 1997.
10. *Sunday World*, 9 February 1997.
11. *The People*, 1 September 2002. William McCaughey made similar remarks on the BBC Radio Ulster programme 'Talkback' on 11 July 2003.
12. *Belfast Telegraph*, 9 April 2004.

Chapter Four: *A Prelude to Disaster*

1. Marianne Elliott (ed.), *The Long Road to Peace in Northern Ireland* (Liverpool, 2002), p. 8.
2. See Chapter One, note 10.
3. Review of the Parades Commission and Public Processions (NI) Act 1998 (2002), p. 83, n. 1.
4. Haddick-Flynn, p. 131.
5. Blacker, *The Formation of the Orange Order*, p. 108.
6. Chris Ryder, *The RUC: A Force under Fire* (London, 1992), p. 330.
7. A. T. Q. Stewart, *The Narrow Ground* (Belfast, 1977), p. 83.
8. David Sharrock and Mark Devenport, *Man of War, Man of Peace?* (London, 1997), p. 259.
9. *Sunday Independent*, 21 July 1996.

Chapter Five: *The Drumcree Debacle*

1. William Brown, *An Army with Banners: The Real Face of Orangeism* (Belfast, 2003), p. 4.

Chapter Six: *'Wheels and Deals': the Spirit of Drumcree*

1. Douglas Jerrold, *The Wit and Opinions of Douglas Jerrold* (London, 1859).

2. Chris Moore, *The Kincora Scandal: Political Cover-up and Intrigue in Northern Ireland* (Dublin, 1996), p. 46.
3. Statement issued by the Spirit of Drumcree under the seal of 'Holdfast' LOL 1620.
4. Dr Clifford Smyth, in the November/December 1995 edition of *Awake*, a magazine produced by the British–Israel World Federation dedicated to the promotion of British Israelism.
5. Ryder and Kearney, *Drumcree*, p. 129.
6. Ibid., p. 322.
7. *Belfast News Letter*, 4 July 2000.

Chapter Seven: *Parades and Strategy*

1. Graham Montgomery and Richard Whitten, *The Order on Parade* (Belfast, 1995), p. 34.
2. Ryder and Kearney, *Drumcree*, p. 145.
3. *Sunday Times*, 30 January 2000.

Chapter Eight: *To Talk or not to Talk*

1. *Belfast Telegraph*, 26 June 1999.
2. Select Committee on Northern Ireland Affairs, Minutes of Evidence – Examination of Witnesses, Question 108, 15 November 2000.
3. *Belfast Telegraph*, 4 July 2000.
4. Ryder and Kearney, *Drumcree*, p. 353.
5. Ibid., p. 354.

Chapter Nine: *'Bricks without Straw'*

1. *Belfast Telegraph*, 9 December 1997.

Chapter Ten: *In Office but not in Power*

1. Address to the Duncairn Unionist Association, 3 February 1921, quoted in the *Belfast News Letter*, 4 February 1921.
2. Dudley Edwards, p. 390.
3. Sibbett, vol. 2, p. 603.
4. James Winder Good, *Ulster and Ireland* (Dublin, 1919), p. 270.
5. *Irish Times*, 10 July and 13 August 2002; *Irish News*, 26 July 2002.

Chapter Eleven: *'Egg on our Face'*

1. The Grand Orange Lodge of Ireland Minute Book 1798–1819, p. 55.
2. Sibbett, vol. 1, p. 442.

Chapter Twelve: *A Heritage Lost?*

1. Harbinson, p. 93.
2. Select Committee on Northern Ireland Affairs, Minutes of Evidence – Examination of Witnesses, Question 77, 15 November 2000.
3. Houston and Smyth, p. 84–5.
4. Haddick-Flynn, p. 353.
5. Recollected by the Rev. William Bingham, as quoted in Ryder and Kearney, p. 265.
6. Kennedy (ed.), *Steadfast for Faith and Freedom*, p. 35.
7. Quoted in David Boulton, *The UVF, 1966–1973* (Dublin, 1973), p. 1.

Select Bibliography

Beckett, J. C., *The Making of Modern Ireland 1603–1923* (London, 1966)

Blacker, William, *The Formation of the Orange Order, 1795–1798: The Edited Papers of Colonel William Blacker and Colonel Robert H. Wallace* (Belfast, 1994)

Boulton, David, *The UVF, 1966–73: An Anatomy of Loyalist Rebellion* (Dublin, 1973)

Brown, William, *An Army with Banners: The Real Face of Orangeism* (Belfast, 2003)

Bryan, Dominic, Fraser, T. G. and Dunn, Seamus, *Political Rituals: Loyalist Parades in Portadown* (Coleraine, 1995)

Cadogan Group, *Picking up the Pieces: Northern Ireland after the Belfast Agreement* (Belfast, 2003)

Cusack, Jim, *UVF* (Dublin, 1997)

Dewar, M. W., *Why Orangeism?* (Belfast, 1958)

Dewar, M. W., Brown, J. and Long, S. E., *Orangeism: A New Historical Approach* (Belfast, 1967)

Dillon, Martin, *God and the Gun: The Church and Irish Terrorism* (London, 1997)

Dunlop, John, *A Precarious Belonging: Presbyterians and the Conflict in Ireland* (Belfast, 1995)

Dwyer, T. Ryle, *Big Fellow, Long Fellow: A Joint Biography of Collins and De Valera* (Dublin, 1998)

Edwards, Ruth Dudley, *The Faithful Tribe: An Intimate Portrait of the Loyal Institutions* (London, 1999)

Elliott, Marianne (ed.), *The Long Road to Peace in Northern Ireland: Peace Lectures from the Institute of Irish Studies at Liverpool University* (Liverpool, 2002)

Flackes, W. D. and Elliott, Sydney, *Northern Ireland: A Political Directory, 1968–1999* (Belfast, 1999)

Garland, Roy, *Gusty Spence* (Belfast, 2001)

Godson, Dean, *Himself Alone: David Trimble and the Ordeal of Unionism* (London, 2004)

Good, James Winder, *Ulster and Ireland* (Dublin, 1919)

Gowan, Ogle Robert, *Orangeism: Its Origin and History* (Toronto, 1859)

Haddick-Flynn, Kevin, *Orangeism: The Making of a Tradition* (Dublin, 1999)

Harbinson, John Fitzsimons, *The Ulster Unionist Party, 1882–1973: Its Development and Organisation* (Belfast, 1973)

Holmes, Finlay, *The Presbyterian Church in Ireland: A Popular History* (Dublin, 2000)

Presbyterians and Orangeism, 1795–1995 (Belfast, 1996)

Houston, Cecil J. and Smyth, William J., *The Sash Canada Wore: A Historical Geography of the Orange Order in Canada* (Toronto, 1980)

Hyde, H. Montgomery, *Carson: The Life of Sir Edward Carson, Lord Carson of Duncairn* (London, 1953)

Keogh, Dáire and Whelan, Kevin, *Acts of Union: The Causes, Contexts and Consequences of the Act of Union* (Dublin, 2001)

Jackson, Alvin, *Colonel Edward Saunderson: Land and Loyalty in Victorian Ireland* (Oxford, 1995)

Home Rule: An Irish History, 1800–2000 (London, 2003)

Ireland 1798–1998: Politics and War (Oxford, 1999)

Sir Edward Carson (Dundalk, 1993)

Jarman, Neil and Bryan, Dominic, *Parade and Protest: A Discussion of Parading Disputes in Northern Ireland* (Coleraine, 1996)

Jordan, Glenn, *Not of this World? Evangelical Protestants in Northern Ireland* (Belfast, 2001)

Kelly, James, *Sir Edward Newenham, MP, 1734–1814: Defender of the Protestant Constitution* (Dublin, 2004)

Kennedy, Billy, *A Celebration, 1690–1900: The Orange Institution* (Belfast, 1993)

(ed.), *Steadfast for Faith and Freedom: 200 Years of Orangeism* (Belfast, 1993)

Kilpatrick, Cecil, *William of Orange: A Dedicated Life, 1650–1702* (Belfast, 1998)

McBride, Ian, *Scripture Politics: Ulster Presbyterians and Irish Radicalism in the late Eighteenth Century* (Oxford, 1998)

McDonald, Henry, *UDA: Inside the Heart of Loyalist Terror* (Dublin, 2004)

Marjoribanks, Edward, *The Life of Lord Carson* (London, 1932)

Moloney, Ed, *A Secret History of the IRA* (London, 2002)

Montgomery, Graham and Whitten, Richard, *The Order on Parade* (Belfast, 1995)

Moore, Chris, *The Kincora Scandal: Political Cover-up and Intrigue in Northern Ireland* (Dublin, 1996)

Ryder, Chris, *The Fateful Split: Catholics and the Royal Ulster Constabulary* (London, 2004)

The RUC: A Force under Fire (London, 1990)

Ryder, Chris and Kearney, Vincent, *Dumcree: The Orange Order's Last Stand* (London, 2001)

Senior, Hereward, *Orangeism in Ireland and Britain, 1795–1836* (London, 1966)

Sharrock, David and Devenport, Mark, *Man of War, Man of Peace? The Unauthorized Biography of Gerry Adams* (London, 1997)

Sibbett, R. M., *Orangeism in Ireland and throughout the Empire* (London, 1938)

Storey, Earl, *Traditional Roots: Towards an Appropriate Relationship between the Church of Ireland and the Orange Order* (Dublin, 2002)

Stewart, A. T. Q., *A Deeper Silence: The Hidden Roots of the United Irish Movement* (London, 1993)

Edward Carson (Dublin, 1981)

The Narrow Ground: Aspects of Ulster, 1609–1969 (London, 1977)

The Ulster Crisis: Resistance to Home Rule, 1912–14 (London, 1967)

Tanner, Marcus, *Ireland's Holy Wars: The Struggle for a Nation's Soul, 1500–2000* (New Haven, 2001)

Taylor, Peter, *Loyalists: Ulster's Protestant Paramilitaries* (London, 1999)

Index